3RD EDITIO

THE BACK STAGE GUIDE TO

STAGE

MANAGEMENT

Traditional and New Methods for Running a Show
from First Rehearsal to Last Performance

THOMAS A. KELLY

BACK STAGE BOOKS
AN IMPRINT OF
WATSON-GUPTILL PUBLICATIONS
New York

DEDICATED TO THE MEMORY OF

Robert D. Currie

my friend and mentor

AND

Gilbert V. Helmsley

An artist and friend

Copyright © 1991, 1999, 2009 by Thomas A. Kelly

Published in 2009 by Back Stage Books, an imprint of Watson-Guptill Publications, the Crown Publishing Group, a division of Random House, Inc., New York

www.crown publishing.com
www.watsonguptill.com

BACK STAGE is a registered trademark of Nielsen Business Media, Inc.

Library of Congress Control Number: 2009920537

ISBN: 978-0-8230-9802-6

The principal typefaces used in the composition of this book were Gotham and Mercury.

Printed in the United States

First printing, 2009

3 4 5 6 7 8 9 / 17 16 15 14 13 12 11

ACKNOWLEDGMENTS

I would like to offer special thanks to all the wonderful assistant stage managers I have had the good fortune to work with, especially Chuck Kindl, Grady Clarkson, Lani Ball, and Ken Cox. I would also like to thank my wife, Memrie, and my children, Tom, Lydia, and William, for their love, support, and patience over the years (and for letting me have the computer and quiet when needed for this book); John Istel, the original editor of my ramblings here; Bill Wilson, without whose guidance and example none of this would have been possible; Amy Vinchesi, the patient editor of Back Stage Books; project editor Ross Plotkin; Tony Moore, the copyeditor of this third edition; Francesca DeRenzi for her contribution of paperwork; and especially Frank Hartenstein, for his help and advice on the automation chapter.

CONTENTS

FOREWORD

It is impossible to make good theater without good stage management.
I speak as a director who has occasionally endured bad stage management,
and I know, believe me, what that means. I've also known bad productions
with good stage management—and, alas, in these circumstances, however
professional they may be and however hard they try, stage managers
cannot finally save poor writing, false acting, indulgent designing, or inept
direction. But I have never known a really good production with bad stage
management.

The trouble is that directors tend to take stage management for granted.
When it is good, they don't notice it—like service at a first-class hotel. But if
it is bad, they notice soon enough, because their job is made impossible.

What makes good stage management? I will leave the science to Tom
Kelly and his book (he is one of the best I have encountered in thirty-five
years of directing, incidentally). I will take for granted the ability to cue
shows impeccably, organize props with efficiency, and keep a clean and
lucid "book" or record of the production. All this is the science. As director
and head of the Royal Shakespeare Company and the National Theatre of
Great Britain, I have, I know, accepted these skills as the norm for many
years. I will concentrate on the art—or, if you like, the intangibles.

The stage management team—and particularly the head of the team—
establishes a mood and an atmosphere of work. The stage managers have
to make a team of the whole theater staff—actors and technicians—and
they must also liaise with the front-of-house staff. From them comes a
sense of discipline: being on time, not wasting time, working hard. Yet this
discipline has to be in the air and accepted by the whole community—not
imposed by rules and regulations or by any kind of tyranny.

The stage management must think ahead. They should never explain
why something doesn't work or isn't there as a justification for failure; they
have to get it to work, and they have to create an atmosphere in which
everything is possible.

A director is particularly dependent on the stage management to
organize the breaks in rehearsal. The various unions have organized the
theater so that the break requirements are all different. They therefore

increase the difficulty of getting a play on. If the day ever comes when the director and the designer and the stage managers are bound by breaks as well, it will be impossible to do a play at all. Or so I sometimes think.

Stage managers have to be diplomats. They have to deal delicately with actors, understanding the stress and strain of creation. And they must not treat the star actor with deference and small parts with disdain. An even-handed understanding is essential.

They must have the confidence of the director and be able to tell him gently when he is being unreasonable or a fool.

And above all they have to create an atmosphere of enthusiasm and hard work and belief.

The most difficult situation for stage managers must be the need to be loyal to a bad director and a bad production. If they allow their own judgment to obtrude or even to show, they will undoubtedly make it worse.

Why on earth should anyone want to do such a job? I can only say that I am glad they do, otherwise I could neither create a production, nor know that it would be re-created loyally every night of a long run. Perhaps, therefore, ideal stage managers not only need to be calm and meticulous professionals who know their craft but masochists who feel pride in rising above impossible odds. I thank them for making my work and the actors' work possible.

SIR PETER HALL, 1991

PREFACE TO THE
THIRD EDITION

"Retire?! You'll never be able to adjust," scoffed many friends at the notion of my doing so. Well, I have. This spring, after the 2007–2008 season at the New York City Opera, having served as their PSM for six years, I decided the time had come. In some form or other I have been working in show business as a stage manager, actor, lighting designer and electrician, carpenter, producer, production manager, teacher of stage management, staging supervisor, scenery shop general manager, etc. for forty-seven years, since 1962, and quite frankly, I am tired. Pleased, happy, and proud of my work, I wanted to stop before I became too tired to keep up the pace or in the end too cynical to be a positive energy force. I have also always wanted to travel, especially to study ancient civilizations, and it made sense to do so while I could still get around well. My life has been deeply blessed by working in production and by the immensely talented and exciting creators and cohorts I have worked alongside, and I am grateful for my experience and career because I know how rare it is to be able to make a living solely in the arts for so many years.

Of course, as soon as I decided to retire, the fine people at Back Stage Books called and asked for a third edition of *The Back Stage Guide to Stage Management*, so here you are with that in hand. It includes some updates on job seeking, networking, and technical improvements and also a whole new chapter dedicated to opera. Stage managing opera was the final mainstay job of my career, and I loved the size, the scope, and the variety of it. Again, I was able to fall back on and use all the stage managerial techniques as discussed in the first two editions, at the same time adapting and learning new and different ways that are specific to the production of opera, and I will be sharing that with you in this edition.

The growth, development, and use of the Internet makes job seeking, networking, and information sharing far more accessible than in my early days. Back then, the only way you knew what other stage managers were doing, thinking, or feeling was by working together or the occasional social meeting. Now I participate in forums and chat rooms in which young and old stage managers share experiences, tools, feelings, and emotions that are basically of interest only to those crazy enough to seek stage management as a profession.

The single most important element in any form of production is *communication*. It is amazing that the more we develop systems like email, voicemail, iPods, cell phones, spread sheets, high-speed internet, Wi-Fi, etc. the *less* we actually communicate. One of the continuing problems is that the more "systems" we develop, the less face-to-face communication occurs, and that is a great loss, especially in the production and creation of any art form. There is little or no spirit of creative collaboration when people sitting alone in front of a computer make decisions on the process of production in a vacuum.

By reducing human input and interaction, every production decision and creative act becomes more mechanical and less volatile and exciting, at least in my opinion and experience. While this mechanical communication may reduce wasted time in some cases of pure information transference, often I have seen hurried emails with errors in them result in mass confusion and bad feelings, etc. Abraham Lincoln is quoted as saying, "One man tells a lie, a hundred repeat it as truth." Well, the same can be said of an email that goes out with wrong dates, measurements, timings, schedule, etc. Chaos is sometimes created by the fact that seldom do people proofread emails that are widely distributed. The pressures of time and the desire to have one task of communication finished so as to get on with another in production can thus snowball so quickly it is alarming. As stage managers, it is wise to always have someone look over schedules, cue sheets, presets, etc. before they are "published" and distributed as gospel.

As I am writing this, we are having a financial crisis and have just sworn in a new president. Economic woes are hitting the performing arts in every area. The costs of commercial Broadway theater have gotten so huge that few exciting or controversial plays or musicals are tried; everything must have "payback" potential. Marketing has become such a driving force in both commercial and not-for-profit theaters, and the marketing strategist is now more highly sought after and thought of than talented creative artists. It seems to me that marketing departments raise expectations and demands of the audience to impossible heights without thought or appreciation of what they are marketing. The sales gimmick or promotional tool is the new star, or so it often seems. Certainly in not-for-profit institutions, if you look at any playbill or program, you will see hugely increased staff numbers and listings for marketing, sales, promotion, finance, and fund-raising and a diminishing number of listings in production and artistic departments.

Development used to mean discovery and working on new projects from new artists and creators; now it means cocktail parties and wooing the rich and the corporations to support the arts. In doing so, institutions often grant way too much decision making and executive power to their boards and donors. This can lead to people with little or no knowledge of production making decisions that innocently enough can end up having disastrous effects on the institutions they represent and try to support. There should be a healthy balance on any board of finance and artistic knowledge so the money raised is not in turn wasted.

How does any of this relate to stage managers? Well, in any producing situation, the stage manager's responsibilities will grow more and more into cost control, bare-bones approaches to production, and dealing with limited personnel and equipment. In plans for new theaters or renovations of existing facilities, often too much priority is given to "branding" opportunities for corporations, lobby design, video capabilities, etc. Meanwhile, spaces for rehearsal, equipment for dressing room monitors and communication systems, costume and scenery shops, and storage facilities may not be included. This will seriously affect stage managers, as will new demands to cut staffing both in their own departments and also the wardrobe, prop, sound, and other technical support staffs.

Stage management is still the most central and exciting position in the mounting of productions, and I hope readers will continue to seek to improve conditions and communications to best facilitate the creation of whatever form of production they choose to pursue.

THOMAS A. KELLY, 2009

PREFACE TO THE
SECOND EDITION

"The Pope is in the Park!" The words crackled over the ubiquitous walkie-talkies surrounding the 130-foot stage that had been erected on Central Park's Great Lawn for the Papal Mass. I hung over the rail at the back of the stage with a huge band of workers with whom I had spent the better part of a month preparing for this moment, watching the whirlwind of movement and excitement that the Pope's arrival caused: security people running hither and yon calling out last-minute directions, stagehands getting ready at the foot of the elevator we had installed to bring him to the stage checking in with me on the stage, television cameramen hearing their assignments and preparing for the shot, and, everywhere, people talking into a variety of headsets, walkie-talkies, wireless phones, their wrists. It struck me once again what all production at any level is about: *communication*.

The Papal Mass in Central Park was one of the highlights of my ten years since the first edition of *The Back Stage Guide to Stage Management* came out, and it reflects a continuing change in my life and career that have moved away from the more standard stage management of theater productions and into production management—first of a variety of television, live events, and presentations and then into general and production management with one of the New York area's busiest scenery and production companies, Center Line Studios. Everything I ever learned or experienced as a stage manager has been directly translatable and useful as my job and responsibilities have changed because stage management teaches so many basic requirements about the organization and handling of any event, production, or challenge.

My experiences over the last ten years have included MTV's *Unplugged* concerts, outdoor events at Shea Stadium, Central Park, Times Square, and Bryant Park, as well as shows and concerts at Madison Square Garden and at a host of TV studios, hotel ballrooms, and meeting rooms. Throughout all of them the basic principles of stage management were my guide.

Every time I thought, "What do I do now?" I was able to find a step in the rehearsal or performance process of stage managing that related to what I was doing, and I could proceed. Like any theater piece, the preplanning and preproduction process is vital, and establishing and being the instrument of communication, scheduling, information dissemination, design, and artistic decisions are the central core of one's responsibilities. There can never be too much advance planning for any production, be it live theater or a fashion show or a news conference. The systematic planning and organizing of technical elements and communicating the schedule and necessities for a smooth event or production follow all the steps and advice outlined in this book for the specific purposes of a theater show.

Differences can emerge in the specifics, such as site planning for a play versus site planning for an outdoor event. But the thorough checking out of a rehearsal studio and theater space for a play involves looking at the same kinds of problems and requires the same process of problem solving as checking out Central Park for a Papal Mass. There are just more complications. Basically, no matter where you are, the stage or production manager's primary responsibility is to create the environment in which the final presentation—whatever it may be, play or concert, TV show or live event—can happen smoothly and with as little interference as possible. In a rehearsal studio, you may be checking for proper lighting, floor space, and rest room and phone facilities, whereas outside for a larger event the focus may be on weather protection, getting basic power, feeding large numbers of people, checking out truck routes and accessibility, etc. However, if you do what I suggest later in the book, seeing yourself at the successful conclusion of an event or production, then tracing back through the steps that got you there, it will give you a great perspective on planning for later jobs.

I have included some basic schedules and guides to production in Appendixes 13–17 that cover large outdoor or nontheatrical indoor events, as well as some site surveys and agendas for meetings relating to such events. These will give you a glimpse into this world and show that planning these events is much the same as planning for theatrical shows and events, except for the need to design in terms of different spaces and differing performance priorities.

However, this book is dedicated to the art of stage managing in theater, and most of the added material in this new edition touches on changes and developments in the theater that have reshaped or changed some responsibilities or needed knowledge for managing certain types of shows. Specifically, theater is entering into two very new worlds: The first is likely to affect mostly the limited world of commercial Broadway and Off-Broadway theater in New York and on the road, and the second is likely to affect all theater.

The first new world is technical—the world of automation and computers. We have seen the use of both advance faster in theater than some of us "old guard" can keep up with. I provide a simple guide to basic automation for the stage manager in one new chapter titled "Automation." In a second new chapter, "Stage Managers and Computers," I cover computer use as it affects the manager's job, with examples in such important areas as the preparation of paperwork involving schedules, prop lists, etc., as well as the keeping of prompt scripts and text changes. Advanced use of some drawing and computer-aided design, or CAD, systems can even allow you to plot scene changes or truck loading in three-dimensional plans. I don't claim to know how, but I have seen others do it!

Obviously, this new reliance on computers and automation puts new requirements into a stage manager's list of necessary knowledge, but it is the purpose of this book to explain that it is *new* and *additional* knowledge that is required. Being a computer whiz does not make one a good stage manager. A stage manager must have personal relating skills, sensitivity to the creative process, and a personality that can combine diligent disciplined control with an ability to handle situations that puts at ease the diverse emotional forces involved in a highly charged artistic environment. In other words, none of what already exists in this book and in the qualities of a stage manager that have been taught and handed down for years is made obsolete by computers and automation. The latter are merely added components of knowledge and skill that must be addressed and included in a stage manager's job qualifications—they do not supplant or replace those that already exist. It does no good for a stage manager to brilliantly help with the automated cueing of a show and then communicate so badly with directors and actors that time and energy are wasted in technical rehearsals. In the end, it is always the performer who must be on stage in front of the audience, who must understand and be fully aware and comfortable with what is happening technically to make for a fully successful show, and it continues to be the stage manager's primary responsibility to secure that comfort for the performer through a combination of patient communication, care for safety, technical knowledge, and reliable cueing.

The second new world that theater is entering has to do with the nature of the theater business. It is a change that in time will filter down to even the remotest community theater, because it affects the creative process and the creation of new work for the theater so much. There is a growing corporate structure to the production of theater that has replaced the legendary and creative theatrical producers and managers who grew up in and with theater, had a real knowledge of and love for the excitement and energy that can only exist in a live theater situation, and felt a respect for the writers, performers, designers, and directors who create theater.

This corporate structure has introduced a new breed into theatrical productions that finds more inspiration in the bottom line than in the chorus line or well-written line of text. It affects everyone connected with theater, but in terms of this book, how does it affect stage managers?

Corporate types in the managerial hierarchy of Disney, Hallmark, Continental Airlines, Cablevision, etc.—some of the companies producing stage productions these days—know a position called "Stage Manager" exists because it is included in their Actors' Equity agreements. But because they may not have had any experience whatsoever in theater, they probably do not know anything about the traditional set of responsibilities and talents required for the job. They are thus easily led into making perhaps inadequate choices by people who are "connected" and want to get a job for a friend or into choosing people with less experience because "they are not so set in their ways and are more open to the new way we have of doing theater" (translation: "not threatening to those inexperienced in theater productions").

Also, experienced stage managers need such a variety of skills and abilities to handle diverse sets of artistic, technical, and managerial functions that corporate types tend to doubt anyone can do it all. So, in a fit of seeming efficiency, they will hire two or three people to do the job that was formerly done by the production stage manager. Look at the program of any theatrical production or theater ad in the *New York Times* these days and you will see the titles technical supervisor, production supervisor, associate director, artistic coordinator, production manager, etc. The corporate mind has blown one job into so many that the right hand doesn't always know what the left is doing, and specialization has replaced placing all final authority and coordination into one position, thus leading to more communications breakdown and confusion.

I was working as a stage manager when the change began, and I am glad I have not had to try to run a show as I think it should be, as described in this book, since the new situation has taken full control of much of commercial theater. There is still a place for the talents and broad range of responsibilities I describe here for stage managers, and those interested in stage managing at any level should be fully aware of all the facets of the job as it evolved over the years so they can function in any theater environment. Even if a particular job does not call upon them to fulfill the whole range of a stage manager's responsibilities, they will at least know what to look for from others.

One of the strangest examples I have seen of this new division of responsibility by the corporate departmentalizing of shows occurs when the stage manager's and the newly created artistic associate's or assistant director's functions coincide over technical or safety issues. For instance, if an actor is not arriving in his or her light at the point of a cue or is standing in the dark, the stage manager is not allowed to give the note, because it might involve a "creative" instinct on the part of the performer. If an actor is abusing a prop or piece of furniture, it is no longer up to the stage manager to correct that individual; rather, it is the artistic associate who approaches the actor from a "performance point of view."

These kinds of restraints on stage managerial functions and responsibilities are truly alien in my mind and experience, and insulting in that they assume stage managers do not have the sensitivity to deal with the combined performing and technical requirements of an actor's approach to the nightly performance of his or her role, when the ability to do so should be a basic foundation of any good stage manager's skills.

Although much of what is "new" in this book deals with the technical changes and advancements made over the past few years, I still believe that personal approaches to the job are what make a stage manager's contribution to the creative process unique, that being involved with every facet of a production makes the stage manager the only person really capable of the overview necessary to ensure, in the end, a smooth, safe, and successfully running show.

I recently completed a workshop at the University of Missouri, and over the course of class discussions involving many questions and answers, we evolved a definition of stage managing using adjectives and experiences and responsibilities that we had identified during our sessions. I think it is an appropriate addition to the definition created by my students at Rutgers eight years ago that appears at the beginning of chapter 1 in this book. It shows that time and geography do not greatly alter what is the basis of good stage managing, and I will use it to conclude this preface:

> Stage managers are calm, meticulous optimists who, through supportive and quick-thinking flexibility, are able to create a pleasant working environment by supplying creature comforts and preparing the space for rehearsals or performance. They achieve this by informing and updating people on all scheduling, patiently resolving or arbitrating conflict, and keeping track of many things at once.
>
> Technical knowledge combined with open, honest communication helps the stage manager adapt quickly to new situations and handle unexpected problems, resulting in the accurate cueing of a show and a creative, diplomatic approach to establishing and maintaining artistic integrity.

This is obviously quite an order, but, I hope, this book can help lead people desirous of achieving the goal of becoming a stage manager at least to the start of the path to this ideal. Experience is still the best teacher. No book can prepare someone fully for the experience of taking a show from the printed page to a fully realized production, but judging by reactions I have received over the last ten years to those who read the first edition of *The Back Stage Guide to Stage Management*, it *can* help!

THOMAS A. KELLY, 1999

INTRODUCTION

Tensions were high during the last days of rehearsal for the opening of David Mamet's play *Speed-the-Plow*. At one point backstage, Madonna, the pop superstar who was making her Broadway debut in the show, turned to her production stage manager (me), and said, "You were put on Earth for me to abuse, Tom."

This anecdote is an appropriate departure point for a book on stage managing because, basically, in their own way, most people share Madonna's attitude toward stage managers. If accepting lots of the pressures and responsibilities for a theater project while receiving little of the glory is not something you are willing to do, perhaps you should return this book before you crease it any further. However, if you are that rare person in the world of theater who has the talent, as Rudyard Kipling said, to "keep your head when all about you are losing theirs and blaming it on you," then read on.

I should note here that Madonna was speaking affectionately; she had come to understand and appreciate my ability to not only take her abuse but excuse it and let it go. I was able to do this because I, in turn, understood the pressures and insecurities that she was experiencing. This is a big part of successful stage managing.

In the simplest sense, stage managers create an environment within which highly volatile people can function freely, devoid of petty distractions and stumbling blocks—other than those of their own creation. The stage manager must execute the creative vision of each production, supporting and assisting the directors, designers, writers, and performers in the achievement of their artistic goals. The stage manager's creative energies should be focused on finding as many ways as possible to make the theatrical process simple and enjoyable, and much of this book's focus will be on ways to do just that.

My hope is that this book will be read not only by prospective stage managers but anyone who ever comes in contact with a stage manager—whether director, designer, actor, or producer—and that each reader will enlighten others regarding a stage manager's functions. In this way all theater professionals will be able to take better advantage of stage managers as a resource and support system.

People backstage often ask me how I stay so calm, and like the musician asked how to get to Carnegie Hall, I answer, "Practice." I've been "practicing" the craft of stage management for a while, ever since I went off to summer stock in Upstate New York with fantasies of acting stardom pirouetting in my head. After all, I had been the lead in all my high school plays, I had just turned eighteen, and anything was possible. My dream of becoming a successful actor continued for several years, in spite of discouraging signs to the contrary. But starting with that first summer in stock, I *always* seemed to find success and encouragement in the backstage and production end of the theater process.

Those first years of stock served as the ideal training ground for becoming a stage manager. I built scenery, hung and focused lights, ran sound and edited tapes, ran props, served as an electrician, worked in a box office, directed, and acted. I learned theater by doing it—all of it. These days such a regimen might be considered exploitative, and few would think of creating a training program like the one I found waiting for me in a small barn in Upstate New York. But I have always been grateful that my firsthand knowledge of every production facet has made stage managing so much easier. I would advise everyone who wants to stage manage to try as many jobs in the theater as possible.

Gradually, more and more people asked me to work in a technical or production capacity while few even *hinted* they might want to hire me as an actor. I took up stage managing as a career, and I have now been working as a stage manager or production manager for over forty years.

In this book I will attempt to share not only *what* I have learned but also a little of *how* I learned. Of course, reading a book will not make anyone a stage manager. The more I stage manage, the more I know it is unteachable, unless the teaching includes hands-on training. Only the experience of taking a show from the preproduction phase through the opening night will give you the knowledge you will need. You will have to make your own mistakes. You, too, will have to forget to turn the house lights off one night or call the cue for a telephone ring instead of a scene-ending blackout. Every show, every rehearsal, every conflict resolved is one more lesson, and so your experience grows. All I can do with this book is attempt to spare you some pitfalls and help you identify some ideals and goals. And perhaps my practical experience will help make the concepts and principles you read about more real.

Stage managing has been a very rewarding experience for me. Personally, I find the discipline of calling a show and the all-consuming process of rehearsing a play or musical to be a profound source of satisfaction and, at times, a great escape. (It is hard to worry about much of anything else when you're calling cues for a big musical or feeding actors lines as they struggle through those first tenuous days off-book.) Stage managing has taken me to many states and a few foreign countries, has exposed me to some of the greats of our time and some of the lowlifes, but it has always kept its original promise that, unlike an office job, it would never be boring or the same every day. Best of all, if a show or situation ever seems unbearably bad, you're guaranteed relief: No show lasts forever.

If you are interested in becoming a stage manager, at any level of professional or community theater, what follows will provide some help and support. If you already are stage managing, read on, take what tips you like, and leave what you don't. I can't promise to answer all your questions—no book can—but by sharing my varied experiences, whether good, bad, or ugly, I hope to illuminate the many facets of this complex and constantly challenging profession.

1

WHAT DOES A STAGE MANAGER DO?

Defining exactly what a stage manager does is difficult because the definition must include so many tasks and responsibilities. To be sure, a stage manager takes blocking notes, calls the lighting and sound cues during performances, and gives acting notes once the director leaves. But such a simple list of physical activities does not completely describe the stage manager's real role in a theater project.

After several hours of discussion on the qualities and requirements of a good stage manager in the stage managing class I teach at Rutgers University's Mason Gross School of the Arts, the students and I settled on what I believe is a good job description. It will serve well as a foundation from which we may explore the various aspects and responsibilities of the position:

Stage managers are responsible and adaptable communicators who have the ability to handle and coordinate diverse groups of artistic personalities with tactful discipline and a sense of humor. They establish a creative environment by combining the ability to prioritize and anticipate and solve problems, with calm sensitivity and grace under pressure.

Their ability to do the above stems from organizational ability, acquired technical knowledge (sound, music, lights, design and construction, typing, use of computers, and so on), familiarity with union requirements, and an inspirational personality that creates positive energy.

This is obviously an ideal definition. It includes a number of topics that will serve as jumping-off points for more completely defining and understanding the job of stage managing. Appendix 1 contains several other attempts at defining stage managers, including some by other theater professionals.

You'll also find the Actors' Equity Association's definition of the duties and obligations of a stage manager, which will further help you to focus on exactly what a stage manager must and must not do.

It should be noted here that all professional theater stage managers in the United States are members of Actors' Equity Association. This alliance with the actors' union illustrates the collaborative and mutually supportive relationship that should ideally exist between actor and stage manager. At times, however, stage managers are placed in an awkward position because their managerial functions may involve to some degree the disciplining, hiring, and firing of actors. In television and movies, by contrast, those with a job description most resembling stage managers are members of the Directors' Guild.

Through my own evolving experience with the job I've come to believe that there is no fixed definition of a stage manager, only precepts and guidelines, because every show, every theater, every situation—whether it be geographic, contractual, or artistic—changes the scope of the job.

Of course, it is always a good idea to know what the person who hires you thinks the job is. That may seem like simple advice, but every director, producer, or general manager I have worked for has had slightly different views on the role the stage manager plays in a production or in the hierarchy of a resident or community theater's operation.

Usually, the higher the level of theater at which the stage manager is functioning, the more contained his or her job description is. For example, it is not unusual in some summer stock and Off-Off-Broadway situations for the stage manager to run light and/or sound cues while calling and watching the show. At some resident theaters, the job of stage manager may include everything from casting to dealing with the transportation and housing of actors.

In each new production, a stage manager will have varying degrees of responsibility depending on his or her relationship with the director or producer. The stage manager may function as an assistant director on some shows and have broad artistic control.

On other productions the producer or managing director may depend on the stage manager to be his or her eyes and ears, keeping firm managerial control over expenses and limiting the waste of time and money on artistic indulgence. At best, the job will fall happily into both camps and the stage manger will not have to "take sides" but will be able to best serve the director and the management by facilitating clear communication between the two.

Now let's get back to our ideal definition, take a look at some of the qualities it mentions, and see how these characteristics translate into actual tasks like scheduling, running rehearsals, and passing notes, all of which seem simple on the surface.

The definition begins by stating that stage managers are "responsible." This means that they are willing to take responsibility and that they will initiate actions that will have a direct bearing on much of the production's ability to move ahead and succeed. Some people resist taking such responsibilities or find they can only function when given orders or directions by someone else. Sometimes it is better to start as an assistant stage manager or a production assistant until one builds up the knowledge and confidence to take responsibility. However, if it is totally outside the realm of a person's nature to take responsibility, then he or she should probably not seek stage management as a career.

Taking responsibility presupposes that the stage manager knows the limits of that responsibility—outlined in the chart shown in Figure 1-1. You will notice that the arrows on the chart flow in both directions, because most often the stage manager is the central clearinghouse of information

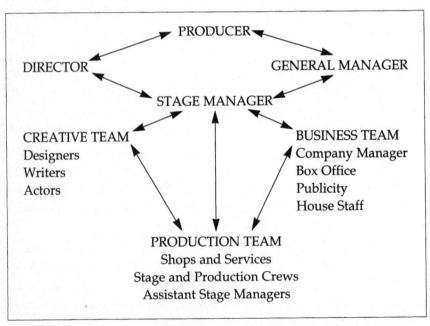

FIGURE 1-1

between the creative and the managerial forces. It is important for the stage manager to communicate clearly the changing needs and requirements of the artistic and managerial personnel to all departments if a theater or a production is going to run smoothly.

A fairly standard example of this occurs regularly in the Broadway theater. Suppose that during a production meeting it is decided that the sound operator must set up the console in the house (the audience seating area) in order to hear and balance the sound properly. The sound operator and his or her equipment, therefore, will occupy a number of seats. Until the box office is notified of this decision by the stage manager, tickets could inadvertently be sold for those seats. Box office personnel should also be informed of any obstructed or partial views that result from a certain set-design choice. Catching these potential problems early will result in less aggravation later.

Stage managers should also double-check the performance schedule. Sometimes due to holidays or ticket sales patterns, playing schedules may change. If the actors and crew are not informed, it is possible to have either no one present but the audience for a performance or a cast and crew sitting around an empty theater. This actually happened during the run of Howard Korder's *Boys' Life* at Lincoln Center Theater. Everyone in management thought someone else had told the stage manager, cast, and crew, but we all showed up for a Sunday matinee that no longer existed. Confirming schedules with management on a regular basis is a good idea.

Obviously, the chart in Figure 1-1 is a simplified structural representation of the stage manager's relationship to all others working on a theater production. What should be immediately noticeable is that the stage manager is "in the middle" and that there are people to whom the stage manager is ultimately responsible—namely, the director for all artistic and creative choices, the general manager for all business and contractual choices, and hopefully the producer, who will meld these two sometimes disparate forces into one clear direction. The stage manager, therefore, must be able to combine creative integrity with practical and efficient budgetary consideration. This means balancing the artistic vision of the director with the financial limitations imposed by the producer or general manager.

The chart also illustrates how crucial it is for a stage manager to be an "adaptable communicator," the next phrase after "responsibility" in our ideal definition. Since the stage manager holds the central position in the structure of theater production as shown by the chart, communication is as vital a part of stage managing as memorization is to acting. There is, however, no one to feed the stage manager the line if he or she doesn't communicate fully. That makes expressing oneself clearly and without editorializing of vital importance. A stage manager who transmits a note to the design staff, for instance, in such a way as to reflect his or her personal feelings about the subject or sender of the note, will ultimately create a volatile and destructive (instead of constructive) creative atmosphere.

Let me give you an example. Suppose your leading lady feels her costume for a certain scene isn't right. After she discusses it with the director, they decide to go for something else. As the stage manager, you jot down a note about the objections and tell the costume designer at the next meeting.

"What do you mean, she can't wear the sweater?" the designer fumes. "Tell her she has to, and I don't care what she thinks."

Now . . . take a deep breath and then tactfully remind the person with whom you are speaking that you are simply the stage manager (i.e., the messenger) and as such are only imparting the wishes of the actor, director, or whomever. Most important, you must make sure that the costume designer understands exactly what the request was, and you should repeat it clearly and unemotionally. Lastly, if the costumer is still upset, you should ask if he or she would like to speak to the offending party in person to voice his or her feelings directly. Usually, this will result in acquiescence, and two days later the idea to make the change in sweaters will have become the designer's and everyone will be congratulating them-selves on their creativity and ability to get along.

Although many do, stage managers must never take sides, play mind games, or call the personnel names. Transmitting a note with a preface such as "Guess what the nutcase-egomaniac-monster wants today?" is no way to get a designer or director in the mood to listen to a request that may have more validity than you imagine. There are enough short tempers and unbalanced egos backstage without the stage manager getting involved. A wise old stage manager with whom I worked for a long time, Robert Currie, once told me there are two rules of stage management: The first rule is that stage managers should have no opinions; the second rule is that they must know when to break rule one.

Adaptability is another vital part of this job. There is no "one way" to do something; each rehearsal may call for a radically different approach. A three-character drama does not go by the same rules or have the same rehearsal environment as a musical or large-cast Shakespeare, and the stage manager must be able to adapt. A comedy will require a different attitude and handling of rehearsal than a heavy drama. The former may allow for a carefree and easygoing environment, whereas the latter may become so charged with the emotions being dredged up by the actors that the same jocular style would not be appropriate.

Adaptability is always required in dealing with the creative process because there is never a foolproof way to predict how long or how difficult certain work is going to be. Schedules, work calls, presets, running orders— all are subject to change at a moment's notice. It is the stage manager's job to organize and communicate the changes as quickly and clearly as possible. The stage manager must avoid editorializing or creating a sense of negativity, no matter how tempting, especially when he or she must tell a group of designers or carpenters who have been working like zealots to complete a project that the director has now decided to cut it. If at all possible, a stage manager should emulate Sergeant Friday from the old television show *Dragnet* and maintain a "Just the facts, ma'am" attitude.

I remember with some chagrin the first time I was faced with a tolerance tester of the highest magnitude. I was the original stage manager on *Sugar Babies*, the burlesque musical that eventually enjoyed a long run on Broadway starring Mickey Rooney and Ann Miller. It was the first big musical I had ever worked on as production stage manager—often abbreviated PSM—from the first rehearsal straight through the initial technical rehearsals, when all the scenery, light, sound, prop, and costume changes are first worked out.

The pre-Broadway tryouts began in San Francisco, and I spent days and nights in my hotel room writing out cues for every department, figuring out where the many flying and moving pieces would be stored. At this point, a crucial task was to decide what traveler or drop would have to be onstage at each moment to mask the scene change behind it. (Travelers are the curtains that open and close on the stage level; drops fly in and out from above.) To complicate matters, there were about thirty-five different scenes and songs in the show.

I was then informed that over half the drops in the show would not be ready for the first technical rehearsal and that they might not even be ready until we after the first preview. Don't worry, I was told by the management, just use what you have. I was despondent; I felt I was the only one who recognized the impossibility of their request. Fortunately, the assistant designer was also aware of the folly of this notion, and as we commiserated and despaired a solution dawned. We both had friends at the San Francisco Opera, and we knew they had a warehouse full of drops. So we convinced our general manager to rent a bunch of them to substitute for our missing ones. In this way, at least we would be able to tech and open the show with some semblance of order.

As the afternoon of the first tech approached, I went over the cue sheets with every department head. They went off to lunch, and the lighting designer and I sat down to have a sandwich and put the first act's cues in my prompt book. We were about halfway through when the director arrived and announced that he had decided to completely change the running order of the show: Songs from Act 1 were put into Act 2 and vice versa. Whole sequences of costume changes were switched. All the scene changes that I had planned out so meticulously were now rendered worthless on what seemed like a whim.

Well, as I said, this was my first big one, and I lost my composure. An hour to go to the first big tech of my life, and whatever flimsy belief I held that I could pull it off vanished. I broke every rule of stage managing in about thirty seconds. I told the director off, advised hiring someone else, and fled upstairs to the boxes to ponder why I had ever thought I could do this job in the first place. I felt very sorry for myself and very alone and very stupid.

Fortunately, the lighting designer on this show was Gilbert Helmsley, a friend with whom I had worked many times. Gilbert was also a teacher and a mentor, and in the next hour he taught me how it should be done.

The solution was simple: I would start with my first cue—house lights to half—and I would just rewrite every cue until I got to the end of Act 1 and not concern myself with the merits of the decision. I followed Gilbert's advice and the tech went beautifully, because as I settled down and did it I realized much of the work I had done was still sound. Since the crew had never run the show in the original running order, they weren't thrown by the new changes. Thanks to the miracle wonders of cutting, pasting, and photocopying, the cue sheets soon became as workable and valid as they had been a few hours earlier.

Of course, with today's computer technology it would be even simpler, and a few strokes of the actual "cut and paste" function on the old laptop would have made those changes seem much easier. The new chapter on computers and stage managers shows several cue sheet examples where a major change in running order can be effected rapidly. However, it is important to highlight the changes and print large "UPDATED Q SHEET" titles on everything, so people will know which cue sheet to work off.

Adaptability. If this happened to me now, I know I would just smile at the director before setting out to make the requested changes. After that afternoon in San Francisco, everything seems simple.

The other key elements of the ideal definition are organizational ability and the need to prioritize; they come into play in almost every facet of the stage manager's job. Scheduling, laying out cues, and judging the need for rehearsals and techs can only be accomplished with these basic abilities, as we will learn as we investigate each step of production in future chapters.

2

PREPRODUCTION

Preproduction on a show at any level is an exciting time. On Broadway, every show is going to be a hit; in stock and community theater, every new show will be better than the last. It is also an important time for the stage manager to be functioning with every bit of his or her ability to foresee problems and work toward creative solutions. One must be delicate during these early days and not undermine the wide-eyed optimism and abounding creative energy with such statements as, "That will never work," or "You must be out of your minds!" It is better to work along with the creators, raising any important budgetary and logistical problems gently and clearly as you go.

Analyzing the Script

All stage managerial preproduction work begins with the reading of the script. If you have the time, it is a good idea to read it through once without taking any notes. This will give you an idea of the tone and style of the play before you start seeking out detailed information. Also, in reading a full play, you can save time and guesswork as you prepare lists and notes by knowing how intricate and vital to the plot various props and furniture pieces are and if they have any special needs. For instance, the first scene may require a chair for an actor to sit in, but in Act 2 stage directions call for that same chair to be thrown or tipped over, and therefore it will need special attention in building and/or placement. Having read the script once to get a general idea of the plot and technical requirements, a good stage manager will go back through it like a detective, searching out every possible technical clue and every acting or stage direction that could cause problems.

At this point it is a good idea to do a production analysis. It will serve as a starting point for discussions at later production meetings with directors, designers, and the management or producer when trying to work out a budget. The more thorough the stage manager is at this point, the better for everyone. It is dangerous to allow designers and directors to go along assuming that everything in their script is possible technically and financially if you foresee problems that may crop up later on. For instance, the script may have been written by someone with a cinematic background and have lightning-fast changes that are going to require either advanced and sophisticated (read: expensive) machinery or a larger number of stage crew and personnel than may be feasible under the theater's or show's budget. Solutions and compromise can be reached more easily in the early stages of production, before the director has assumed that every instantaneous change will be possible.

The analysis will be of ongoing use to the actors and stage manager as they figure out the space required for costume changes, the time needed for crossovers, and so on. The analysis allows the stage manager to assist the director and actor in figuring out which entrances and exits may become complicated by a quick costume change or by the character's need to reappear from another side of the stage. The stage manager must keep his or her eye on all departments' requirements by constantly referring to the analysis; this attention will prevent members of the company from wasting time and energy working on something that is later discovered to be technically or logistically impossible. With the help of this analysis, the director won't spend hours blocking a group's entrance from a wing space that must remain free for a large set piece.

Creating a Production Analysis

Another of the major purposes of a production analysis will be to assist in creating the agenda for production meetings. Therefore, it is important to include all areas of the production in the analysis. This form can be set up on a spreadsheet program on a computer in Microsoft Excel or a similar program. Keep your original electronically and then make changes and updates as the meetings are held and decisions are made in production. With some simple cut and paste and editing, you can easily adapt this first analysis into a Costume Plot, Props Preset, and Running Sheet. You might want to look at the similar Who/What/Where example for *Il Matrimonio Segreto* on page 270. Column headings should include placement in the script or score, costumes, scenery, lighting, props, sound, and a column for special effects and notes.

The first column designates the page in the script where a certain technical requirement arises. This column will keep you "on the same page" with everyone else as you discuss the show. It will also help clarify where the bulk of the show's technical requirements will fall, as well as where actors make entrances and exits. This is crucial in the preparation of schedules and scene breakdowns. Use a Roman numeral for the act, an Arabic numeral for the scene, and "p." for the page. For example, the sixth page, which is in the second scene of Act 1 would be written I/2/p.6. This is also the style used to number pages in a script.

The second column should contain all the information you need for the costume plot and for an actor-scene breakdown. The latter will be useful for scheduling rehearsals and will form the basis of any discussion of understudies or covers. As you read you should carefully note every entrance and exit of each character and include a basic description (age, character type, etc.), pointing out whether this changes at any point. For instance, if a character ages or becomes extremely wealthy between scenes, this will no doubt require costume and makeup changes for which plans must be made.

Indicate where costume notes are provided by the writer ("elegantly attired" is a favorite), but also be aware of the costume changes not specifically spelled out. Passage of a day or more will probably indicate a change of costume, as will any change in season or weather. Also note any action that an actor must perform with a costume. A fight, a fall, or the use of stage blood are examples of stage business that must be discussed and planned for artistically and financially. You should also look out for more subtle uses of costume. Does the character need any pockets or lots of pockets? Does a shirt or coat have to be taken off or put on during the action? Does one actor use a costume piece to tie or blindfold another performer? Does a costume have to be torn or ripped off?

These are just some of the things to be watchful for in preparing your analysis.

The cast and costume section will also show right away if there is a need for quick changes that must take place in the wings. By using this eight-column, "across the page" approach, instead of a continuous list, you will be able to look directly over to the set and prop columns and see if there will be any traffic problems. If there are scenery or prop changes happening simultaneously, plan adequate room for both at the production meetings.

The next column is for the set, and it should have each setting and all scenery shifts marked here. Be thorough: It is from this initial analysis that you will get an idea of the size of the running crew you'll require. The designer will work out a lot of the shift problems with you, hopefully, but think ahead. For example, try to determine what scenery and furniture could be put on a pallet or winch and what could be flown, if you have a fly floor. By bolting one or two large pieces of the furniture to the pallet floor and putting some sort of glide strips on the bottom of the pallet, two people can push off a whole living room of furniture instead of running around moving each piece. Wagons are larger variations of the pallet and often contain whole sets with walls and furniture. These are often moved by winches, which allow one man to turn a crank, reeling in a cable that has been attached to the wagon, and, due to the laws of physics, he moves far more weight than one person could by pushing or pulling. The stage manager should be aware of the following elements of the set:

- Doors and their locations
- Whether the door frames are large enough to allow costumes, hats, trays, and other props to fit through
- Any indications of a raked stage (a stage floor that slopes down toward the audience)
- Anything that moves onto or off the stage during the course of the action that will have to be handled by actors
- Any playing areas that are elevated and that may require railings and escape stairs so the actors will be able to exit
- Any flying pieces that come in or out during the action
- Any curtains or blinds pulled by actors

Mainly, the stage manager should be ready to discuss and plan for anything about the set that will affect the actor. From the outset, safety should be a primary concern so there are no unfortunate surprises once on the set.

The light column is fairly self-explanatory. Look for changes in the time of day and season. Keep an eye out for practical lights, mood or effect lighting like lightning, and so on. The lighting column should also denote the position of any blackout. This is a time when the stage goes completely dark, and the stage manager has to plan ahead to assure that all backstage and house lights are out. If a blackout is indicated, the across-the-page form will be very helpful in ascertaining what else is going on in the dark: what actors have to get on- or offstage and what scenery or props have to be moved. All of this must be carefully discussed and planned in ensuing production meetings.

The prop column should contain every prop mentioned or indicated by the script. For instance, if the actor says, "Why don't you mix some drinks while I whip us up some dip for the crackers," there are a whole lot of props indicated by this line of dialogue that may not appear in the stage directions.

Carefully look at how any prop is used (or abused) in the script. A book or a newspaper seems simple enough, but a book or newspaper that is thrown, used as a weapon, sat on, or manipulated in some way makes the prop's requirements a bit more complex. (That's why you must be a detective while completing this analysis.) This fifth column will form the basis of your preliminary prop list, so try to include preset positions wherever possible and some indication of whether a prop is a "perishable." (Preset positions are the initial placements of a prop on- or offstage; perishables are those props that are eaten, beaten, or destroyed every performance and will have a great bearing on the cost of the props for the show.)

The sound column should include every audible effect, whether doorbells, phones, sirens, cars honking, doors slamming, or what have you. Also note any offstage voices that may require actors using microphones. In many large theaters, the question of whether to amplify the actors arises for every production. It should be dealt with as early as possible, and especially when body mikes are being considered, since they will affect the use of costumes and the ease of costume changes.

Try to indicate, wherever possible, the source or location of a sound effect, so the necessary speakers and size of equipment can be accurately budgeted. Let's say a play calls for a radio that must broadcast a news report from stage left, a car horn that must be heard when the front door is opened stage right, and a dog howling in the backyard, up center. This may necessitate at least three speakers.

It is also important to note any mention of music, either practical (onstage sound emitted by a real radio or music that is sung, hummed, or whistled by actors), or underscoring or effect music (offstage sound such as heralding trumpets or a band passing by). Two considerations are important here. First, if the song or music is copyrighted, you must alert the management so they can secure the rights to use it; second, you must find out from the author and director what music they envision as live and what will be on tape. This becomes further complicated if a character plays an instrument onstage but the actor doesn't know how to play it—you will have to discuss and plan this in your production meetings. Of course, with musicals the question of sound amplification becomes larger and far more complicated, as levels must be set according to the orchestra size, and body mikes distributed according to chorus and/or principal designations, and many other factors.

The category of special effects covers a wide range of problems that are important to note when you prepare the initial analysis. Although weapons are usually under the jurisdiction of the prop department, effects people often handle charges or explosive devices—anything more complicated than a standard blank-firing pistol.

I stage managed a play on Broadway called *Accomplice*, a murder mystery by Rupert Holmes that ran briefly at the Richard Rodgers Theatre in 1990. The show had electrocutions, retractable knives, blood bags, a flaming umbrella, and an exploding lamp. All these effects required close coordination between the effects designer and the prop, electric, and set crews and designers. For instance, there was a scene in which a man took a foot bath and was then electrocuted when his wife tossed a hair dryer into the tub. The prop man had to find a bathtub big enough for all the wiring and effects to be hidden in. The set designer had to make sure there was a spot in the floor where a small trap door could be opened under the tub and that was also close enough to an electrical outlet to allow the wife to throw the hair dryer into the tub without pulling the cord out. And the electric and prop shops had to rig and wire the tub while still having it look believable as an antique that might be found in a quaint remodeled English farmhouse. Every element in the show had similarly complicated multi-department requirements, and throughout the production and rehearsal periods it took endless visits to the various shops and many, many phone calls and faxes to achieve the desired effects.

Rain and running water are examples of other stage effects that involve several production departments and must be carefully coordinated through meetings and discussions.

In the "Special Notes" column of your analysis, you should include anything that occurs to you that might involve extra planning, expense, or personnel. If there are accents or dialects in a play, there may be a dialect coach, and if so, when and how often does the director wish to give up rehearsal time so actors can work on their accents? Or should you try to schedule the coaching around the rehearsals on the actors' free time? If there are fights, will there be a fight director? Are there any special cueing needs that should be discussed right away?

As soon as I read *Accomplice*, I knew there would have to be additional television monitors mounted to ensure the cast's and crew's safety. These simple TV cameras, like security cameras in a bank, would allow the stage manager and crew to see the exact position of the actors during various explosions and when trap doors opened.

It is also important to note anything that might require special licensing, such as open flames (torches, candles, kerosene lamps), explosives, or any scenery or effect that will involve the audience. On Broadway and in all New York theaters, every firearm used must have a permit, every open flame must have a permit from the fire department, and every pyrotechnic or explosive device must be inspected, approved, and operated by a licensed pyrotechnic. In whatever town or city you are working, it is a good idea to check what the licensing requirements are for any fire, firearms, or special effects that you may have in your show. Don't forget that it is much simpler to deal with these elements in advance rather than have an inspection after opening night and discover that implementing safety devices will take time and delay your performances.

Figure 2-1 is a sample preliminary production analysis covering the first dozen pages of *Death of a Salesman*.

After you've completed your analysis, it will be easy to devise preliminary prop lists, sound effect lists, costume plots, rehearsal and scene breakdowns, scene-shift plots, and initial rehearsal and tech schedules. More important, if done correctly, a production analysis gives you the security of knowing all the elements of a production as you enter into meetings and discussions with the creative and technical personnel. It will

ACT SC., P.	CAST/COST	SET	LIGHTS	PROPS	SOUND	SPECIAL EFFECTS	SPECIAL NOTES
I, 1	Willy Loman 50's suit, hat. Linda Loman 50's-nightgown robe	2 or 3 level cutaway of house (w/ kitchen) 2 bedrooms	Dim/Night. Practical lights in kitch. and B.R.	2 Heavy salesman cases. Refrigerator. kitchen table 3 chairs	Music/Flute. Car arrives. Door slam. Linda/off stage. Does she need microphone?		
I, 4	Willy - slippers "-suit jacket on			Pens, etc. for Willy's pockets to empty on table			
I, 7				Milk bottle in refrigerator with milk			
I, 8				Cheese in refrigerator			
I, 11		An exit from kitch. USC					
I, 12	Biff 30's Happy 20's in pajamas	upper level is Boy's B.R. - Note: Must be quick escape for fast transition + cost. change later	Moonlight thru window and bedside lamp	Cigarettes (period) ash trays, lighter			

FIGURE 2-1 *Sample Production Analysis of* Death of a Salesman

make them feel immediately secure that you are organized and capable of taking charge. There is nothing worse than a stage manager being caught unprepared or forced to play catch-up and fake it. As the executor of the creative vision, the more thorough a job preparation you do, the more confidence and fun you can have in commencing the journey from printed page to production reality.

Meeting the Director

Often your first meeting with a director will be in the form of an interview to gain his or her approval of your hiring by the producer or general manager. Sometimes you may be the resident stage manager and the director is a guest director. In the best of all possible worlds, the director has asked for you, and you can cut through all the preliminaries and get to work.

If you don't know each other, the first meeting with a director is vitally important. The hardest part of these first meetings is being yourself and not trying to impress or overwhelm the director with your brilliance. The director needs to get a sense of the person with whom he or she will be dealing on a daily basis.

Listening is a good practice in a first meeting. Let the director tell you about the script and the concept even though you may be bursting with questions and hard-earned observations gleaned from your production analysis. Often directors will get into exactly what they expect from a stage manager and how they want things run. If not, it is important to ask your own questions. Here is a sample list of questions you should ask and issues that you should raise during your first meeting with the director:

1. At the beginning of the rehearsal process, how long will actors remain at a table reading and discussing? How soon does the director expect to start blocking? Does the director want you to call places and formally begin each rehearsal and scene, or would he or she prefer to ease from informal small talk into the rehearsal work without abruptly shifting the mood?
2. What level of rehearsal props and furniture does the director expect and at what point?

3. Does the director want strict blocking kept from the outset, or will there be a period of improvisation?

4. How does the director want breaks called—five minutes in an hour, or ten minutes every hour and a half? Does the director wish you to call a reminder ten or fifteen minutes before the scheduled break?

5. What policy would the director like to establish regarding visitors at rehearsals?

6. How would the director like to structure the basic rehearsal schedule, and how should you break up the script—by scene, page number, act? Your production analysis should serve as an excellent tool to devise an actors' scene breakdown, detailing the acts and scenes and which actors appear in them.

7. Would the director like to establish any guidelines for prompting actors with their lines? How soon does the director want actors off-book? And should you correct them word-for-word or allow them to paraphrase at first if the scene is moving along?

8. How are rewrites to be handled—e.g., passed out and read through outside rehearsals or held to be distributed all at once by the director? It is also possible to email new script pages to the actors' homes between rehearsals or when they have a day off? This allows the actor to get over any bad feelings and the playwright and director to send along any explanatory notes regarding the cuts, changes, or rewrites without interruption or emotional reactions from the actor.

9. How much discussion and leeway does the director want to allow before you prod him or her to move on and stick to the scheduled work for the day? This is a delicate and very important point that should be agreed upon in advance, because there should be no sign of quarrel or disagreement between the director and stage manager in front of the cast.

10. Establish a time when the two of you can talk privately each day so you continue working on the same wavelength while not having to discuss questions or problems during rehearsal periods.

The director and stage manager should emerge from the first meeting with a genuine feeling that they can work together. The basic ground rules should be set.

A stage manager should further inquire whether there is any research or background material the director would like in rehearsal. In regional theaters, dramaturges will often provide these materials, and sometimes the director may have an assistant who will help with the extra research work. Find out if these positions exist on your show and set up a meeting as early as possible to discuss everyone's responsibilities. Clarify where the responsibilities and authority of the stage manager's position will overlap and/or supersede these often helpful, but sometimes meddlesome, additional staff.

Make it clear, for instance, that no schedule should be presented to the actors or crew by anyone other than the director and stage manager, that notes to the crew must be handled through the stage manager, and that any script or major blocking changes given to actors must go through the stage manager to avoid chaos. Often the director's assistants will give out the director's notes, thinking they are sparing you the trouble when in fact they are creating a nightmare by giving out information and changes that affect your ability to call cues and run the show.

It may also be useful to ask the director if he or she has any previous knowledge of the cast and any advice about the most effective and helpful ways to work with the cast members. Finally, seek out any personal likes and dislikes—smoking rules (smoking herbal cigarettes is currently allowed onstage—at the opera, they cannot be *lit* onstage unless the costumes are flameproof but can be carried on already lit (as in *Carmen*), food and drink favorites to have on hand, or certain words that the director may prefer using. (Directors often use different terms to describe the same thing. For instance, they may prefer that everyone use *company* instead of *cast* when addressing the actors.) Let the director know you are available to make life as pleasant as you and the budget possibly can allow.

Meeting the Producer

Presuming all is well with the director, and you want the job, it is now time to discuss it with your employer. No matter what kind of theater you may be working for, it is important to have a full and clear concept of what is expected of you, especially in terms of work hours and duties outside of rehearsal and performance. There are "traditions" in a lot of theaters that you should find out about ahead of time so you're not surprised when someone informs you that the stage manager always did the sound before, or drove the actors, or organized company parties or softball games, and so on.

There are fewer of these added-on responsibilities in a single-show, commercial-theater stage management job, but it is still valuable to set boundaries. Basically, I always try to convince management to allow me to handle everything from the curtain back—actors, running crew, dressing rooms—while they deal with everything and everybody from the curtain out—house manager, box office, concessions.

This is a good basic premise, but it gets complicated. While you should try to divorce yourself from financial responsibility as much as possible, it is still necessary for management to deal with actors and crew members concerning salaries, expense money, and overtime work. Also, the need for specific work or additional expense is often requested by the stage manager.

There are many different types of management for which you may work as a stage manager. In a regional or resident theater there is usually a managing or producing director who is in charge of the business end of the theater and with whom you discuss your contract and the initial budget and contract necessities of the show. This position is comparable to the general manager in the commercial theater.

The general manager or managing director often has an assistant who may be called the company manager in the commercial arena, or the business manager or assistant managing director in a resident theater. These assistants are the functioning day-to-day business representative on the show, handling payroll, petty cash, and other financial matters, and through whom the stage manager will communicate directly to the producer, general manager, or managing director.

It is very important that this communication be clear, open, and devoid of misrepresentation. Work to establish a common vocabulary, and be sure that the company manager understands when you are joking and when you are serious; otherwise confusion about a show's progress can abound in the front office. Remember that business people don't always fully understand artists' eccentricities and strange demands and therefore may not always see things the same as you. What seems like a reasonable demand to an actor working under pressure for eight hours a day, like doing personal banking since he or she is stuck in rehearsal during banking hours, may seem excessive to a business manager.

In the first meeting with an employer, the stage manager should proceed much as with the director, listening to the manager's description of how he or she wants the theater or show run. Then augment the manager's basic outline of responsibilities with ideas and needs of your own.

Your first meeting with the producer or manager should also include a discussion of any unusual expenses you have discovered through the development of your production analysis and through your previous meeting with the director. Mention any hidden costs you have unearthed (the previously mentioned need for additional video monitors for *Accomplice* is a good example). If you feel the crew size will need to be larger than average, or if the nature of the casting or scene changes will preclude doubling roles or understudying within the company, make sure you bring it to the producer's attention.

You should also mutually establish the production's important preliminary dates:

- The deadlines for the submission of the designers' completed drawings
- The date by which the shops will bid and/or begin work
- The days of auditions
- The projected date of casting completion
- The beginning date of rehearsals
- The dates the company will move into the theater
- The date of the first performance

As with the director, you need to establish your lines of communication with the manager. What are the forms and reporting systems he or she is used to? Is there a best time every day to talk and update each other on progress and problems? Producers and managers don't want to be burdened with everyday conflicts that you should be able to solve, but they do appreciate early notification of major problems or decisions that only they can handle or make. For example, in *Speed-the-Plow* we were constantly dealing with overzealous Madonna fans who would jump onto the stage in the middle of a performance. Fed up with their potentially dangerous interruptions, Madonna told me clearly, in her own inimitably forceful tone, that there had to be additional security men hired. I called the general manager immediately, so that by the time the songstress and her people reached him, he was aware of the situation and had agreed to hire more security men. It was far better for him to have talked to me first than to have had to meet her fury head-on, ignorant of the full details of the situation; in this case he already had a plan and a solution ready to calm Madonna.

Finally, you must discuss your own working requirements. This includes salary, billing, assistants, and the establishment of a petty cash fund for your purchases and expenses. You should agree on the limit and extent of this fund and how far you can go in terms of hospitality (coffee, tea, food, and other assorted sundries for auditions and rehearsals) and additional creature comforts (dressing room supplies, lozenges, varieties of juices, mineral waters, and so on). Every producer has different limits, and it is best to be clear at the beginning, so you don't do more or less than they want you to.

Production Staff

The next step is the selection of a production staff. The amount of input you have in the choice of production personnel will vary depending on the type of theater in which you are stage managing. Resident theater companies and a great many community theaters have long-term staffs; the job here is to meet with them and discuss how they function and how it would be best to communicate with them in terms of schedule, notes, and other information.

In any production situation, you must form as positive a team effort as possible. The stage manager is like a catcher on a baseball team, involved in every play, giving the signals, and positioning the players. It is the stage manager's/catcher's responsibility to be sure everyone is working with the same signals and is very clear about the activities of the rest of the team.

In a theater where you are the new person on a team that has been playing together for a long time, be sure you learn their particular ways of working, but don't be afraid to introduce enough of your own methods to take charge. I don't mean that you should arbitrarily demand changes in a theater staff's work methods, but often people have fallen into habits that make no sense, and it is up to you to ease them into new routines that work better or ensure clearer communication for everyone.

For example, I once worked in a Broadway theater where the crew proudly told me they never looked at the callboard. To me, the callboard of a theater is the center of communication. If you post a schedule or notice there, then everyone who works in that theater will see it on the way into work, and everyone begins the day with the same information. More important, the stage manager does not have to explain the day's schedule a hundred different times. I explained this to the crew and showed them a sample schedule that would always indicate when they were involved, and they finally grew to like it. (They also began to notice that, by checking the board, they could find out about free tickets to various shows, including our own.) Other resident staff people have told me, "I only take verbal notes," or "I only take written notes." This usually stems from past communication problems, and it is always best to suggest that perhaps you can improve upon whatever system fouled them up before. For a while, until trust is established, you may want to work with both written notes and a daily talk.

In the commercial theater, the general manager or technical supervisor often hires crew people that he or she has worked with previously. However, your input may be sought when the regular person is not available, and you could have the opportunity to suggest, or even hire, personnel for one or two departments. In any case, it is important to know the functions and duties of each backstage department. Let's look at an average production staff of a Broadway show and what each position entails.

PRODUCTION SUPERVISOR

This position is becoming more and more of a necessity, especially on big, technically complex musicals. Usually this person has functioned previously as a production person in either sets, lights, or props. To be clear here, a "production" staff member is someone who assumes initial responsibility for some aspect of the mounting and creation of a show. He or she works directly for the producer and with the creative personnel. There are also "house" staff members who work for the theater and execute the daily running of a show with those people in the "running crew," hired by the "house" department heads.

Production supervisors take overall responsibility from the outset for the coordination of the technical elements of a show. They help with the budgeting, scheduling, selection of scenic shops for the building of sets and costumes, and rental of sound and light equipment.

It should be noted that, in almost all commercial theater situations, the rental of the theater is on a "four wall" basis. This means literally what it says: You get the four walls, and everything else must be built or rented, delivered, and set up by the production. The production supervisor usually oversees all the elements of the design and construction period and remains on the job until all the technical aspects of the show are running smoothly. Working closely with the production department heads, the production supervisor ultimately leaves it all in their hands.

PRODUCTION CARPENTER

The production carpenter is responsible for everything having to do with the set and scenery for a show, including its rigging, hanging, and movement. He or she is also responsible for the hanging plot, which establishes where everything that must be hung will be flown above the stage—scenery, lights, curtains, special effects. The fly floor, a large grid above the stage from which these technical elements are hung, is usually divided by 6-inch sections, each with a pipe, and the carpenter works out which pipe gets what.

Basically, the production carpenter runs the load-in of a show, deciding in what order the work will be done so that everything keeps moving as swiftly and sanely as possible. The production carpenter may also be involved in the building and use of wagons and winches and will establish the need for a production flyman or winch operator if the complexity of the show demands it.

PRODUCTION ELECTRICIAN

The production electrician is responsible for everything that relates to the lighting of the show. Using the lighting designer's plot, this person prepares the rental order in the lighting shop, making sure all the instruments are to the designer's specifications and in good working order. He or she cuts all the color gels for the lights, checks that the theater's power supply is sufficient for the show's requirements, and orders any necessary lighting board equipment or ensures that the one in the theater is adequate and functioning.

The electrician also oversees the installation and wiring of the sound equipment and usually is the one to hire a production sound person to whom the electrician delegates responsibilities for this area. The production electrician must coordinate the hanging of the lights with the carpenter and supervise the internal wiring of any set pieces or installation of outlets for practical lamps and appliances.

On a musical, there will often be a production followspot operator who may also function as an assistant to the electrician. The followspot operator is usually chosen by the master electrician.

PRODUCTION SOUND SUPERVISOR

The production sound person, often hired by the electrician, supervises the preparation and installation of all sound equipment. The stage manager must work closely with the sound person on the ordering and installation of the internal communication systems and headsets, all of which will be discussed later. On a show that requires lots of sound effects, music, or other aural elements, there usually will be a sound designer. The production sound supervisor's relationship to the sound designer is analogous to the relationship between the production electrician and the lighting designer: They are responsible for the technical execution of the design.

PRODUCTION PROPERTY MASTER

This staff member works closely with the set designer on the location and procurement of all furniture for the show and with the director and stage managers on the hand props used by the actors. If there are special props that must be built, he or she will coordinate this with a shop and supervise its work. Props also include rugs, curtains, and upholstery, as well as all food and liquid requirements in a show.

WARDROBE AND HAIR SUPERVISORS

The wardrobe supervisor coordinates all maintenance and changing of costumes in the theater. The designer and the costume shop construct, or "build," the costumes; the wardrobe supervisor oversees their use. Often in a regional or resident theater these two functions will overlap more, and the wardrobe supervisor will manage the construction or rental and the running of costumes during the show. The supervisor establishes the need for dressers and hires them for each production. Here is another valuable use of your initial analysis. You can draw from it a preliminary quick-change plot that will help establish the need for dressers. The dressers will assist actors getting in and out of costume and coordinate the cleaning and washing of the wardrobe.

The hair supervisor functions much as the wardrobe person does. He or she hires those hairdressers needed for the preparation and running of the show.

CASTING THE CREW

Having done as thorough a production analysis as possible, you as the stage manager should be in a good position to help ascertain the desired number of crew in each department. Further, if possible, discuss with the department heads the particular needs and style of each show and how that might affect the choice of various production personnel.

Try to "cast" a crew a little bit. The work will go far more smoothly, and the end result will be more successful. Hire people whenever possible who have track records in the type of production you are staffing. For musicals, try to hire people who have experience with musicals or big-cast shows; for dramas with small casts, try to employ staff who are used to the detail and closer personal contacts of an intimate show. Pay attention to teams of people who have worked well and harmoniously together in the past; it helps under pressure. Sir Peter Hall once told me that the experience of mounting *The Merchant of Venice* in New York was one of his happiest ever. This resulted from the positive "can do" attitude of the crew, who, because of the ease of communication and a shared respect and understanding of responsibility garnered from working together in the past, allowed no problems to get out of hand.

Assistant Stage Managers

Every cliché in the world holds true when discussing assistant stage managers (ASM's). Your success will be greatly affected by your choice of assistant and your ability to effectively delegate responsibilities. Sometimes the choice is yours, and sometimes it is made for you. When discussing your job requirements with a prospective employer, one of your strongest requests should be choosing your own assistant. In some instances, your assistant will also head up or be part of the running crew, another reason you want someone whose diligence, tact, and reliability are unquestioned.

Now, let's look at the need for assistant stage managers. There should always be one assistant, and most of the time, on a musical or large-cast dramatic play, you must have two. If you look back over the analysis you made charting the entrances and exits of cast, scenery, and props, you will begin to get an idea of how many assistants are necessary. Ideally, every entrance, exit, and scene shift should have an ASM present, both to cue and help execute the change, as well as to alert you if there are any problems in terms of running the show: an actor missing for an entrance whom you will have to page, a piece of scenery that must be moved or adjusted necessitating a longer blackout, and so on. Your assistants are additional eyes and ears, and without them you are flying blind when calling a show.

Sometimes on a simple play, it is possible for a stage manager who is calling the show from the wings to also run and check his or her side of the stage, but it is better not to have to do this. One reason that this is not a good idea is that it eliminates the possibility of the stage manager occasionally watching the show from the front (a necessity that is discussed in detail in chapter 9). Many newly designed theaters have booths from which the show can be cued and watched, but watching and trying to maintain a show directorially over a long run from the wings is impossible. So it is almost always necessary on a long-running show to have at least two assistants. Sometimes you open a show with one assistant and then add either a combination understudy/ASM after the opening or hire an additional outside ASM once the show is established, so the PSM can go out front to watch.

In allocating responsibilities, discuss with your assistants which areas they feel most comfortable with. Some ASM's may feel more confident about technical matters than they do about artistic ones; others may love working with the director and actors but feel intimidated by the technical side. Your rehearsal and technical period will function best if your assistants are confident and happy with their assigned tasks.

I try to divide the responsibilities into general areas, so that one assistant is handling all "actor-oriented" jobs, such as recording blocking, cueing lines, taking all costume and prop notes and routing them through me, and assisting me in the creation and communication of the daily schedule. If I have two assistants, I will ask the other to focus on the more technical functions. This assistant should watch for changes and developments that will affect anything in the areas of set, lights, and sound and help me establish the proper cueing and scheduling of technical work and rehearsals.

From the outset of rehearsals, I assign initial responsibility for one side of the stage to each assistant so that, as the production process unfolds, they both learn what will be the offstage and technical requirements of their sides during the actual running of the show. Some other responsibilities that need to be divided depending on the number of assistants and the complexity of the show are the following:

- Care and feeding of cast—providing and replenishing coffee supplies and food
- First aid—keeping the kit stocked and remaining aware of actors' needs
- The maintenance of the script—tracking changes and rewrites, and dispersing same (more on this later)
- Security—supervising the storage of actors' valuables (wallets, jewelry, watches) and keys to dressing rooms
- Scheduling—typing and communicating rehearsal and fitting schedules

On a computer, the rehearsal schedule can be started in the morning and added and changed during the day as needs evolve. Ideally, it is approved, printed, and posted by the end of the day. The completed schedule should then be emailed to everyone involved in the production.

The more clearly you define each assistant stage manager's area of responsibility, the smoother the production will run. Remember, however, that in delegating areas of responsibility on a show, the stage manager does not relinquish full authority for them. It is important to work with your assistants constantly, checking on their progress, and sharing observations in every area.

There are other advantages to having ASM's. Because assistants will provide the production stage manager with better information, it will be easier to foresee and stave off potential problems. Furthermore, if much of the detail work is being handled by assistants, it allows the PSM to have more time with the director and other creators and thereby better understand and appreciate their needs.

As with every member of the production team, it is vital to keep communication open, easy, and honest. No one on the stage management staff should feel paranoid about making a mistake, asking questions, voicing an opinion, or making an observation. The more the stage managers are keeping up with each other, the better the whole process will flow.

Production Meetings

From the moment you are hired to stage manage a show, you should be pushing the major creative contributors to get together at the earliest possible time for a production meeting. Smaller design and casting conferences can continue, but until you bring together everyone involved in the creation of a show, many questions remain unanswered. Time is wasted because many people wait until this meeting to really begin thinking about and focusing on the problems of a particular project. The initial full production meeting becomes a "reality check" for everyone, the point at which collectively everyone says, "I'd better get to work, because this looks like it may really happen."

A good stage manager functions as a combination of host and master of ceremonies at these meetings, always referring back to that valuable first production analysis to make sure that everything that needs to be addressed is properly discussed. Let's look at a list of who should be at the meeting:

1. *The Director.* Check his or her schedule first. Once you know the director's available dates, you have a starting point from which to schedule as many other people as possible.
2. *The Producer(s).* Often, however, they will just meet and greet everyone at the outset of the meeting and then leave, knowing the stage managers and general manager will fill them in on the details discussed.
3. *The General Manager,* or someone with full budget knowledge and authority. The presence of this person is vital lest much time be wasted coming up with design solutions and/or casting schemes that are well outside the realm of fiscal possibility.
4. *The Playwright (play) or Librettist, Lyricist, and Composer (musical).* Often in these meetings a difficult technical transition can be solved by the writer adding or amending certain material. Sometimes this individual or team must be present to answer casting or costume questions.
5. *Designers.* Every design decision affects each designer. For example, the colors of costumes, sets, and lights are all interdependent. Often designers work with assistants on a show; it is important to include those assistants, too, if possible.
6. *Production Heads.* The production supervisor, if there is one, and all the individual department heads should be there. Frequently, this is the only time the production staff gets to hear the creative ideas behind the project and to meet some of these people before the show is in the theater.
7. *Casting Staff.* These people need to have input from the creative team in order to make a realistic appraisal of casting needs, understand the creators' expectations, and determine their own staff's ability to find performers willing and able to do certain roles and/or understudy.

This is a basic list, and it will expand or contract depending on the circumstances of the show that you are stage managing. (Shakespeare no longer attends production meetings, for instance.)

PREPARING FOR THE PRODUCTION MEETING

As you prepare your "guest list" and contact those on it, be sure to record the vital contact information—everybody's name (correctly spelled), address, and phone number—that everyone will need at the meeting. This information will form the basis for a contact sheet—the single most important tool that stage managers prepare. Its maintenance is essential to a production's successful communication. Accuracy and thoroughness are paramount here. The first contact sheet should include everyone attending the production meeting and list their job titles or descriptions and any other pertinent names and numbers, such as secondary offices, the scenery and lighting shops, as well as any known cast members.

The stage manager must also prepare a preliminary production schedule that includes days during the preproduction period when people are and aren't available for meetings, conferences, or casting. Frequently, designers and directors are working on other projects, so it is crucial that the stage manager take responsibility for gathering this information.

Once a date is set, everything will begin to fall into place. One week before the meeting, send out a reminder to everyone; this will also serve as a check on the accuracy of your contact sheet. A day or two before the meeting, telephone everyone to confirm their attendance, again working from your contact sheet to be assured of its accuracy.

Heading into the meeting, it is important to talk to the director and prepare an agenda with him or her, as it will be useless to try to discuss topics that the director doesn't want to approach at this point. Be sure you also agree on the formality of the meeting: Does the director want to run it or have you handle it? Write up an agenda, and go over it carefully with the director and the producer/general manager to make sure it includes everything they want discussed. Figure 2-2 is an example of an agenda for a meeting. Check Appendix 2 for a sample of a production schedule that I've handed out at production meetings. It is essential that you date everything you hand out, especially schedules and script pages, so that people can readily know whether they have the most current versions.

In creating the agenda for the meeting you should draw heavily from your production analysis as well as from any notes taken during your meetings with the director or designers. Every department and designer should have a place on the agenda. This will also help keep the meeting moving, because all those attending will see that they will have time to offer their input and ask questions and therefore won't be trying to get a word in before they are scheduled to speak.

The temptation at these meetings is to move too quickly due to the time pressures of everyone present. The stage manager must gently try to keep everyone focused on the agenda and avoid endless stories and bad jokes that sometimes flow if people are avoiding facing the problems that exist. The stage manager should structure the agenda so that everyone necessary for any particular element of the production is present at the time it is brought up. Some people may have to come late or leave early, so make sure their departments, and any others that will affect their work, are discussed while they are present.

It is helpful to start the meeting with introductions and a quick look at the preliminary schedule and then have the director make his or her remarks before getting into the specifics of the meeting. I try to alternate the agenda so that somewhat routine matters are interspersed with the more complicated areas of discussion so that people don't get burnt out too soon. If possible, schedule a break before the most complicated or tense matter on the agenda so that people have a chance to meet privately before launching into messy waters. You may know, for instance, that the director and set designer want to radically alter the look of the show and need approval and support; give them a chance to talk to each other or to other people involved before formally presenting the ideas at the table.

Casting is an area that will involve fewer of the people present, like the crew and some of the designers, so schedule those discussions before or after the bulk of the meeting. Keep careful notes or minutes detailing what is said, with exact quotes when possible, so that agreements, desires, and finalized decisions can be acted upon. It is a good idea to draw up these notes as soon as possible after the meeting and get copies

ACCOMPLICE PRODUCTION MEETING   FRIDAY, MARCH 9

AGENDA

I.   INTRODUCTIONS AND OPENING REMARKS:
     Rupert Holmes and Art Wolff

II. THE SET
     1. Progress report and any questions on construction/Roy
        Sears
     2. The Trap/All effects rigging and requirements
     3. Foot bath/Look, style, and effects coordination with
        lights, trap operator for electrocution effects 1, 2, and 3
        including sound
     4. The Wheel/Operation and use: How controlled on and off the
        stage; actor and operator coordination, etc.
     5. Fireplace/Practical? Revolve/How does it operate? Can
        actor just push, is it crew operated?
     6. The Chair/Discuss fully its use, operation, and safety;
        any provision for him getting stuck up there?
     7. Discuss AEA involvement and report to them in advance on
        all effects, flying, smoke, and knives, etc.
     8. Discuss all rain and coordination with costumes, etc. Will
        rain effect give enough sound or must it be enhanced?
     9. Rundown on load-in and coordination with the Luncheon, etc.

III. SPECIAL EFFECTS
     1. General progress and concept update/Greg Meeh
     2. Discuss each major effect (Foot bath, Umbrella fry, and
        "The Big Wow") and their relationship to all other
        departments—sets, props, costumes, sound, and lights
     3. Other effects: All blood problems and knives coordinated
        with props, costumes, etc. Include "Jacob's Ladder" lamp
        effect

IV. COSTUMES
     1. Progress report/Alvin Colt
     2. Discuss all blood problems and special rigging for effects
     3. Discuss understudies, also Hair and Makeup
     4. Quick-change booth necessities

FIGURE 2-2 *Sample Production Meeting Agenda*

ACCOMPLICE PROD. MTG. 3/9/90   2.
―――――――――――――――――――――

V.   LIGHTS
     1. General progress report/John Monaco
     2. All coordination with effects, also rain, lightning, and
        sink
     3. Board and racks location, Q lites, practicals, and
        coordination and schedule of load-in, etc.

VI. SOUND
     1. Discuss effects (thunder, electrocutions, etc.)
     2. All music discuss with Rupert
     3. Discuss operation and effect of onstage tape recorder and
        the cues played on it; schedule recording session
     4. Communication systems and console location

VII. GENERAL AND MISC.
     1. Everyone reminded of confidential aspect of keeping
        script's surprises a surprise/Rupert and Art
     2. Go over schedule/All invited to 890 Broadway on Thurs. 3/15
        at 4:30 to "meet and greet" cast
     3. Run-thrus, discuss concept of cast on stage Sat. March 31
        without "tech"
     4. Discussion of all program and front of house coordination
        with Gel Gatto, etc.
     5. Questions or additional information

NOTES:

to the principal people attending. Appendix 3 contains some examples of post-meeting notes that illustrate what I mean.

Basically, if a production meeting can answer more questions than it raises, and everyone emerges feeling a basic surge of positive energy, it is a success. Most often, it is the stage manager's diligence and thoroughness of preparation that will have been prime contributors to that success.

The Audition Process

Stage managers should be involved as much as possible in the casting and audition process. By listening to the discussions between the casting agent and the director, you will gain important insights into the show. By watching the director's reactions to various actors' auditions and interpretations, you will get a sense of his or her tastes and working style.

The primary function of a stage manager during auditions is to prepare the space, making sure the room for the audition is well lighted and that there is a place for the auditioners to wait and prepare or freshen up. The stage manager should also maintain accurate lists for the director if there are appointments and make signs and/or notices that will help people find the entrance to the room, studio, or theater.

Remember that this is a time when everyone involved is nervous and on edge—the creators are anxious that they might not find what they are looking for, and the performers are often tense about their auditions. It is helpful to maintain a formal but calm air in your handling of both groups. If you can, provide as much information as possible for the auditioners. Perhaps print up a sheet that includes the production's title, dates, creative staff, and—most important to auditioners—whom they will be meeting or performing for that day. Make sure you or your assistant checks each auditioner for name and contact number, and collect a picture and resume from every actor who hasn't submitted one previously.

Keep an accurate list of who is seen and in what order. Work closely with the casting director, if one is working on your production, checking for any changes on the audition schedule. If you are running an open call, keep an accurate list and schedule, collecting all information from the auditioners when they arrive and giving them an idea of how long it will be before they are seen based on whatever time span you have arranged with the director (usually two to five minutes for each performer).

Throughout the audition process, whether it is at the highest level of agent submissions and appointments or a large group call, the stage manger can do much to help humanize and ease tensions. Have water and tissues handy. Treat people as courteously as possible, and try to avoid condescension when answering their questions. Try to introduce each person individually whenever possible, after having checked the pronunciation of their name. Double-check that they are ready; sometimes that one extra breath or straightening of clothing is necessary to give them the confidence to go out and put themselves on the line.

If actors are reading from the script, be sure they are absolutely clear about what section is to be read. Sometimes the stage manager is called upon to read with the actor. If this is the case, always stand or sit to one side of the stage and face away from the director, thereby keeping the focus on the actor. Try to avoid any excessive acting; remember that it is the other person's audition. However, it is helpful to give some character to the reading so that at least it makes sense. Make an effort to stay in the tone or style of the piece. Listen to the directions and comments the director makes to each auditioner so that you can help people prepare as the day goes on. Two frequently asked questions at auditions are: Does the director want to hear an accent? Should the actor play older or younger if indicated?

Also indicate on the stage with tape where the actor should stand for the best light and acoustics. The audition process will be the first contact you have with the future cast of your show, so let the performers see from the outset that stage management is well organized, supportive, and aware of their needs.

DANCE AUDITIONS

On a musical, there will often be large chorus dance auditions. These take a great deal of organization to avoid chaos. It will be necessary to sign up a large number of dancers, and the best way is to have stacks of numbered cards in two different colors (one for men and one for women) and have them filled out and returned by the dancers after they arrive. The cards should contain names, phone numbers, height, weight, hair color, and not much else; initially they are a tool for you and the choreographer to organize large groups of dancers.

The next step will usually be for groups of twenty or thirty dancers to go into the audition space and learn a dance number with the choreographer. You can call for numbers one to twenty or thirty, based on their card numbers, collect their cards as they enter, and divide the cards into groups of six to ten each, depending on the wishes of the choreographer. After teaching the combination or dance to a large group, the choreographer may dismiss some people and then start auditioning the smaller groups. At this point it is valuable to have the groups line up so that you may line up their cards in the same sequence in front of the choreographer. He or she can then address them by name, work with the group, and hand you the card or cards of those he or she wants to keep for further auditioning.

This screening process will go on until all the smaller groups have been seen, then those who have been asked to remain will return to learn what is usually a more extensive combination or dance number and perhaps to be seen individually as well. Again, you should organize the cards and the dancers so that the choreographer always knows who is auditioning in front of him or her. This may also be the time to hear the auditioners sing, and sometimes men will be called back to be paired with different women and vice versa.

It is vital that the cards and lists be kept accurately so at the end the choices and their identification and notification match up. It is terrible to tell someone they are chosen and then have the choreographer tell you he or she meant the one in the yellow shirt, not the red. Work as quickly as you can, but don't lose track of who's who. It is also vital to have assistants and be clear with them and the choreographer about exactly how the call is to be organized.

The Production Schedule

The single most important preproduction responsibility of a stage manager is the preparation of the production schedule. A veteran Broadway general manager and producer, Roy A. Somlyo, once told me that the test of a good production schedule was whether he could ascertain on a daily basis whether we were behind or ahead in every area and department. Therefore it is important to include deadlines, delivery dates, and completion dates for everything involved in the production. By the time production meetings are completed and the work is progressing, the stage manager should have assembled enough information to accurately assess the time needed in the theater for the technical preparation of the show prior to the addition of performers (load-in, hang and focus time) and the directorial and technical requirements in terms of time needed with the actors (technical and dress rehearsal time).

In preparing a schedule for a professional theater, the stage manager will have to be aware of the rules of the Actors' Equity Association. In a community or university theater, the stage manager must ascertain the basic time and energy restrictions of the cast and crew.

As the level of production goes higher, the number of unions with varying work rules escalates. On a Broadway musical, the stage manager may be dealing with time requirements of four or five different unions in making a schedule. (I will discuss all this in more detail in the section on technical rehearsals in chapter 7.) To demonstrate the variety of possible production schedules, a sample may be found in Appendix 2.

It is the quality of the preproduction work that will lead to either a smooth, well-run rehearsal and creative period or a chaotic, hair-pulling experience. Every bit of preparation and planning will pay off tenfold once rehearsals start. On a personal level, the stage manager will be much more relaxed and confident if he or she has done a thorough job. Because of the stage manager's knowledge of the script and familiarity with all the creative staff gained through production meetings and discussions, he or she will also be better able to answer questions from people new to the production. Most important, if the preproduction period has been well organized, everyone involved will feel secure with the stage manager, making the job far easier and more rewarding as rehearsals begin.

3

STAGE MANAGERS
AND COMPUTERS

The world of computer use has blossomed during the twenty years since the first edition of this book came out, and the stage manager's need to understand and use a computer is certainly a fact of life today in the preparation of paperwork, script updates, etc.

There are so many computers on the market that I will not attempt to campaign for one make over another. I am a Macintosh person, so much of what I speak of will come from my experience with Claris 4.0, Calendar Maker, and MacDraw. However, all brands of computers and their associated software programs can produce spreadsheets, calendars, and basic forms and organizers that are just as useful as the ones I create on my computer. I will try to generalize the concepts and areas of computer use rather than describe the detailed functioning within a particular program. A laptop of any kind is very valuable because you can place it next to you at rehearsals or meetings and make immediate entries about prop list and preset changes, rehearsal schedules, line notes for actors, etc. At the end of the day, much of what previously had to be transcribed from written notes on yellow pads into more readable form via typewriter can just be looked over and expanded or corrected, where necessary, then printed and circulated to others.

One useful tool on computers for stage managers is the differences in font size and style they allow. First, find a font (i.e., a print style) that reflects the character of your production, and always use it for the title on all paperwork, schedules, sign-in sheets, etc. connected with the production. This will help give your show instant recognizability on a callboard or in a mailbox so people will not have to wade through various shows and reports to find your information. Being able to use differing sizes and bold or italic print also allows a stage manager to emphasize certain kinds of information. When I am doing updates of notes, cue sheets, prop lists, and presets, I always italicize and make bold all new information so it stands out. This avoids the "Where's Waldo?" of people receiving notes or changes but having to compare them to the last set before being able to figure out why you have sent the memo.

Dates are vital, and almost any computer will page and date all your work if you tell it to. So you should set that up first, and then you never have to think about it again.

In addition, all computers come with word-processing programs and have spreadsheet functions that are an invaluable tool for stage managers. With the ability to set up forms of differing column widths and row heights and assigning titles to the columns or rows, almost every piece of stage manager's paperwork can be done in spreadsheet form. Figures 3-1 and 3-2 show two examples of spreadsheets produced by Claris 4.0, but their style and content could just as well be produced by any other spreadsheet program.

Figure 3-1 is a FLY Q sheet. Note the use of "logo" type font for the title, the "tall" orientation of the page, the various sizes of columns and rows, and the dating of the sheet's printing. As the tech rehearsals for this show had not yet been held, note that cue numbers were left unused so they would be available when moves were added during those rehearsals.

A basic sound plot like the one shown in Figure 3-2 can evolve as it develops into the final cue sheet. The illustration is a good example of the way well-organized plot and cue sheets done in this format can include a lot of information in a compact, neat, and very useful fashion.

Most computer programs also have a basic drawing program that will allow stage managers to create simple versions of their floor plans for use in blocking and/or marking presets and plotting scene shifts.

Many stage managers now enter their entire scripts into a computer, so they can prepare a prompt and cueing script that allows them to expand and contract the size of the material on the pages as necessary. For instance, if two or three pages of dialogue are going to go by with no cueing, the material on them can be entered in a smaller font. With its tight margins and/or small amounts of space at the ends of scenes or acts where the stage manager may have huge amounts of cueing and set change notes to enter, the full printed script may be cumbersome at times. When the cueing is fast and furious, the script material can be printed in a larger font and arranged so that the cueing or blocking is allowed more space than on the

All in the Timing FLY Q SHEETS   p___of___

	A	B	C	D	E
1	TRANSITION	LINESET #	FLYING PIECE	SPEED	ACTION
	PRESHOW	#1	DROP BOX	* *	LOADED
		#9	PHILLY COAT		COAT ON WIRE
		#11	PAYPHONE		HIGH SPIKE
		#12	BRICKWALL		" "
		#17	CALENDAR		
		#21	SWING		
		#23	NUMBERS		
2		#28	DOOR		
	Into TROTSKY	#28	DOOR/WINDOW/MIRROR	FAST	Down to Low Floor
3		#17	CALENDAR	FAST	Down to Low Spike
4					
	End TROTSKY/Into	#12	BRICKWALL	MEDIUM	Down to Floor
5	PHILLY	#11	PAYPHONE	MEDIUM	Down to Low Spike
6					
7	During PHILLY	#9	Mark's JACKET	FAST	Flys up and Out
8					
9	During PHILLY	#11	PAYPHONE	FAST	Up to High Spike
10					
	End of PHILLY/Into	#23	SWING	MEDIUM	Down to Low Spike
	WORDS, WORDS,	#3	DROPBOX	FAST	Open
	WORDS	#12	BRICKWALL	MEDIUM	Up to High Spike
		#28	DOOR	MEDIUM	Up to High Spike
11		#17	CALENDAR	FAST	Up to High Spike
12					
	INTERMISSION	#23	SWING	----	Up to High Spike & tied off
13					w/slack in the line
14					
	Out of INTER/Into	#21	NUMBERS CORNICE	MEDIUM	Down to Low Spike
15	UNIVERSAL				
16					
	End UNIVERSAL/Into	#21	NUMBERS CORNICE	MEDIUM	Up to High Spike
17	PHILIP GLASS				
18					
	During PHILIP GLASS	#12	BRICKWALL	MEDIUM	
		#21	NUMBERS	MEDIUM	ALL 3 PIECES FLOWN OUT
19		#28	DOOR	MEDIUM	TOGETHER
20					
21					
22	TRANSITION	LINESET #	FLYING PIECE	SPEED	ACTION
	During PHILIP GLASS	#11	PAYPHONE	MEDIUM	OUT First
		#23	SWING	MEDIUM	OUT Second
23		#17	CALENDAR	MEDIUM	OUT Third
	End PHILIP GLASS	#8	"NO CHANGE" SIGN	FAST	Down to Low Spike
24					
	Into SURE THING	#8	"NO CHANGE" SIGN	MEDIUM	OUT
25		#32	BLACK SCRIM	MED/SLO	Down to Floor
26					

subject to change   mark piotrowski/sm   10/2/96

FIGURE 3-1 *Sample Computer-Generated FLY Q Sheet* (Form Generated on Computer by Mark Piotrowski, 1998 MFA Graduate, Rutgers University)

All in the Timing   Master Sound Plot

	A TRANSITION	B PAGE	C SOUND	D DIRECTION	E DURATION	F SOURCE	G NOTES
2	Preshow	- - - -	"Einstein on the Beach" music	Full	approx 35min.	Recorded	
3	Into TROTSKY	89	Russian music x/fd to mariachi music	Full	approx 2min.	Recorded	
4	Top of TROTSKY	89	Tubular Bell	Full	- - -	Recorded	Begins scene
5	In TROTSKY	90	Tubular Bell (chromatic)	Full	- - -	Recorded	End of Variation 1
6	In TROTSKY	92	Tubular Bell (chromatic)	Full	- - -	Recorded	End of Variation 2
7	In TROTSKY	92	Tubular Bell (chromatic)	Full	- - -	Recorded	End of Variation 3
8	In TROTSKY	93	Tubular Bell (chromatic)	Full	- - -	Recorded	End of variation 4
9	In TROTSKY	94	Tubular Bell (chromatic)	Full	- - -	Recorded	End of Variation 5
10	In TROTSKY	95	Tubular Bell (chromatic)	Full	- - -	Recorded	End of Variation 6
11	In TROTSKY	95	Tubular Bell (chromatic)	Full	- - -	Recorded	End of Variation 7
12			NOTE: There are 8 (eight) bells total. I lied when I said there were 9!!!!				
13	Into PHILLY	75	Restaurant muzak	Full	approx 12min.	Recorded	Underscores entire scene
14	Into WORDS	27	Jungle sounds x/fd into office sounds	Full	approx 3min.	Recorded	
15							
16	INTERMISSION	34	Music	Full	approx 20min.	Recorded	
17							
18	Into UNIVERSAL	41	Instrumental Christmas music	Full	approx 3min.	Recorded	
19	Into GLASS	61	Glass-type music (Being recorded by Mike Smith & will have to you ASAP)	Full			Per our conversation, go ahead & put a pre-recorded piece of music on the master tape as back-up
20	In GLASS	61	Bell	Full	approx 4 min.	Recorded	
21	In GLASS	70	Bell	Full	- -	Recorded??	
22	End of GLASS	70	same as #19 above	Full	- -	Recorded??	
23	Into SURE THING	13	Busy restaurant sounds	Full	approx 4min.	Recorded	Ends the scene
24	In SURE THING	thru-out	Bells - 44 in the entire scene	Full	approx 21min.	Live	Underscores entire scene
25	Curtain Call/Outro		Upbeat section of "Einstein on Beach"	Full	approx 10min.	Recorded	From microphone SR

subject to change   mark piotrowski/sm   10/3/96

FIGURE 3-2 *Sample Computer-Generated Sound Plot* (Form Generated on Computer by Mark Piotrowski, 1998 MFA Graduate, Rutgers University)

full printed script. Remember when doing this, though, that it is vital to number your pages the same way they are numbered in the printed script that everyone else is using, so you can turn to the correct pages as requested to start or find blocking or cueing. One page in the original printed script may end up being three or four pages in yours, or you may condense two or three pages into one, so mark them in the top right-hand corners either as pp. 6a, 6b, 6c, 6d, etc., or pp. 3, 4, 5, depending on whether you have enlarged or condensed the material.

Having your own "personalized" script will also make changes in cueing or dialogue easier to keep track of neatly, because you can always "save" the original p. 5, for instance, and then "save as" the new p. 5 and make your changes without all the hassles of erasing, printing out new pages, etc. You will also always have the original pages to answer the inevitable queries, "What did we use to do—or say—or have lit—here?"

Computers have taken a lot of the tedium out of stage management paperwork by making it simpler. But the truth is still that (a) *the paperwork must still be done*, and (b) *it must be accurate*. It is all too easy for stage managers today to look really organized and complete in their paperwork, but when you go to apply it or investigate its content, you find out it is bogus. Computers should make it easier to keep up-to-date with all preset and cueing sheets, schedules, etc. The danger is that the stage manager can start rushing things to get a particular form or sheet completed and give out false or misleading information. One of the best ways to avoid this problem is to include in the paperwork large italicized TBD ("to be decided") or DTC ("decision to come") or TBA ("to be announced") notes wherever decisions have yet to be made. These will draw everyone's attention to the decisions that are needed and help prod those responsible for making them to do so, as well as give the stage manager a quick checklist of what needs to be updated and what requires more information every time he or she goes to the paperwork.

Do not leave out any reference to valuable information on your paperwork because you do not have the specifics yet, but *do not guess* or surmise what the information might be, either. It does no good at a production meeting to have to answer the request for a date or piece of information with, "Well, I don't know yet." Your inclusion of the item as an issue to be decided with the designation TBD, DTC, or TBA lets everyone know that you are aware of the need for an answer—you haven't forgotten or overlooked the necessity for the piece of information; you just don't have it yet. The first day of tech, the start of rehearsals, the first public performance of a production—for a myriad of reasons—all are points in a production schedule that favor late decisions. But there is no reason for you not to turn out your paperwork with all the decisions that must be made accounted for in an accurate way.

Communication of information is such a huge part of the stage manager's job, and the computer is an advanced tool for fulfilling that responsibility, but a computer cannot think for you or ferret out the hidden problems in a schedule or determine the use of a prop or piece of scenery. That is the stage manager's responsibility; let the computer help you to clearly and accurately dispense information, but never lose sight of the fact that you are the gatherer of that information and the controller of who gets it and when.

There are many uses of computers still evolving that will affect stage management, like email, the use of modems to fax your producer's office directly with reports and schedules, truck-loading programs that will take your scenery load in shapes and sizes and suggest the perfect way to load it. But *you* will have to decide what goes into your email messages and what to fax. *You* will have to add the variable of deciding when you want the scenery to come off the truck at the next stop!

Hopefully, computers will never replace the need for stage managers, and the advance of technology will not eliminate the incredible need for personal attention to detail or looking after the emotional and physical well-being of the performing and creative artists stage managers serve. Hopefully they will only enhance our ability to give those areas more attention by eliminating the mundane aspects of our job and allowing us fresher spirits to deal with the personal and creative sides of theater production—not to mention the associated values of a shorter workday!

THE FIRST REHEARSAL

As the preproduction process continues, the stage manager gets closer and closer to what should be regarded as his or her opening night: the first rehearsal. It is vital to the stage manager and the production's success that everything goes as smoothly and peacefully as possible on the first day. The tone for the production will be set, and the actors' willingness to trust the stage manager to look after all necessary details will be established at the first rehearsal.

The Rehearsal Space

Long before the actual day arrives, the stage manager should try to get into the rehearsal space (room, hall, theater) and familiarize him- or herself with the facility. Here is a partial list of items to check:

1. The location and accessibility of the men's and women's rooms.
2. The availability of drinking water (perhaps a cooler will have to be provided).
3. The adequacy of the room's furniture. Are there enough tables and chairs?
4. The entryway or lobby area. Is there a place for hanging coats, etc.?
5. The availability of dressing or changing rooms.
6. The adequacy of the lighting: bright enough, too bright, etc.?
7. The condition of the walls. If there are enough mirrors for dance rehearsals, they must often be covered for a nonmusical play. This is most easily accomplished with rolls of brown packaging paper and masking tape.
8. The condition of the floor. Decide whether you will be able to use tape to mark out the set. Make sure it meets the requirements for a dance floor if necessary.

9. The size of the room. Make sure it is large enough for the set to be marked out on the floor, while leaving space for the director to sit a few feet away and for the actors to make entrances and exits. Ideally a rehearsal space should be 10 feet bigger in each direction than your set; i.e., if the set extremities are 40 x 30 feet, you need a space 50 x 40 feet. Sometimes it is possible to cheat on the depth or width if the set's playing area is less than its actual dimensions. For instance, if there is a porch that people will be seen crossing before entering an upstage front door, there is no need to mark out the veranda on the floor. However, it is vital to give the director some room to get perspective in front of the set.

10. The access to and availability of the space. Find out what time it opens and whether you will be allowed in early to set up. Don't schedule a rehearsal to begin the minute the place opens; always allow at least a half hour between the opening time and the first call to get set up and organized.

11. The size of the access to the space. Make sure there is a loading dock or freight elevator if you need to get large furniture or rehearsal set pieces into the space. Try to figure out what hours and manpower expense this may involve.

12. The adequacy of heat or air-conditioning and how it is controlled.

13. Telephone availability. In today's world, almost every performer carries a cell phone; payphones, with their limited availability and other hassles, are a thing of the past. However, a land line with a couple of extensions should be available to stage managers and others in the office production and management staff at both rehearsal and performance locations. A fax machine is important when rehearsing for the transfer of drawings and all other material difficult to email. The production should have a computer and printer; and the office should be either set up for high-speed wireless Internet or at least have a hardwired hookup so that the daily dispersal of schedules, reports, script pages, costume-fitting needs, public relations requests, etc. to a set email distribution list can be easy and quick. A very good idea is a website for the posting of important news, schedules, etc. so that everyone can check the latest information on their own home computers. Another excellent tool is the "rehearsal hotline." This is a

dedicated line with voicemail onto which the stage manager puts the schedule and any pertinent notes at rehearsal's end every day. Then everyone from producer on down can check when various scenes are run, and when various actors will be in rehearsal or fittings, without having to track down a printed schedule or call the stage manager.

14. The availability of copying equipment. Copying is a daily and ongoing need in rehearsal and production. When in a rehearsal studio, there will usually be large-capacity copy machines, and the studio will provide you with a card or a code to charge you for their use. It is important to discuss in advance when and how script changes will be handled. If there are going to be massive rewrites, be sure the stage management does not end up with the responsibility unless you can have an added person brought on as a production secretary/PA to handle all the copying, writing, and distribution responsibilities.

Try to keep the main access door behind and to the side of the director's vision to avoid distraction. If you can, have the director or choreographer meet you at the space to see it and decide exactly how they want the room set up.

After the rehearsal room has been chosen and you have familiarized yourself with it, you can begin gathering the materials and information you will need to start using it. Once, while working at Lincoln Center's Vivian Beaumont Theater, the stage managers decided to tailor the space to the specific project we were rehearsing. The play was *In the Matter of J. Robert Oppenheimer*, a dramatic recreation of the trial of atomic bomb inventor Oppenheimer on grounds of treason and being a possible Communist sympathizer. As the stage managers, we immersed ourselves in the idea of "living history" theater as discussed with us by Gordon Davidson, the play's director. Because the play's subject was thick with paranoia and suspicion, we decided to make the atmosphere of the rehearsal environment as close to that of the actual hearing as possible. We made the waiting/lounge area cold and sterile and covered the walls with pictures and posters of the period. The waiting-room table was neatly stacked with *Life* magazines and newspapers of the period, as well as history and pictorial books on the bomb, the Communist threat, and other related topics.

When people arrived for rehearsal, they were treated as witnesses or government experts, as the case warranted, and were formally signed in. They were then directed to wait quietly because "the hearings were in session." Overall, it was a very successful exercise that helped create the necessary atmosphere for discovering the play.

The Ground Plan

With the arrival of the ground plan of the set, the future of the production suddenly becomes more real. Stage managers learn a lot from the ground plan and must refer to it constantly. Basically, the ground plan is like an architect's floor plan, delineating the location and size of all walls, doors, windows, stairs, steps, and the other necessary structural details of the set. It is usually drawn in half-inch scale, which means that every half an inch on the drawing will represent one foot on the stage. For example, a door that measures 2 inches on the ground plan will be 4 feet wide on the stage.

To work on the ground plan and figure out the dimensions of doors, furniture, and offstage space, it is necessary to use a scale rule. This is a triangular-shaped ruler that has different size calibrations on each face and from each end. By laying the side marked ½" (one half inch) on the end alongside the lines on the ground plan, the scale rule will give the number of feet for any dimension, with fractional lines representing inches.

Study the floor plan for the show *Accomplice* (Figure 4-1) for a few minutes. Some of the first elements you should check for would include:

1. *The actual playing dimensions of the set.* For example, on the *Accomplice* ground plan, the kitchen, exterior area, and dining room are all out of the playing area and would not have to be included in the floor marking in the rehearsal hall.
2. *The offstage space.* This will indicate whether there is a crossover, where there will be room for the stage manager, prop tables, quick-change booths, and the like. Notice on the *Accomplice* drawing that

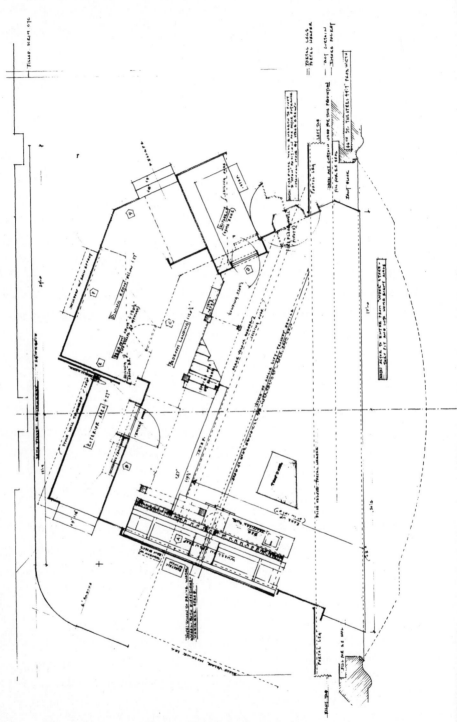

FIGURE 4-1 Accomplice *Ground Plan by David Jenkins*

there is no space between the scrim and back wall, so all crossovers had to be made through the basement.

3. *Furniture location and size.*

4. *Different stage levels.* Notice the indication that there is a "rake" to the stage. A floor that is raked usually is slanted or tilted gradually upward as it goes upstage. This helps audiences see better and is often a standard feature on sets in theaters where the audience sits below the level of the stage, as in most standard proscenium houses. Note the indication 6″ in 10″0″. This means that every ten feet, the stage will become six inches higher, so over twenty feet, an actor standing all the way downstage at the edge of the stage would be one foot lower than an actor standing all the way upstage. Other indications of level changes are shown by the indication of +9″ and +27″. These indicate how many inches from the deck or stage floor each level is, so looking offstage left, we can see there are two 9-inch steps leading to the dining room, which is then 27 inches high.

5. *Location and path of any moving pieces.* In *Accomplice*, there was a moving fireplace downstage left and a trap door stage right. These had to be carefully plotted and laid out in the rehearsal hall so that the placement of furniture and the movement of the actors didn't impede these moving pieces. It is vital that these measurements be accurately plotted in big musicals in which large sections of scenery are tracking on and off and could run over people or other scenic elements. Imagine the wasted time and energy if the director stages a scene or musical number only to find out that he or she has to redo the work because a traveling piece of scenery or a moving wagon wasn't indicated on the rehearsal room floor. The stage manager must carefully mark such paths and be sure to point them out immediately to the director or choreographer in rehearsal. Then, if there is not enough room to stage a large chorus or crowd scene, the stage manager can suggest that the director and designer meet and solve the problem while changes are still relatively easy to make.

6. *Location and size of any rugs, carpets, or other floor coverings.* This is important for actors to know in rehearsal. For instance, a woman

can walk quietly on a carpet in heels but will start to "clack" when she crosses onto wood. This may make a difference in the staging.

7. *Location of all practical lamps that will be turned on and off by the performers.* Also check with the designer on the type (pull chain, switch, button), as this will affect actors' blocking and timing.

8. *Location of the "act curtain" (the curtain that closes to signify the end of each act).* It is always a good idea to mark this on the rehearsal floor, so the director and actors know where they must stand to allow the curtain to fall.

MARKING THE FLOOR

Having thoroughly examined the ground plans, the stage manager should proceed to lay out the floor of the rehearsal room or rooms. This means that the set's outlines must be replicated on the rehearsal room floor. This is one of the most valuable functions a stage manager performs and should be executed with a lot of care and thought. It is helpful to have two assistants and the following:

1. Three 50-foot tape measures and two 25-foot tape measures
2. A ball of string (for making circles if necessary)
3. Three or four rolls of cloth tape, 1 inch wide and in various colors
4. Knee pads (for crawling around on the floor)
5. Scale rule, copy of the ground plans, and pencils
6. A T-square

Frank Hartenstein, the original PSM of *Starlight Express, Into the Woods, The Who's Tommy,* and *The King and I,* among others, taught me a time-saving device that you should make for yourself: a sheet of clear acetate the size of the ground plan, marked with a grid of one-half-inch or one-inch boxes, depending on whatever scale the designer used. By placing this transparent grid over the ground plan you will be able to quickly plot points that would take a good deal longer if you measured every line with a scale rule. Instead, you can simply count boxes. The acetate then serves as a good way to keep the ground plan protected and available during rehearsal in case the director needs to refer to it or make additional measurements.

If the design calls for more than one level or set unit, before plotting or marking any specific points, choose different colors of cloth tape for each. Now place one of your 50-foot tape measures down the middle of the room, so that it extends from what will be downstage to what will be upstage, and secure it firmly: It will serve as the center line of the room or floor plan. Give your director the maximum amount of room by placing the "0" on the tape measure as far as possible from where the director will sit, while making sure there is enough room to lay out the whole usable set in front of him or her. Make sure this line is square and straight, or all your other marks will drift.

Now place another 50-foot tape measure horizontally across the front of the playing area (with the "0" stage right), lining up the 25-foot mark with the "0" on the vertical tape measure or center line that you have already run up and down the stage. Check that it is square and fasten it securely to the floor. Secure another 50-foot tape measure across the floor in the same manner halfway up the center line so that the 25-foot marks on both tapes cross. Your floor should now look like Figure 4-2.

You and your assistants are now ready to lay out the floor. With the ground plan in front of you and either the acetate cover or your scale rule, you can find each point necessary to transpose what is on the paper in front of you to the rehearsal floor. Basically, you are going to create a floor full of dots that, when connected with the cloth-backed marking tape, will render the outline of the set. (Never use packing tape to mark a floor, as it will never come up.)

Your assistants should each have a 25-foot tape measure and rolls of the floor tape in a variety of colors. They can work together or individually to place the marks you call out. Every mark will be taken out from the center line, up from the base line, or up or down from the halfway line, whichever will make the measurement shorter. Typical points for a chair that plays center stage might be, "At four feet, six inches on the center line, go out seven inches stage right, and at five feet, two inches on the center line, go out one foot, three inches stage left." This would pinpoint the two upstage legs of a chair straddling the center line at about five feet from the edge of the stage and facing slightly to stage left. Every set will require different markings, but these are the most important:

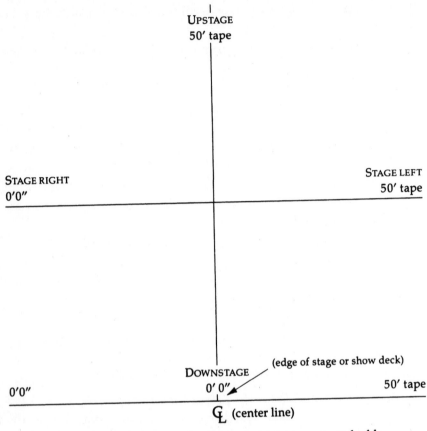

Note: Leave room in front for director, stage manager, and table.

FIGURE 4-2 *Preliminary Rehearsal Floor Layout*

1. The beginning and end of every wall and the point where it joins the next
2. The openings for all doors and windows
3. The upstage legs or edges of every piece of furniture
4. The four corners of any platform, rug, or other floor covering
5. The four corners of any steps, staircase, or riser
6. The four corners of any trap or other opening in the floor

Different levels should be in different colors; so the bedroom in *Accomplice* would be outlined in a different color than the dining room, and the tapes would cross each other. Musicals and multi-set shows require different and more involved techniques but always begin with the same basic concept.

If a play has many unit sets, it may be better to have ground cloths for each set, with the different wall and furniture markings on each one. Then on your basic floor only the upstage corners of each such cloth need to be marked. A ground cloth should be a sturdy material like canvas that won't tear when actors rehearse on it and should lie flat for safety. On the sides of the rehearsal room, in their proper position, the masking wings called portals should be marked. Any drop that will be flown in and out should be indicated by a mark with a piece of tape on the side so that you can point it out to the director or choreographer during staging.

These are some of the basics of laying a floor; every stage manager has different methods and tricks of the trade discovered through trial and error, and every show will have different demands. The floor should end up looking a lot like a big version of the ground plan in terms of shape and relative sizes and dimensions. After the job is complete, it should be possible to walk around the rehearsal room and get a spatial sense of the set's size and feel. Be sure you and your assistants check everything quite carefully before the actors or director get on it, so if a door ends up being six inches wide, you discover your own mistake and correct it.

When doing complicated tasks in the theater, remember the basic rule or axiom: If you don't know, ask. When I was young and relatively new at stage managing, the production manager at the Vivian Beaumont Theater asked me to tape out the floor for rehearsal. He asked me to do it as if I would obviously know how, and being eager to please, I didn't want to disillusion him by telling him I didn't. He gave me an assistant who also took it for granted that I knew what I was doing, and away we went. However, I had never marked a floor before or helped anyone else mark a floor. I didn't even know how to read a scale rule. Basically, I didn't have a clue.

In retrospect, what we produced on that floor was hysterically funny. We "eyeballed" the measurements, making rough estimates of the dimensions and tried to make it look as much like a big version of the floor plan as possible. But we ended up with steps three inches deep and doors less than a foot wide. Finally, we realized this could not be faked. We confessed, got a lesson in laying out a set properly, and started again. The result was far better, and we both learned not only how to lay a floor but how much easier it is to ask how to do something than to waste everyone's time faking it.

Many people starting out make the same mistake. In our desire to appear knowledgeable and on top of the job, we take on tasks that are way over our heads. Today, I have no compunction about asking for help and appreciate when assistants ask me questions instead of plowing into work that I will either have to redo myself or have them do all over again.

Before taking up the tape measures, it is a good idea to mark the center and the front of the stage with a piece of tape in whatever color you used for the ground or deck level of the set, putting small pieces at each foot mark for quick reference later on. If you are doing a musical, the choreographer will probably want each foot in large numbers across the front of the stage for staging purposes. These should be absolutely accurate for spacing purposes in a dance and can be done with tape or stencils bought at most stationery stores. If you have several rooms or are moving a lot with a musical, it is handy to make a roll of canvas with the numbers that you can easily and quickly spread out anywhere. Often, those are the only marks a dance rehearsal will need.

Rehearsal Props

Props are one of the first items that actors will need in rehearsal. The timing of stage business as well as the meaning and memorization of lines is contingent upon their use of props.

The stage manager should create a preliminary prop list, which may be drawn from the original production analysis and any further developments and notes from staff meetings. This prop list should be written up in the preproduction phase so that it can be used in preparations for the first rehearsal. Prop lists may also be kept on a computer. This will greatly facilitate additions and corrections, as well as simple preset changes, and make it possible to keep completely up-to-date at all times.

The first prop list should be as thorough as possible, as this will make it easier to keep up-to-date later on. Set a meeting with your prop master or prop department as early as possible to discuss rehearsal props. Try to cajole, beg, and demand as many of the actual items as possible, since this serves the actors the most. However, there is great reluctance on the part of prop people, designers, and managements to have actors use real props in rehearsal. The reasons are understandable; they feel props will get lost, stolen, misused, broken, or otherwise damaged more easily in rehearsal than in the more directly controlled environment of a theatrical performance. There is also the jaded belief that if you give an actor or director a prop too soon, he or she will get bored with it and change it. I have listened to these arguments often, but the few times I've worked on shows that had real props in rehearsal, none of the arguments seemed to hold water. More often, problems were solved early, and inexpensive, well-thought-out solutions were found that would not have occurred to people while in the heat of a tech week.

Once you have established what actual props are available, the remainder must be duplicated or in some way mocked up as "rehearsal props." Use every bit of ingenuity and care to make these props as much like the real ones in form, style, weight, and function as possible. It is a frustrating waste of time to have a lot of business and action worked out with a rehearsal prop, only to find out the real one is bigger, doesn't open the same way, or doesn't work the way it was supposed to. A good stage manager makes sure that whatever rehearsal props and furniture are used are close in every detail to what will be used onstage. This simplifies everyone's transition during the move to the theater and during technical rehearsals.

The stage manager's greatest allies in getting props early are star performers and directors with clout; they can make demands that would be laughed at by the prop department if made by a stage manager. For Mike Nichols's Lincoln Center production of *Little Foxes*, every prop was in place for the first reading, which is extremely unusual. This allowed the actors to immediately feel the environment of southern elegance and style that is so strongly present in Lillian Hellman's play.

The Actors' Information Packet

As I have emphasized before, the first day of rehearsal is the best opportunity for stage managers to gain the trust and confidence of the cast.

As the cast arrives, you should hand each of them a folder, with his or her name correctly spelled on it, and inside of which is every bit of information that could be helpful to the cast members, as well as all the forms they need to complete. More often than not, they will be greatly impressed by your organization and consideration. Each actor's folder should include, but not be limited to, the following:

1. *The cast list.* This item should detail each actor and the character he or she is playing. It will help the cast get to know one another more comfortably, without the awkwardness of having to ask, "Who's playing the butler?" and so on. This list, if done in the form of Figure 4-3, may then be used for a myriad of other purposes: You can give it to the costume people for size and fitting information; to the press people to check off who has submitted their bios and headshots for the program; and to the stage managers and company manager, who can use it to check off whom they need to collect

ACCOMPLICE

W/E

CAST
in alphabetical order

JASON ALEXANDER								
PAMELA BRULL								
MICHAEL McKEAN								
NATALIA NOGULICH								

UNDERSTUDIES

Note: Each column may be used for a variety of purposes: to check off receipt of materials (bio, W-4, picture); for time of first-call; or as a sign-in sheet, in which case each actor would put his or her initials in the box under appropriate date.

FIGURE 4-3 *Sample Cast List Form*

paperwork from or distribute it to. With a few additional lines, it can also serve as your sign-in and first-call sheet for rehearsals.

2. *A contact sheet with every conceivable number needed.*

3. *Two schedules: one in calendar form and one a more detailed day-to-day plan.* Be as specific and complete as possible. If the director has committed to certain calls, spell them out in detail. Include first run-throughs, deadlines for script memorization, completion of fittings and costume calls, and any other relevant events. Also be very clear about the days when attendance is mandatory. Try to indicate how committed the director is to keeping to the schedule in terms of days the actor is not called initially. Include on every schedule the address and phone number of the rehearsal hall, theater, and production office, as well as your own. Also date all schedules and indicate that they are always subject to change. Sample calendar and linear rehearsal schedules are shown in Appendix 4.

4. *All forms that the actor must fill out, with as much of the information already entered as possible.* If this is an Equity production, Equity insurance cards and membership information sheets must be included, as well as whatever employment forms the company manager might need. Fill in blanks like the producing company's name and address, the date of the first rehearsal, type of contract, etc., not only to save time and endless questions and repetition, but also because it is a nice thing to do for them. Make sure you have many pencils on hand.

5. *Basic information sheet.* This will vary in every situation, but some of the facts it should include are, once again, the stage manager's phone numbers and those of the rehearsal hall and theater, a guide to how to get places: transit information to the rehearsal and theater, any tips on dining and entertainment in the area, any rules you want to formally set about lateness, use of the phone, refrigerators, smoking, and any other information that might be valuable. I stage managed the Broadway production of *The Merchant of Venice*, and because half the cast was from England, we prepared a "visitor's kit" that include subway and bus maps, visitor's brochures, etc. This is also a good idea on tour. The more thorough

you are, the fewer cast members will get lost, and rehearsals and performances won't be messed up by absenteeism and lateness.

6. *A wallet phone card.* Laminate wallet-size cards with the phone numbers of stage managers, theater, rehearsal hall, and production office.

The style and artistic level of these information packets can run the gamut, but there are always folders with two pockets in them on sale at stationery stores that can easily be labeled with everyone's name. Give packets without the specific actor forms to all production personnel, and make sure everyone's is complete and the same. A good test of what to include in the packets is to think of every question you have been asked on the first day of rehearsal or can imagine anyone asking, and see if it can't be answered from the information you hand out. The more times you can say the first day, "It's in your packet," the more you will be able to deal with unforeseen problems, and the higher regard everyone will have for your professionalism and caring.

Preparing the Contact Sheet

Somewhere in the great mysterious tradition of "it's how things are done," the stage manager was given the responsibility of the contact sheet. It probably began when some well-meaning stage manager, frustrated by the out-of-date and inaccurate contact sheets issued from the producer or general manager's office, suggested he or she take it over. Actually, it is practically impossible for anyone else to do it as well as the stage manager, because he or she, as the liaison between the technical, artistic, and management staffs, is the only person who has constant access to most of the people connected with the show and is therefore best equipped to get the latest addresses or telephone number changes, additions, and corrections.

I discussed briefly in the Production Meeting section the basis of the contact sheet. This is a document that should go on computer if at all possible, as it will make changes and updates so much simpler. Everyone has a preferred format, and the stage manager should always check with the producing office to see if the staff there have a particular style they prefer.

It is also very important to have the management and producer check the contact sheet carefully for correct titles and order of importance.

One producer I worked for solved the ordering problem by doing all contact sheets alphabetically; others like to carefully divide management and office personnel from creative staff.

Another careful consideration on the contact sheet is privacy; the stage manager should check very carefully about the inclusion of stars, directors, and producers, many of whom prefer to have only an office or agent's number listed. It is often necessary to create two contact sheets: one for a select group including the producer, the general manager, and the stage managers, and another of everyone in the company.

On the formal list, I always begin with the producer and management personnel, partially because they are usually established first and change the least. Second, there is the "Creative Staff" section: the director and author and their assistants; all designers and their assistants; and any additional writers, composers, choreographers, fight directors, etc. The "Production Staff" section should include stage managers, crews, and all assistants, interns, and volunteers. The next section is the "Suppliers": the names and addresses/phone numbers of all shops, unions, rental agents, cleaning companies, and trucking companies. The "House Staff" is the listing of people employed by the theater for all shows: the house manager, the box office personnel, ushers, and doormen. In a regional repertory theater or a community theater, these listings go in the first section, as the theater is both producer and management, but in a commercial situation, they are usually distinct.

Finally, keep the "Cast and Understudies" list completely separate, because most likely it will change more than any other due to the normally nomadic nature of performers. This section, as with the creative staff, should include the actors' agents and managers, along with the cast's home and service numbers.

These divisions have grown out of use; the people who you combine in a group are often people who have to be contacted at the same time, so you don't have to keep flipping back and forth. Two warnings: Be sure that everyone's name is spelled correctly, and be certain that their titles, positions, or character roles are right. These mistakes cost more in terms of morale and goodwill than almost any other; identity is so important to everyone in theater.

Before distributing a contact sheet, try to confirm the information, either by calling the phone numbers or double-checking them in directories, on old contact sheets, or with agents. If you can get through the first rehearsal without anyone telling you that you messed up his or her name, address, or title, you will have gone a long way toward unifying a company's trust and confidence in you as a stage manager.

Preparing the Script

The stage manager is often responsible for obtaining the show's scripts and putting them in the proper shape for all company members. The easiest is, of course, a revival of a play that has already been published, such as those available from Samuel French, Inc., or Dramatists Play Service. In such cases, the stage manager can assemble the scripts and/or see that copies are made at a duplicating studio. If the play or musical is to be done "as is" with no changes, then the job is basically just counting up the necessary number of scripts and ordering and distributing them.

If a script is going to be reworked or cut considerably, then it is a good idea to reenter the script in a computer with all the changes and cuts in it, so everyone starts working with the same manuscript and rehearsals won't get bogged down with some people having some cuts and others not. Once on computer, subsequent cuts and/or changes can be made easily and new pages printed and distributed. All pages of a new or evolving script should be numbered and dated for clarity. For movies and television, they use different colored pages for different versions or rewrites, but often with a play or musical that is being worked on, you would run out of colors all too soon. Figure 4-4 is a sample page from the working script of *Speed-the-Plow* by David Mamet, listing all the rewrites made during the rehearsal period. Fortunately, due to the small cast of this play, it was possible to update everyone daily with new pages and corrections and keep the rehearsal process running smoothly, with a minimum of comments like "But my script says . . ." It is also necessary to keep updated scripts available for all design and production people. I usually keep the new pages and rewrites in folders on my desk in rehearsal marked for designers, sound, and prop people, as well as anyone else who needs periodic updates. When they come by, they can sit down and update their scripts.

It is also a very good idea to keep one script completely up-to-date that belongs to no one and is not used for anyone's notes or blocking. This script

```
Revised 3/26/88



GOULD        I wanted to do Good . . . But I became
             foolish.
FOX          Well, so we learn a lesson.  But we aren't
             here to "pine," Bob, we aren't put here to
             mope.  What are we here to do (PAUSE) Bob?
             After everything is said and done.  What
             are we put on earth to do?
GOULD        We're here to make a movie.
FOX          Whose name goes above the title?
GOULD        Fox and Gould.
FOX          Then how bad can life be?


             _____


END.

SPEED-THE-PLOW

DRAFT JUNE 1987

Copyright © 1987
Copyright ©, by David Mamet
Revised 2/23/88
Revised 3/9/88
Revised 3/15/88
Revised 3/17/88
Revised 3/20/88
Revised 3/22/88
Revised 3/26/88
```

Note: Last revision date should appear at the top of every script page.

FIGURE 4-4 *Example of Script Revision*

can then be copied for anyone in its entirety or may be referred to by one of the actors or creative staff to help the person update and insert new pages into his or her copy of the script. Often during rehearsal, the most up-to-date script is needed by people outside of rehearsal, like the producer, publicity department, or designers, and it is good to have a free one to copy or lend briefly. Too often, the stage manager ends up being the only person with a totally accurate script, which can't leave the rehearsal because of all the other blocking and cueing information that is included in it.

If a play is still being written while rehearsals are going on, it is invaluable to the production to have the playwright and the production office have compatible software. The cost of renting or even buying these will be a worthwhile investment because of the time, money, and energy saved by not having to do endless mailings, retyping jobs, and photocopying. It also means the playwright can work right at rehearsals or at home and instantly have access to his or her work as well as the ability to pass it on to the stage manager for printing and distribution to the cast. This will eliminate the awful hours or rehearsal sometimes wasted waiting for rewrites that then need to be copied and distributed before rehearsals can continue.

Too much efficiency in this area can squelch some of the fun, too. For much of the rehearsal period of *Speed-the-Plow*, Mamet was secluded deep in Vermont, far from a fax machine or computers. He would write on his typewriter, call me on the payphone at rehearsal, and read me sections of new dialogue. I would dutifully write the new lines down and read them back to him with as much of the flavor of the cast's current performances as possible. He would listen, make sure I had it right, and make some changes. I would read them again. As anyone who has seen or read a Mamet play knows, his dialogue is often colorful and full of epithets and dysphemisms. Often when I got off the phone, the theater doorman would be laughing or shaking his head in wonderment at what he had just overheard. Little did he know that he had become our first critic.

It is important to have plenty of scripts. The list of the people who need one varies from show to show, so it is a good idea to do a script list for each show and mark down the number of each script and the date it is given to each person. Scripts are expensive, and sometimes it is easy to lose track of where they all go. There are people who may only need to read the script once and then can give it back, so if you keep a record of the people who have taken a copy, you can occasionally call in the extras. Here is the beginning of a list of people who will need initial copies as well as copies updated with changes (it's only a start, so be prepared with plenty):

- The producer and any of his or her staff or backers whom he or she might indicate
- The director, choreographer, and any assistants they might have
- The writers (playwright, composer, lyricist, book writer) and their assistants
- The publicity department
- The general and company managers
- The designers and their assistants
- Various crew members, especially props, sound, followspot, and wardrobe supervisors
- All actors and understudies
- All stage managers
- The house manager
- The rehearsal pianist and conductor on a musical

The Stage Manager's Script

There are many different ways to prepare a stage manager's script, and most stage managers eventually develop a technique that is best for them. Usually, the stage manager will require several scripts. I like to keep one with blocking/staging notes, acting comments given by the director, and any other notes of a creative and directorial nature. This script may also include comments on specific lines that I jot down during run-throughs or rehearsals and my own timing and pacing notes. This is generally the book that I use in rehearsals, before and after opening.

I also immediately start a second book that is far more neat and formal, which will evolve into the "prompt" script. In this book I will begin to note any cues or technical descriptions that the director might give regarding mood or sequencing of house lights, curtains, sound effects, and so on. I also will keep track of everyone's exits and entrances in this script for warnings and checks later on. Finally, I will enter important, finalized blocking and stage groupings so as to be able to help the lighting designer and wardrobe people prepare for technical rehearsals.

Some people do all this in one book, combining the blocking indications and acting comments with the technical notes and the cues, but I find it far too messy and confusing. In the end, I want the prompt book to have only the information I need for the running of the show and the other book to have everything I need for the rehearsal or staging of the show with the actors.

Stage managers' scripts should always be on three-hole paper in a binder so new or additional pages can be easily added and taken out. I always keep a large stack of blank three-hole paper with the script so I can quickly put notes on cueing or new lines of blocking into the script without erasing and changing everything. If you are handed a small booklet-sized script of a show you are stage managing, go to a copy shop and get them to enlarge it onto three-hole paper. Then, get it into a binder. Even if you have to pay for this yourself, do it—it's worth it! Your life will be far happier.

Try to start the cast off with some form of bound script that makes it easy to insert pages and changes as well. A folder-like notebook with three rings or posts is available at all stationery stores. A particular favorite of mine is a simple three-ring binder made by a company called Acco International from a material they call Accohide. The binders come in a variety of colors, are sturdy, and make it possible for the actor to clip pages in and out with relative ease. Put the actors' names on their scripts for the first day of rehearsal.

Some stage managers now put their scripts on computer. I still do not trust computers enough to ever use them even briefly with the amount of information I need to record. I also "think" with a pencil; I can write a note in any place on the page, make a mark, a squiggly line, a circle, an arrow, etc.—which I could never be as flexible with on a computer. As to calling a show from a computer, it just seems to be courting disaster with power failures, overload, or any of the still-rampant foibles of computer operation.

Notification of First Rehearsal

Referring to your contact sheet, now notify everyone on it of the time and place of the first rehearsal. (This is an excellent opportunity to check the contact sheet for absolute accuracy.) If there is time, mail everyone notification with whatever other schedules or information may be pertinent, and then call three or four days later as a backup. Better yet, ask them to confirm receipt of the package and let you know if they are coming. If you write or talk to everyone before the first rehearsal, you should be able to correct any contact-sheet errors before the first mass distribution.

If you have an Equity company, the union must be notified at least a week in advance so they can send an Equity representative to the first rehearsal to go over AEA rules, collect unpaid dues, and hand out membership and insurance information. It is important to mail AEA a cast list, production schedule, and the date of the first rehearsal as soon as you have them. Many people on the contact sheet may not be able to be at the first rehearsal, or they may not find it necessary to be there, but everyone should be informed of when it is occurring, and the stage manager should know exactly who is and isn't coming in order to supply enough chairs, refreshments, and other items that will be needed.

HOSPITALITY

Check with the producer or general manager on how elaborate a spread you can put out for the first rehearsal. It is traditional in the morning to at least have coffee, tea, and bagels or rolls. Make sure there is enough of everything. You don't want to have to keep making new pots of coffee or running to the store for food. Fruit is always nice to have, and more and more people are avoiding caffeine, so try to have both regular and decaffeinated coffee available. If there is to be a reading around a table, it is nice to have some mints and nuts on the table for snacking. Remember: The point is to make everyone feel secure and taken care of at a point when their anxieties and vulnerabilities are most acute.

The First Rehearsal's Agenda

A lot of people will demand time and space on the first rehearsal's agenda. This is because the next few weeks may be devoted exclusively to work on individual scenes and/or musical numbers and the first day is often the most opportune time to address the cast as a whole. Also, many people need information or input from others connected with the show. Of course, the director will always say that he or she needs to get going as fast as possible and cannot afford to waste a lot of time, so the stage manager's task is to schedule everyone as compactly as possible.

On a professional production, there are three people who will often need to conduct business at the first rehearsal:

1. *The Actors' Equity Association Representative.* The stage manager must schedule about an hour for the "Equity meeting." This meeting is for all AEA members involved with the production, and its main purposes are to review the pertinent Equity rules, to have the actors fill in any necessary insurance and other work-related forms, to collect any outstanding membership dues, and to elect an Equity deputy. Because this meeting is mandatory and all non-Equity members are excluded, the stage manager must try to make the meeting as undisruptive as possible. One solution is to schedule everyone else to come after this meeting or try to set up other necessary meetings simultaneously—between designers and the director or between the public-relations people and the producer—anything that will keep the non-Equity attendees busy, hopefully in a separate room. Sometimes producers and press people will want to conclude their business before the union meeting, so they can get back to their offices. Another solution I have tried is having the AEA representative meet with the cast directly after lunch the first day of rehearsal. This means the cast can meet, greet each other, get most of the formalities out of the way, read the play, have lunch, and then have their Equity meeting.

2. *The Producer/Manager.* Production managers usually like to address the companies at the first rehearsals and also may have to collect last-minute contracts or employment forms. Include as much of the necessary paperwork as possible in each actor's packet, so the cast must suffer through only one session of filling in forms.

3. *The Press Representative.* Often the public relations director needs approval of program biographies and will want to set up interviews

at the first rehearsal. Try to have this happen during the time set aside for the actors to fill out forms. Remember that the publicity or PR person is often functioning under tight deadlines already and must have time with the cast if necessary.

With the business taken care of, the company can move on to the "art." Often the director and writers will want to talk about the show and then have the designers present set drawings and models, costumes sketches, and any other elements of the production that are ready. Plan ahead for this by talking with the director and designers before the rehearsal, asking them how much time they would like and whether they will need any assistance. Stage managers often help with the designers' "show and tell"—setting up tables, clip lights, or whatever will enhance the presentation. Even with careful planning, however, unforeseen circumstances may intrude. When we did *King Lear* at Lincoln Center, the set model was so large that we could not get it into the rehearsal hall. It had to be disassembled and rebuilt for display to the cast.

If the director intends for the actors to read the script while sitting in chairs or around a table, check to see if there is any arrangement he or she prefers; otherwise use your own best judgment based on the characters' relationships in the script and use the labeled scripts as "place cards" for the cast. They will usually pick them up and all move around anyway, but at least you started with an organized concept in mind. Along with their scripts should be the aforementioned packets of information, a pencil or two, and maybe a small pad for taking notes, as well as anything else you feel would be helpful.

Here is a sample first rehearsal schedule:

10:00: Full cast called/coffee and introductions
10:15: Equity representative meets with cast; director free for design meetings with costumes, sets, and props in separate rooms
11:30: Full cast meets with producer, PR reps, director/opening remarks and greetings
12:00: Design display of set model and costume renderings
1:00: Lunch break
2:30: Full cast/read-through of play
6:00: Break for day

Basic Necessities

Every theater production should have some essential items present at all times. Of primary importance is a first-aid kit that should be readily available during rehearsals and performances. The following is a list of necessary supplies to include:

- Headache relief medicine (aspirin, non-aspirin substitute), stomach relief medicine, throat lozenges
- Ankle, knee, and elbow braces for minor sprains
- Ice packs, assorted bandages, peroxide, and antiseptic sprays
- Needle, tweezers, and matches for splinters
- Eye wash and contact lens solution
- Orajel and oil of cloves with cotton swabs for toothaches
- Smelling salts, small oxygen tank

It is a very good idea for all stage managers to take a basic first-aid and CPR course. Almost all hospitals offer one. In New York, St. Clare's Hospital and St. Luke's/Roosevelt Hospital both offer courses to the public at various times, and they are very familiar with theater professionals and the problems they are likely to encounter because they get most of the emergency calls from the theater district.

Depending on the circumstances of the production, a stage manager may have more or fewer resources. I always make sure to have the following rehearsal supplies on hand:

- Dozens of pencils (basic No. 2 with an eraser); pencil sharpener
- Legal-size pads and 8½ x 11-inch pads of three-hole paper
- Extra three-hole binders, paper, and a three-hole punch
- Notebook dividers
- File box and file folders
- Scale rule and rulers
- Stopwatch(es)
- Scotch, masking, and cloth-backed (floor) tape
- Push pins
- Scissors

- Phone with answering machine or voicemail for setting up rehearsals; phone line may also be used for email and Internet access if wireless or cable-modem connection is unavailable.
- Computer with email access, printer, and fax, all available in rehearsal office. Computer setup should ideally include printer, paper, writable CDs, a flash drive, and any other necessary supplies. No one should be using the production computer or email for personal needs; it is too vital to communication that these resources are always available for both outgoing and incoming calls, emails, transmission of drawings, schedules, script pages, etc. Any stage manager in today's world without his or her own laptop, email account, and cell phone should plan on spending his of her first paycheck to update their supplies.
- Calculator (every computer comes with a calculator, if needed).
- Basic stationery and stamps.

This is only a start, and most stage managers will add and subtract items, tailoring the list to their own needs and requirements.

Finally, while the first rehearsal is happening, the stage manager and assistants should be able to be the most relaxed people in the room if they have anticipated everything correctly. Arrive at least an hour before the first call to make coffee and handle any last-minute details. Thereafter, full attention can be turned to the production's participants as they arrive. Again, the more the stage manager has prepared the information and assembled packets of needed forms to fill out in advance, the better the first day will go. People will be occupied with the information and forms, leaving stage management free to deal with the unexpected. Positive energy and good-natured efficiency and control will kick the show off to a strong start. In this way, the stage manager becomes the calm center of the storm of emotion that will inevitably arise as the creative process begins.

5

THE REHEARSAL PERIOD

The rehearsal process of a show is a period of constant exploration, readjustment, improvement, and accommodation. The stage manager must be responsible for keeping track of all changes in the script, any new technical requirements, and the development of the staging. The stage manager is also a primary source of help, support, and confidence for the actors and director during this time.

There are many varieties of rehearsal periods, and every director works in a different way. Generally, a rehearsal period lasts three to four weeks and begins with a careful reading of the text and some discussion. This may be followed by a period of experimentation, where the performers work through the material "on their feet." The director will then begin to set the blocking; the stage manager is responsible for recording the actors' movements. As the staging develops, the cast will approach the deadline for being off-book, which means they will no longer carry the script around, because they are supposed to have their lines memorized. The stage manager will facilitate this transition by providing lines from the script when the actors "go up" on their lines. Thereafter, rehearsals are devoted to a combination of act run-throughs; detailed work on specific scenes, character relationships, and transitions; and full run-throughs. The stage manager's tasks will vary slightly from one type of rehearsal and one type of show to another.

Rehearsing a Musical

On a musical, it is very important that the stage management team divide up responsibility, because there are often multiple rooms in which rehearsals are taking place, with actors and dancers running from room to room. Usually there is a "book room," where the director will work with the actors on scenes. One stage manager must always be present at these rehearsals, watching blocking and noting all entrances and exits to determine where costume changes will be made, props placed, and so on.

In another room, the dance and music elements will be rehearsed. In this room the mainstage managerial function will be to maintain order, call and monitor breaks, and watch the entrances, exits, and staging of large groups, checking that there will be sufficient wing and stage space for the movement being developed. Quite often there is a third room where singers can work on solo and duet numbers with the composer, or where the composer can work out revisions as well as new material. At least once a day there are rehearsals in one room where dancers and soloists are put together, or sections of the show are run, and all stage managers should be together at these. The scheduling and coordination of the various rooms is the responsibility of the production stage manager, and the assistants take whatever rooms they are assigned to and run them, calling all breaks and communicating changes, technical problems, and developments to the PSM. In this way, the PSM is left free to communicate with the outside world, giving notes and getting information from shops and designers, as well as to travel from room to room watching as numbers or scenes are staged to learn their timing and to note any technical or cueing problems for later.

Rehearsing a Nonmusical Play

On a straight play, the director may want to spend several days doing "table work," where the actors spend rehearsal time around a table reading the script and exploring meaning and character and perhaps familiarizing themselves with an accent or style. Other directors want the actors to get right on their feet and make all these discoveries during the staging. The stage manager must know which method the director is going to pursue and be prepared for it. Going from the table to staging is a delicate moment, and the more the stage manager has prepared the taping of the floor and supplied rehearsal props and furniture, the smoother the transition can be for the actors and director.

The beginning stage of rehearsal is also the period in which to check with the actors about how they want rehearsal props, furniture, and costume items set. Remember that they have to be out there in front of the audience, and whatever they need to feel comfortable and safe, within reason, is your job to provide. Some actors will never be satisfied, and some are easily pleased or don't care, but never assume, and always double-check; it will pay off in the long run.

The stage manager should always sit facing the stage playing area so he or she can cue actors when they forget a line or some blocking. Once an actor begins to learn lines, the stage manager must be very alert and stay "on the book," which means watching the text carefully and being ready to "cue" the actor with any forgotten line. It is vital that this be done clearly and without judgment of the actor's success. It is also very important not to give line readings or performance values to the cueing or prompting. The stage manager should simply provide the missed line clearly and with as little emotion as possible.

The stage manager must pay careful attention to everything the director says regarding character interpretation and jot down the most salient points. Notes should be taken as well of any requests or changes the director chooses regarding the design or running of the show. These notes must then be passed on to the proper designer, crew member, or department head (more about this later).

As rehearsals progress, the stage managers and assistants should be able to develop an accurate prop and furniture preset list for every scene. Then, at the top of every rehearsal, all the props and furniture for the scene to be rehearsed can be set by the assistant and checked by the PSM.

Rehearsing During the Director's Absence

Sometimes the stage manager will be called upon to run rehearsals while the director is in a meeting or otherwise engaged, and these sessions can be very valuable for the cast. This time may be used to drill certain scenes in which the cast has had trouble memorizing their lines. Sometimes a stage manager will be asked to lead a "speed-through," a rehearsal in which the actors run through their lines to make sure they know them. The actors usually sit while running the lines and concentrate on accurately speaking their speeches as quickly as possible rather than conveying emotional truth or performing.

In the director's absence, the stage manager may choose to go over certain staging that is tricky or that demands perfect timing. Have a clear idea of the areas the cast should be working on, but also ask them which aspects of the show they feel need attention. There are always scenes that end up getting less rehearsal time, so try to include them. Remember that you are not the director, that the purpose of these rehearsals is to drill and refine the director's work, not redefine it, and remind the actors of this.

Once the routine of the day-to-day rehearsal process has begun, two of the stage manager's most important functions begin—recording the blocking (the actors' movements) and facilitating script changes. Stage managers often handle these tasks their own way, but there are certain standard rules and customs that apply.

Blocking Notation

There are some basic terms and symbols that everyone uses to denote areas of the stage: *Upstage* (US) refers to the back of the stage, the area farthest away from the audience, and it derives from the Greeks, who always raked their stages, making the back of the stage literally "up"; *downstage* (DS) is the area closest to the audience; *stage right* (SR) and *stage left* (SL) are the areas to the left and right of the performers as they stand facing the audience (downstage), so that *audience right* would be the same as stage left and vice versa; *center stage* (CS) is the center of the stage, anywhere on the center line that runs perpendicular to the first row of audience seats.

Given these basic directions, a form of shorthand has developed that simplifies the recording of blocking in rehearsals. Here are some of the areas and their symbols:

USR: upstage right   **USL**: upstage left
DSR: downstage right   **DSL**: downstage left
USC: upstage center   **DSC**: downstage center
X: cross

Thus, if a character named Bill were to cross from one corner of the stage to the other, the stage manager might write "B X USR to DSL," meaning Bill

USR Upstage Right	USRC Upstage Right of Center	USC Upstage Center	USLC Upstage Left of Center	USL Upstage Left
SR Stage Right	SRC Stage Right of Center	CS Center Stage	SLC Stage Left of Center	SL Stage Left
DSR Downstage Right	DSRC Downstage Right of Center	DSC Downstage Center	DSLC Downstage Left of Center	DSL Downstage Left

FIGURE 5-1 *Basic Diagram with Blocking Abbreviations, Proscenium Stage*

crosses from upstage right to downstage left. Figure 5-1 is a diagram of a stage with all the major areas indicated. These areas define a basic proscenium stage well, but thrust stages or arena (theater-in-the-round) theaters require different ways of indicating staging. Sometimes it is based on aisle numbers, or clock or compass positions in the case of theater-in-the-round. No matter the type of situation, the key is to use whatever system is clear, consistent, and used by all departments and designers. It does little good to work out a brilliant symbol system for your blocking and preset lists only to find out the theater staff uses another. This is particularly difficult when touring a show that goes into a lot of different round and semi-round theaters, as they will all have different names and numbers for aisles and positions. Try to develop a key that you can translate for any theater. Figures 5-2 and 5-3 show some basic stage shapes with possible symbols and abbreviations for staging.

Armed with the shorthand symbols, the stage manager must transcribe the actions, movement, and stage business the director is giving the actors. (As discussed before, the stage manager should place the script in a three-ring binder and have plenty of blank three-hole paper available.) If the script pages (those with the dialogue) have type only on one side of each sheet and they are placed on the right only, then the paper on the left side of your notebook will be the blank back of the previous script page. Blocking notes

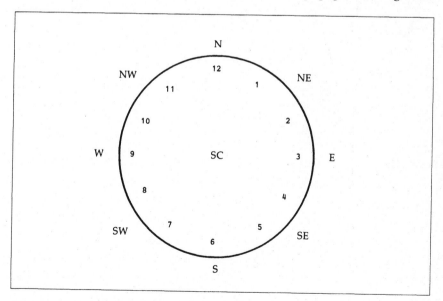

FIGURE 5-2 *Basic Blocking Diagram, Theater-in-the-Round*

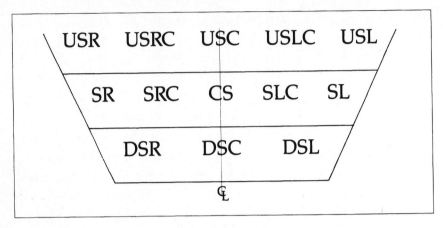

FIGURE 5-3 *Basic Thrust Stage Diagram*

can be written on this back, and if the page gets too messy, neatly copy the blocking notes onto a clean sheet of three-hole paper and insert it into the binder. Some right-handed stage managers find it easier to set up their books with the text to the left, leaving the blank page for blocking and notes to their right. On a new script that is evolving and going through frequent changes, write the blocking either on a new, blank sheet of three-hole paper or on the script page itself (the reasons for doing the latter are discussed below).

Either way, the blocking should be taken by putting a number by the word or line on which the action happens and writing the action down on the blank page across from the number. Start with numeral 1 on each page, numbering each action or bit of stage business consecutively. For each new page, start numbering from 1 again. This is very important, because if you continue numbering past the page, and then one day the director cuts out some blocking, your numbering system will be thrown off.

Early in the rehearsal process, before the blocking is finally set, it may be better to write the stage directions right on the page in the margins or in the space above or below the lines. Figure 5-4 is an example of how I've done this in the past. This will make it easier to follow the script, feed the actors lines, and correct their blocking when they are still learning their roles. Also, if you are working on a new play where the script is constantly changing, don't write any blocking or directorial notes on the back of the previous page—if it is cut you will have to transcribe all the notes on it to a clean sheet of paper. However, for neatness and clarity, it is best

ACCOMPLICE <u>ACT TWO</u>, scene 1   p. II-10

HARLEY: Harley is a totally acceptable name. (XDS to Hal)

HAL: Not when your last name is Davidson! Look: yes, if you had a
⟋XDR   ⟋ x back to her
lousy body or lousy looks, you would not have gotten this
part, but that's not your fault. In this business, the
free rides, the lucky breaks will never compensate for
all the inequity. ⟍ she sits

HARLEY: I'm in equity! — Lean into her

HAL: Harley, you are not the only person who will be standing
naked in front of the audience . . . symbolically
speaking. Should we fail, Erika will be doing "Same Time
Next Year" this year; I will be the permanent punch-line
of the great backstage joke about how Erika's
XDL
of bed ("manager-husband" has written a thriller that would rise
and fall on the summer-stock market if Erika wasn't
taking the lead and footing the bill . . . and Brian
will return to the role he created: 'Understudy' . . .
standing by for the upcoming national tour of "Love
Letters," which Mandy Patinkin will no doubt be
presenting as a one-man show. It seems to me that, of all
of us, you have the very least to lose.

HARLEY: I just . . . I had thought . . . (SHE breaks down in
tears) Hal wander UL

HAL: Harley . . . lets you and me make a bargain, okay. I want to
use your body in my play, (which I think should make you
Sit w/   feel better than if I wanted to use your body outside my
her after   play), but I in turn have a legitimate two-act thriller
crying   "in New Haven prior to Broadway," we should all be so
lucky, with a legitimate cast, of which, I might add, I
am prepared to consider you a full and equal member; and
in which you, (as Janet's accomplice), and later, (as
Jon's accomplice), Harley, you are the title character.
(pause) Okay?

HARLEY: Okay.

LAMP

FIGURE 5-4 *Preliminary Blocking Script Page Sample*

to transcribe the blocking to the opposite blank page at some point later in the rehearsal process when the script is fairly frozen.

Often it is helpful to make small, rough stage diagrams of the set to record blocking, especially for large crowd scenes and for the positioning of chorus and tableaux in musicals. Actual dance staging is taken down by the dance captain or the choreographer's assistant, and they often employ a system of dance notation called Labanotation. However, it is the stage manager's responsibility to record the positions the dancers reach, their entrances, and their exits. This can be notated in the same way that regular stage blocking is indicated—by placing numbers next to the song lyrics where various movements take place and showing the beginning and end positions on the facing page or on a roughly sketched stage diagram.

Script Changes

Script changes come fast and furious sometimes, and they must be carefully and accurately recorded as they happen. If a line or speech is cut after discussion between the actor and director, and it is rehearsed and run that way in a rehearsal, it is best to bracket the cut in the stage manager's script and date the cut. If the author later confirms the cut, the page can be retyped and new pages handed out.

Sometimes, the actor, director, or playwright will later decide that all or part of the cut line or speech must be reinstated, so always keep a file, dated, of all script pages that are changed and amended, so you can retrieve cut material easily. This becomes easier if a computer is used and every change becomes a new document or file, always leaving the complete original text for reference.

The Rehearsal Script

As mentioned before, it is also necessary for the stage manager to keep an accurate record of directorial and technical notes in his or her script. In early rehearsals, I try to write down the exact quotes on character, motivation, and the meaning of the play as stated by the director or playwright during actor discussions or note sessions. These become invaluable later on when training understudies or rehearsing replacements. Even on a short run, you can arbitrate disputes or eliminate unnecessary arguments about changes by reading back an exact quote or a clear summation of the director's and/ or the playwright's thoughts on the moment in question.

An interesting problem arises when the playwright and director don't agree. On *I'm Not Rappaport*, the Tony Award–winning play written by Herb Gardner and directed by Daniel Sullivan, the two often had completely opposite points of view about certain scenes and characters. They worked fine together, however, because their disputes had to do with different means to the same end, and they would work the problems out. But, when only one of them was present, the confusion could become astounding. In this case, I found it valuable to keep their conflicting quotes on the same page in different colors so, as I worked with an understudy or replacement, I could refer to Herb's broader, more intellectual position on discussions of character history and meaning and Dan's more dramatic and directorial quotes on the actual playing of a scene, its pace, shape, and rhythm. Combining these viewpoints gave the actor a wonderfully rich perspective on the role, but balancing these two outlooks often proved a difficult and treacherous tightrope act.

As rehearsals progress, it is helpful to neaten and cut down on the number of notes you make in the book so that eventually your blocking script looks something like Figure 5-5.

The Running Script

In a separate script, I begin to write the cueing and technical notes on a show, transcribing only that blocking that will actually affect a cue or that will have to be carefully watched in the running of the show. For instance, if there is a fight or stabbing onstage, it is important to record how furniture may have been moved or if blood has spilled, even though that particular section may not have a cue. It is the stage manager's responsibility to know and foresee any problems that might develop during performance and work with the crew or actors involved to solve them. Carefully take down any stage business that might affect future cueing or staging so you are alerted to any possible problems. For example, make a note to watch that nothing falls off a turntable during

① Jes enters R. on balcony.

② Lor hangs onto balcony; Jes kneels down - kisses him.

③ Lor drops from balcony.

④ Jes rises, moves off R.- gets casket. Jes hands casket to to Lor thru bars - (kneels)
⑤ Jes rises.

⑥ Lor x's L. to C.

⑦ Jes exits. Lor x's to L.C. - puts down casket, kneels down.
⑧ Graz x's L. to C. Sal x's to below bench.
⑨ Lor opens chest, pulls out jewels. Leo runs D. to L. of Lor holding torch.

Man 2 + Viol move DS.

⑩ Man 2 gives torch to Graz. Leo x's to Man 2, gives him torch.

FIGURE 5-5 *Sample Pages from Finished Blocking Script*

THE MERCHANT OF VENICE   Act 2 Scene 6

Enter Jessica above in boy's apparel

JESSICA

① Who are you? Tell me for more certainty,
   Albeit I'll swear that I do know your tongue.
LORENZO ② Lorenzo, and thy love.

JESSICA
   Lorenzo, certain, and my love indeed,
   For who love I so much? And now who knows   30
   But you, Lorenzo, whether I am yours?

LORENZO
③ Heaven and thy thoughts are witness that thou art.

JESSICA
④ Here, catch this casket. It is worth the pains. ⑤
   I am glad 'tis night, you do not look on me,
   For I am much ashamed of my exchange;   35
   But love is blind, and lovers cannot see
   The pretty follies that themselves commit;
   For if they could, Cupid himself would blush
   To see me thus transformèd to a boy.

LORENZO
   Descend, for you must be my torchbearer.   40

JESSICA
   What, must I hold a candle to my shames?
   They in themselves, good sooth, are too too light.
   Why, 'tis an office of discovery, love,
   And I should be obscured.

LORENZO   So are you, sweet,
   Even in the lovely garnish of a boy.   45
⑥ But come at once,
   For the close night doth play the runaway,
   And we are stayed for at Bassanio's feast.

JESSICA
   I will make fast the doors, and gild myself
   With some more ducats, and be with you straight. ⑦ 50

                                    Exit above
GRAZIANO
⑧ Now, by my hood, a gentile, and no Jew.

LORENZO
⑨ Beshrew me but I love her heartily,
⑩ For she is wise, if I can judge of her;

the scene before it will move, or jot down a reminder to check if a door has been left open or shut incorrectly. (I will discuss the creation of the cueing script and offer sample pages in chapter 7.)

Fight Rehearsals

A whole book should be written about the creation and maintenance of stage combat. Even B. H. Barry, one of the theater's finest fight directors, must sometimes cajole and demand enough time from the director and producers to stage or rehearse the fights. In some productions, fight rehearsals are afterthoughts and stage combat isn't given adequate time to grow and develop creatively and safely. There is always pressure to produce results quickly due to time constraints, and actors may be pushed into performing maneuvers that are dangerous or uncomfortable for them. The result is a fight full of hesitancy and contrived-looking movements, making the moment seem artificial and staged.

As the stage manager, try to schedule plenty of time for fight rehearsals—I find they require about twice as much time as the director thinks is necessary at first. Best of all, see if you can set up an interview or meeting between the director and the fight instructor during the initial phase of preproduction meetings.

Also, make sure the fight director is present when the fights are first run on the set in stage lighting. Sometimes, a designer or director will sacrifice safety for the "look" of the show by having a fight scene staged on a set that is too dark or cluttered for the combat to safely occur. The fight director must be able to have this changed.

The fight director and the actors need time to themselves to experiment and discover what is possible to achieve together before they are judged or censored. In a show that has considerable fighting—sword duels, the use of other assorted weaponry, a big physical brawl—it is mandatory that some time be given to run the sequences every day of rehearsal and before every performance. Like athletes or dancers who must warm up, the actors involved must keep their fight moves and responses tuned to do exactly what has been safely planned, not what their normal reflexes might do to ward off a blow or repel a physical threat.

When I worked on the Broadway production of *Othello* in the early 1980s (starring James Earl Jones and Christopher Plummer), every fight was run before every performance. Even with all the duels and blows exchanged in the show, there were never any injuries. However, it was only after prolonged negotiations with the management and the unions that this extra pre-performance fight rehearsal was allowed. Technically, the crew and actors would have had to be compensated with overtime pay for this extra rehearsing.

After AEA's experience with *Othello* (as well as with other productions requiring extensive stage combat), the union decided to require fight rehearsals, as well as a fight captain. The fight captain must be a permanent member of the cast and is assigned to watch and rehearse the fights. It is his or her job to correct any stray moves, sloppy choreography, or extension of the original limits of the physicality of the fight.

Rehearsal Report Forms

It is a good idea to write up a daily rehearsal report. Try to get as much necessary information onto one page as possible. There are many forms the report can take. An early example of a written report is found in Appendix 5, a report for *The Merchant of Venice*. This can easily be entered as a basic form into a computer program and then filled out and emailed daily. The primary advantage of a computer-generated form is that it can easily expand or contract the various sections to include the different priorities or needs that emerge on a given day of rehearsal.

This form has many functions, for both the creative and management staffs. Its primary purpose is to serve as the only complete log of the rehearsal period. Therefore, its accuracy is essential. The stage manager should record the day's schedule carefully, especially the beginning and ending times of rehearsal, all breaks, and what scenes were rehearsed. This information is vital for resolving any overtime disputes or arguments about whether a particular scene, actor, or musical number received enough rehearsal. Often, the stage manager's log is used in insurance and arbitration proceedings, so it is crucial to be truthful, clear, and concise, without a lot of editorializing or cuteness.

This point was brought home to me while working on the Broadway musical *Cyrano*. Our stage manager's log was subpoenaed by an arbitrator who was searching for factual information about disputed events surrounding the firing of the conductor. Sure enough, all the salient facts concerning certain events and occurrences were there. But we had also included a lot of very colorful editorial comment on the day-to-day romantic and extracurricular happenings on the show. The arbitrator was a bit perplexed as he read through all these extraneous comments trying to find the necessary facts about the conductor during rehearsals. Needless to say, we were also a bit embarrassed to have our work read in public. This served as a lesson not only on the possible serious use of the stage manager's log but also on the style and fitness of its contents.

The log is also essential for bookkeeping. Often fittings and technical rehearsals will involve some overtime payment to actors, and it is important that an accurate record of all calls be kept, including start and finish times, to avoid confusion and debate later on. The log should record whether any actors are absent or late; Equity rules now allow management to dock, or reduce, actors' wages if they consistently don't arrive on time. It is also an important tool for informing the management, on a daily basis, of any growing problems that are eventually going to be costly or in need of control.

The log should give the highlights of all technical notes in a shortened form that will remind you upon review to refer to more detailed notes for discussion with the various designers or department heads and forewarn management of any additions or changes that will result in new expenses. Leaving a space for notes and comments gives the stage manager a daily opportunity to add any particular thoughts, facts, or opinions on the day's work and progress that deal with anything outside the specific categories on the form.

Communicating Notes to Designers and Crew

Another of the stage manager's most important functions during a rehearsal period is relaying to the appropriate departments any notes, comments, and problems that crop up. It is a good idea to keep one daily sheet of blank paper on the rehearsal table, dated, with each department's heading on it, so the stage manager or assistants can add all notes to one specific place. These notes should then be entered in shortened form onto the daily report and kept in a folder for the designers or crew.

Various shows and theaters have different modes of note distribution, but the stage manager must see to it that it happens in whatever form as efficiently, accurately, and completely as possible. Often, in the commercial theater, notes must be phoned quickly to designers and shops to avoid costly progress on work that may have to be altered due to changes made in rehearsal. I try to update all departments at least once a day, and often two or three times daily in the case of props and costumes.

Some notes are easy and clear and can be easily passed on; others require in-depth conversations with those concerned. Always try to get a clear idea about the nature of and need for a discussion before going back to the director with further questions. Try to assess whether there is a need for a meeting or phone discussion with the designer or crew member. Attempt to solve the problem with as little wasted time and emotion as possible, but be sure not to avoid a conflict. It is always better and cheaper to have a designer and director have an argument and resolve it during the rehearsal/building phase of a show than to put it off until dress rehearsals in the theater.

The Golden Rule
of Theater Production

When several different people on a production seem to be making conflicting demands that are impossible to fulfill, it is useful to remember a simple truism. It is the "The Golden Rule of Theater Production" in theater and was first explained to me by one of the theater's finest designers, Douglas Schmidt. There are no exceptions to this rule, and the wise stage manager should be guided accordingly.

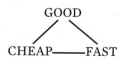

The rule here is that you can have any two, but *never* can you have all three. Let me give you an example. If the director demands a new set piece quickly and the set designer insists in a high-quality job, the producer will not be able to pay for it cheaply. If the producer absolutely won't pay a lot for the piece, then the director must compromise on the speed of delivery or the designer on the quality of its components.

A stage manager's priorities should be guided by this truth. This is why a show like *Sugar Babies* will try to set all its cues during a technical rehearsal even without all its drops; it is just too prohibitively expensive to pay for the added overtime that on-time delivery would cost. In the case of *Sugar Babies*, the management opted for "good" and "cheap"; the company had to live with that decision as the drops arrived after the techs.

There are a variety of reasons why this rule might come into play: The creators procrastinate on finalizing the design concepts for the production; there are last-minute changes during the rehearsal period; the financing of the show lags behind the creation, so the construction shops don't get their start-up money until long after all artistic decisions have been made. The stage manager can positively affect the bottom line if he or she continually enhances communication and agreement among the creators by accurately transferring notes and efficiently scheduling meetings.

Scheduling

The stage manager must be in control of all scheduling by getting everyone's requests for rehearsal time, and balancing these needs with the union requirements and the energy resources of the cast and staff. All Equity contracts dictate the number of hours that their members can work each day and limit the hours that Equity members can work straight (usually five hours) before a break of one or one and a half hours.

Let's take a standard schedule and look at all the different ways of breaking it up. A basic rehearsal rule is that actors can work seven out of eight and a half hours, and five hours before a break of at least an hour must be given. This is optional, and every company votes on whether to make the break an hour or an hour and a half. If they vote for the hour lunch, then the day becomes seven out of eight hours, with the added half hour break at the end of the day.

Working with the rehearsal scene breakdown, the stage manager sets about structuring the day with all the required elements in mind. Often, a list of costume-fitting requests will have come in during the day, followed by the director's desires for the day and, on a musical, the choreographer's and music director's rehearsal time requirements. Frequently, the producer and press agent will request actors to grant interviews or make appearances. Because of all these needs, it is a good idea to establish a deadline for such "outside" requests. Then set a time later in the day to get the director's rehearsal request, as well as those from the choreographer and musical director.

Every day and every situation is different, but basically the stage manager can now progress to the setting of the next day's schedule. First, look at the rehearsal needs and see if there are actors who will not be called at all or called only for small sections of the day. If these are the people needed for fittings or other appointments, then life is easy. This list can also be valuable when you go back to the costume people having found only two possible fittings they requested; maybe they can make use of the performers who are available.

If there are actors needed in two or three places at once, then the stage manager's job gets complicated. Before giving up and telling the costume designer, press agent, and choreographer that their requests are impossible to fulfill, look for easy solutions. In the spirit of a great compromiser, try to work out everyone's needs. For instance, a director may want to rehearse a scene that has a large number of people in it for two or three hours. However, only a few of the performers have a significant number of lines or amount of action. Suggest that the director divide up the rehearsal into three time slots wherein he or she can work with those with the larger roles first, then a period of time with the smaller parts, and finally a space of time to put them together. This will free up some of the people for other appointments.

If a leading player has only a small entrance in a particular scene, or only comes on at the very end, it is often possible to free him or her from a rehearsal because the director would rather lose a lead from that rehearsal than be forced to let him or her go when work begins on the actor's big scenes. Most directors are conscious of the need for the cast to go elsewhere during rehearsals and will work with the stage managers and designers to make it possible. The further ahead the stage manager can make requests and work out the schedule with the director, the better. Some directors fix schedules in advance and stick to them, while others can't decide what they want to do until the last moment. The latter is more true with new plays or musicals, where the time usually devoted to discovery, experimentation, and changes makes it hard to estimate the time requirements.

Always try to keep the actors' energies in mind when scheduling, because it makes no sense to create a timetable on paper that is not realistically achievable by the performers. For instance, try to give a leading player a break between a long costume fitting and the rehearsal of a major scene or number. If possible, after a leading player's fitting, try to schedule scenes or songs that can be worked on without him or her, so if the fitting goes overtime, or if a lead needs time to rest after it, the rehearsal process can continue successfully. This is a good rule any time leading players are scheduled outside of rehearsal. Nothing alienates a company and the creative staff more than sitting around doing nothing, waiting for the star to reappear.

Try to get the schedule finalized in your computer, printed, and posted (always in the same place or places every day) as early as possible. A sample of a daily schedule is included in Appendix 4. It is also helpful to attach a cast list (see Figure 4-3 on page 76) with the time of everyone's first call next to their name so that you don't hear the frequent laments "I didn't think I was in that scene" or "I didn't see my name, so I didn't know" when you phone the next day to find out why someone isn't there.

Program Information

The collection of much of the program information and the actors' biographical material has become a fairly standard stage managerial responsibility. Since the press agent is usually paid on a scale commensurate with the stage manager and is not involved in seven to ten hours of rehearsal six days a week, it is not clear why they can't handle this chore themselves. But the fact is they don't, and if they try, they usually make mistakes, so the stage manager winds up doing it.

Sometimes program bios will have been handled before rehearsal, but if not, get a list of all the bios needed by the press agent, the date he or she needs them, and the allowable length. I like to print this information out at the top of a piece of paper and make copies for every cast member. I make it clear that the bio requirements are set by the press agent so that any requests for more words or extended deadlines may be directed to him or her. Then simply keep a copy of the cast list where you can check off the submissions before turning them over to the press department.

There are other components of the program that the stage manager is sometimes called on to provide: the cast of characters in order of appearance, the act and scene breakdown and descriptions, and the production staff and credits list. The cast of characters in order of appearance is self-explanatory, but check with the director and playwright about whether this should be done by visual or vocal appearance, because often characters appear long before they speak.

The act and scene breakdown should always be approved by the director and playwright. A fairly standard example is:

ACT ONE:
Scene 1: The home of Mrs. Smith, an evening in winter, 1946
Scene 2: Later that evening
Scene 3: The next morning
ACT TWO: A hotel in New York, a few days later
ACT THREE: The same, moments later

The act/scene breakdown descriptions are more or less specific or poetic depending on the play and its nature. Of course, with a musical, it can be quite lengthy and complicated and is often connected with the list of songs in the order in which they are sung. With new works, the proviso "Subject to Change" must appear until a play or musical is "frozen," which means the producer and creator agree that no more changes are to take place.

Careful attention should be given to the production staff and credits. The staff list should include everyone working on the production who does not appear elsewhere. Check and double-check with every department so that no one gets left out. The credits are for businesses and individuals who have provided services or donated props, costumes, or other production items. These credits should be carefully confirmed with every department as well.

Discipline and Order

The tone and atmosphere of the rehearsal process is very much in the hands of the stage manager. A good stage manager must walk a thin line between being the uptight and dictatorial disciplinarian who stifles people's joy and freedom of expression and the lax, easy-going individual who allows the process to bog down due to wasted time and lack of control and communication.

Be as clear as possible about the basic rules of rehearsal with the cast. Ask for explanations of any lateness, but don't attack; just attempt to ensure that whatever caused the lateness will not happen again. Suggest that you will assist with wake-up or reminder calls and will investigate better transportation routes or provide numbers of car services if necessary. Always approach a person who is late as though he or she is more upset and concerned about it than you are, keeping in mind that together you can solve any problem to make sure it doesn't happen again. It does no good to get someone defensive or upset, because then you are further impeding the person's ability to get it together and get on with the work he or she has been called to do.

Make very clear the boundaries of rehearsal decorum in terms of smoking, food, and drink, as well as the rules on the presence of any guests. Try to always have a separate space in which the people who are not rehearsing can mingle, talk, eat, and so forth, thereby saving the rehearsal space completely for concentrated work. There should be a real contrast between the two spaces. If coffee or other refreshments are provided, try to keep them outside the work space, so breaks and socializing occur out of the way.

Try to give breaks of five minutes in an hour or ten minutes in an hour and a half. Announce the breaks clearly and give warnings when they are half over as well as when there is a minute left in the break. All too often, actors and directors stand around talking throughout a break and then go to the bathroom or make phone calls when you try to get them back to work. Try to discourage this, reminding them gently they are on a break, and that they should take advantage of it. Sometimes it is hopeless, so just announce the end of the break and wait. A favorite break-killer is the ten-minute discussion between the director and one or two of the actors about how destructive breaks are to the creative process, at the end of which, as everyone else is returning ready to get back to work, they take a break. No matter how much creative energy is flowing, after an hour and a half of work, almost everyone needs a chance to have a few minutes off.

Part of maintaining order in rehearsal is, of course, having it yourself. Stage managers should be friendly, accessible, and supportive but never the center of too much rehearsal frivolity and joking around. "An iron hand in a velvet glove" is a good model for professional managerial style; an alternative might be "easygoing perfectionism." If stage managers concentrate on functioning and communicating in a kind, clear, and supportive manner instead of trying to be everyone's best friend and the center of the company social whirl, they will be far more successful in the long run.

Visitor Policy

In general, rehearsals are very private work places. It is the only period of time in which a performer can experiment, taking creative risks in private, and experience failure that is not threatening or destructive. The stage manager has a responsibility to preserve and nurture that atmosphere. It is important to reserve judgment and criticism of anyone going through a rehearsal process; try to be supportive in every way possible. In the end, it is the actors who will put themselves on the line in front of hundreds or thousands of people, while the stage manager goes quietly about the backstage business, sheltered from public scrutiny. Always remember this distinction in dealing with actors.

I worked on one production that, unfortunately, made clear the reason why rehearsals should be private and closed to outsiders. The ingénue in this particular musical had a retired vice cop for a husband/agent, and he had never been around a show in rehearsal. Well, apparently he didn't appreciate the way his wife was handled in the show. He threatened to knock one poor chorus boy's teeth down his throat, and he was abusive toward the director, the producer, and me on several occasions. He was finally barred from the theater, and security guards were hired to enforce the ban. Needless to say, this was a particularly ugly exception. But be aware that anyone who is present in a rehearsal situation who doesn't belong may be a detriment to the whole creative process. Avoid it if you can.

Try to set aside a few moments at the end of every rehearsal day to catch up with your assistants and check each other's progress, as well as to divide any work that needs to be done by the following day. Go over notes, schedules, and share any personal insights or conflicts that you or your assistants may have become aware of or witnessed during the day. Often, you will return home to be greeted by phone calls about some problem that an assistant warned you about, and having had time to think it over, you will have a better chance of dealing with it constructively.

As the rehearsal period moves from basic staging to first run-throughs, back to detail work, and then to more run-throughs, the stage manager must be the instrument that allows this process to flow and develop. Whether by careful scheduling, by always having scenes preset, or by getting the accompanist ready, the stage manager should never let the day come to a screeching halt on account of something that could have been anticipated. This usually means working throughout other people's breaks and arriving early and staying late. This is *not* extra work; it *is* the work. Build a secure, creative environment for people to work in, and the process will be more rewarding for everyone involved.

6

AUTOMATION

One of the biggest developments over the last ten years in the theater has been the advent of more and more automated scenery. This development cannot help but influence the way shows are designed, run, teched, and stage managed. A new type of knowledge is required for a stage manager approaching the cueing of an automated show, but the fundamentals remain the same. First, it is necessary to learn a few basic terms that will come up throughout this chapter:

1. *Automated Scenery.* The term applies to any scenic element that is driven by a motorized winch controlled and programmed by a computer. This can include deck or stage scenery or flying scenery as well as tracks and travelers. Another advancement in the use of automated scenery is the development of what is called a "turtle." This is a platform-like device that rides in the base of a piece of scenery or furniture that can be moved by remote control to turn that piece of scenery or furniture. One example might be the raft in *Big River* when it needs to travel across the stage and then turn downstage for a scene, or when it must look as if it is being turned by the actors; the use of a turtle allows all this to occur on a straight track. Another example would be turning a piece of scenery to reveal different angles of a house in the course of a play.

2. *Effect.* This term, usually abbreviated "Eff" or "EFF," applies to each motor or winch that is used in an automated production and controlled or programmed by computer rather than a human being. One effect may control or drive a variety of scenic elements. For instance, in the "dream" automation cheat sheet (Figure 6-1), EFF #3 controls both the gazebo and the train platform, and EFF #9 controls both the train and the bar. In other words, for automated cueing by means of computer, the term *effect* has replaced the term *winch* or *fly line* at the appropriate cue points.

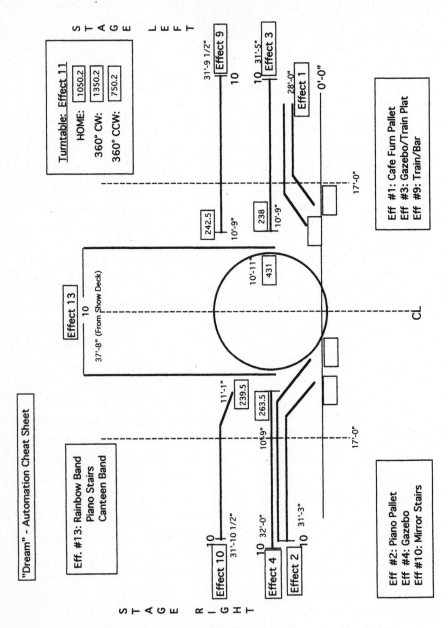

FIGURE 6-1 Dream *Automation Cheat Sheet*

3. *Dog.* This does not refer to the star of *The Wiz* or *Annie.* Instead this is the term for the piece of hardware that rides in a track in the stage floor or deck to which various pieces of scenery or prop palettes can be attached. It is the actual piece that is moved by an effect from one position to another on cue. What is attached to it and when it is attached are the responsibility of the design and stage management teams to determine during the technical rehearsals.

4. *Tracks.* Tracks are various-length cuts in the stage floor in which the guiding cables and dog can ride so as to move the various scenic elements to their predetermined points by their effects. Tracks are usually lined with either metal or hard silicone or plastic so that the repeated tracking on and off of the scenic elements will not damage them. In Figure 6-1, the lines from the effects to the measured and numbered spots on the ground plan indicate the tracks. For instance, Effect 9 travels on a straight track from 31'-9½" off center to 10'-9" off center in a straight line, whereas Effect 10 travels onstage and slightly downstage on a track with a built-in bend in it. Sometimes, a particularly large piece of scenery will have a "drive" track and a "guide" track, the first to hold the dog and do the actual pushing or pulling of the piece and the second to help keep it from going off course or jamming on a bend or curve.

5. *Knives.* These are the pieces of hardware that are inserted through what is called the *receiver* (a reinforced metal slot in the pallet or scenery base) and used, like a ship's rudder, to guide the scenery across the stage. Knives are connected with the dogs that actually move the scenery.

6. *Target.* This is the term for the desired stopping point or limit of an automated scenery move. For example, a piece of scenery is moved from offstage by means of a dog to the target spot onstage, which is its playing position for a scene or song. Note that it is important early on for the stage manager to know the position of the dog and receiver for a given platform, pallet, or piece of scenery since it is their location, not the edges of the platforms, pallets, or scenery being moved, that will have to be programmed. In rehearsals, the stage manager must "spike" or mark the playing position of each piece as it is set by the director or choreographer both for

blocking purposes and to keep track of where the dog will have to move to achieve the desired position. In Figure 6-1, for instance, Effect 9 moves the train; the onstage edge of the train scenery piece may come to 8 feet from center, but the driving dog, which is what the Effect controls and is the computer-programmed limit for the move, must move to 10 feet, 9 inches from the center (the 10′-9″ measurement shown in the illustration).

Automation control systems are set by either velocity or time. For example, in Figure 6-2, Cue 120 for the train moves it from point 51.1 forward to point 241 (its target), accelerating (ACC) for four seconds to a

AUTOMATION CUES   DREAM

SAVANNAH

CUE	EFF	UNIT	FROM	DIR.	TARGET	ACC	DEC	SPD
100	3	Train Platform	20.8	F	202.6	4	5	20
110	4	Gazebo	10	F	175	3	5	14
120	5	Train	51.1	F	241	4	6	5
130	3	Train Platform	202.6	R	169	3	3	10
	4	Gazebo	175	R	145.6	3	3	10
	5	Train	241	R	207.3	3	3	10
140	5	Train	169	R	51.1	3	3	10
150	3	Train Platform	201.8	R	20.8	3	3	10
	4	Gazebo	145.6	F	233.9	4	4	5
160	11	T/T (2 o'clock)	730	CCW	505	8	6	16
170	11	T/T (12 o'clock)	505	CCW	460	3	3	2
	3	Empty Dog	20.8	F	234	3	3	5
	4	Empty Dog	233.9	R	10	6	3	10
180	11	T/T (3 o'clock)	460	CW	550	5	5	4
190	3	Gazebo	234	R	10	4	3	12

FIGURE 6-2 *Automation Cues*

speed (SPD) of 5 and decelerating (DEC) for six seconds. If the controller is set by time, the stage manager and director may time a piece of music that they want to cover the move and then assign that amount of time to the move with the desired acceleration and deceleration, and the computer will determine the required speed or velocity. With the kind of controller used to cue the show shown in Figure 6-2, the stage manager and programmer must work to find the right speed or velocity to accomplish the needed distance of the move and then build in the required acceleration and deceleration. The "from" and target numbers on the cue sheet are the computer's numbers that correspond to measurements on the stage. The computer doesn't work with feet and inches; it is the stage manager's job to translate the desired settings to the computer's numbering system for cueing.

The stage manager's cueing should follow the style of the samples shown in Figures 6-2 and 6-3. From left to right, those include the cue number; the effect number for the motor or winch the computer is commanding; the unit description, telling which scenic element has been attached to the effect; the from number, telling the preset location of the dog before the move; the direction (DIR) letter, telling whether the piece is moving forward (F) or reverse (R), or, in the case of a turntable, clockwise (CW) or counterclockwise (CCW); the target, telling where the piece is moving to; and the desired acceleration (ACC), deceleration (DEC), and speed (SPD) of the move.

The controller shown in Figures 6-2 and 6-3 is set to velocity. If instead it were set to time, the last column would be time, not speed. With time controllers, the stage manager translates the director's or designer's desired concept of a piece's move by basically telling the computer, "I want the house to move from offstage to center stage in seven seconds, a move of twenty feet," and the computer assigns the speed necessary to achieve those parameters, including the required acceleration and deceleration.

Of course, the actual sight of a large piece of scenery moving at a rapid or slow speed may be quite different from what the director or designer envisioned in his or her imagination, so it must be continually fine-tuned. Likewise, if a piece is moving with music or during a certain piece of dialogue, the move must be consistent with the mood or tempo of the stage action or music, and that can take considerable adjusting. The great thing about automation, however, is that once the perfect speed is found and set, it is possible to repeat it exactly at every performance.

DECK - AUTOMATION CUES

DREAM

| CAFE SOCIETY |

CUE	EFF	UNIT	FROM	DIR.	TARGET	ACC	DEC	SPD
200	2	Piano Pallet	10	F	213.1	6	6	9
F:205	7	Bar TVal: 2 @ 125	40	F	237	5	5	8
210	6	Mirror Stairs	10	F	215.5	5	5	10
215	33	Bar Translator	1	F	2	-	-	-
Mirror 1		Mirror Rotate		CCW				25%
230	1	Cafe Furn Pallet	10	F	192.9	3	3	4
	2	Piano Pallet	213.1	F	287.8	3	3	3
240	2	Piano Pallet	287.8	R	246.7	3	3	3
265	2	Piano Pallet	246.7	R	213.1	3	3	3
Mirror 2		Mirror Rotate		CW				25%
275	8	Mirror Blackout	10	F	155	4	4	4
280	33	Bar Translator	2	R	1	-	-	-
285	2	Piano Pallet	213.1	R	10	8	3	12
	6	Mirror Stairs	202.2	R	10	8	3	14
	7	Bar Unit	237	R	10	10	3	9
290	1	Cafe Furn Pallet	192.9	R	10	4	3	8

FIGURE 6-3 *Deck Automation Cues*

The cueing of automated fly floor or rail moves is similar to the cueing of scenery moves. It is basically run off the same type of computer programs, and is also set by either time or velocity. In Figures 6-4 and 6-5, each effect number refers to a line set or position on the fly rail that has been motorized and is controlled by computer command. For rail cues, F (forward) is the command that brings a piece in or toward the stage and R (reverse) is the command that takes it out or up from the stage. Once again there are target numbers, which are the computer's settings

RAIL WORKSHEET

DREAM

CUE	EFF	UNIT	DIR.	TARGET	ACC	DEC	SPD	
	51	Austrian	IN	211				
	52	#1 Chiffon Fly	OUT	10				240.3
	53	#1 Chiffon Travel	Closed	157				15
	54	Ceiling Fly	OUT	10				320
	55	Chandelier	OUT	10				201
	56	#2 Chiffon Fly	OUT	10				237
	57	#2 Chiffon Travel	Closed	165				15
	58	Mirror Hanger	OUT	10				365
	59	Blue Scrim	IN	323				
	60	RP Screen	IN	323				
	61	#1 SL Tab	OUT	162				
	62	#1 SR Tab	OUT	228				
	63	#2 Tabs (SR & SL)	IN	203				
	64	Fly Groundrow	IN	365				
	65	I-Beam Trolley	SR	10				
SAVANNAH								
Q30	62	#1 SR Tab	R	100	2	2	2	Gazebo A110
Q35	51	Austrian	R	10	10	10	10	
Q40	62	#1 SR Tab	F	228	2	2	2	
Q50	61	#1 SL Tab	R	10	2	2	2	
Q55	61	#1 SL Tab	F	162	2	2	2	
Q60	61	#1 SL Tab	R	36	2	2	2	

FIGURE 6-4 *Rail Worksheet*

RAIL WORKSHEET

DREAM

CUE	EFF	UNIT	DIR.	TARGET	ACC	DEC	SPD	
Q65	61	#1 SL Tab	F	162	2	2	2	
Q70	61	#1 SL Tab	R	36	2	2	2	
	62	#1 SR Tab	R	140	2	2	2	
	63	#2 Tabs	R	30	2	2	2	
Q75	61	#1 SL Tab	F	162	2	2	2	
CAFE SOCIETY								A210
Q80	62	#1 SR Tab	F	228	2	2	2	
	63	#2 Tabs	F	203	2	2	2	
Q100	64	Groundrow	R	10	5	5	15%	After LQ 91
DECK Q110	65	I-Beam Trolley	F	402.6	10	10	10%	
DECK Q115	65	I-Beam Trolley	R	10	10	10	25%	
Q120	62	#1 SR Tab	R	140	2	2	2	
	63	#2 Tabs	R	30	2	2	2	
TRANSITION INTO RAINBOW ROOM								
CUE	EFF	UNIT	DIR.	TARGET	ACC	DEC	SPD	

FIGURE 6-5 *Rail Worksheet*

for various "trims," or heights that flying pieces are to play at. There are also the commands for ACC, DEC, and SPD, which are exactly like those already described for deck pieces.

All computer-controlled automated moves could be run off the same computer, but the stagehands' union on Broadway will not allow it, insisting that the deck moves be run by one computer and controller and the fly or rail moves by another. Thus the traditional carpenter and flyman positions are not lost, and jobs are protected. However, the resulting duplication is both an additional and needless expense for the production and another problem that the stage manager running the show must contend with. For instance, perhaps a cue needs to be perfectly synchronized between the deck and fly floor. That can best be accomplished if it is handled by one person at one computer pushing one button on one cue. An example of a cue that needs to be synchronized in this fashion might be moving onstage from the wings a platform with trees that needs a sky backdrop to complete the picture. The director and designer might want all this to happen over a few bars of music, the moves coming to a perfect standstill as the lights change and the first note of a song is sung. With automation, such a cue can be built with the scenery and drop moving to very specific timings so they are at a standstill on an established beat of music. But with two individuals handling the moves, if one of the operators reacts ever so slightly differently to the stage manager's "go" instruction and pushes his or her command button a beat or two before or after the other operator, then either the drop or the platform will still be moving at the desired moment of stillness for the song.

Stage managers have been adjusting to the increased demands of calling highly automated shows for the last ten years. Some of the advancements and changes the process has required have been learned and instituted and today do not seem as startling as when they were first introduced.

One major change is the absolute necessity these days for a stage manager to see what is happening at every point in a show to time movements and changes as perfectly as the advent of automation calls for. During the technical rehearsals for a show, most stage managers have to be in the front of the stage to see the moves and timing of their cueing sequences. This is not only necessary for the purpose of timing cues but for ensuring safety. With the size and complexity of today's automated scenery, a stage manager must see and know that certain pieces have moved before cueing others or cueing performers to move onto the stage. This has resulted in vastly superior theatrical communication and monitoring systems, both audio and visual, than were possible ten years ago. Wireless headsets allow the stage manager and his or her assistants to position themselves anywhere backstage they need to be to get the best view and yet remain in contact with actors or technicians during difficult sections of cueing. Video monitors, including infrared cameras for seeing movement in blackouts, allow a stage manager to see every actor or moving piece of scenery that has to be seen during a shift to achieve a smooth and safe transition.

A frequent early complaint about automation was that it was dangerous because it was not under the control of a person and the equipment would not understand to stop whatever was going on if someone were hurt or there were problems. But today every moving piece of scenery is programmed to shut off automatically if it encounters "resistance" that has not been programmed into a move. In other words, a big piece of scenery moving along its track encountering a fallen actor or another piece of scenery stops until given a new command to start again. Stage managers also have at their fingertips stop buttons to shut down various sections of moving scenery at will if they see or an assistant tells them over their headsets that there is a problem.

There is a lot of good to be found in the ability to perfect a cue and get it to happen exactly the same at each performance by means of automation. But there is still the need to understand and be able to use all the ways of cueing that can be done without automation so one can function in all kinds of theaters. Personally, I would miss the human touch to running a show, but I also know it would be impossible for any group of stagehands and stage managers to achieve some of the dizzying piling on of effects and scenic movement that today's mechanized, oversized, Disneyized, lavish musicals require.

7

LOAD-IN AND TECHNICAL REHEARSALS

There is probably no more intensely involving and rewarding period for a stage manager than when a show loads in to the theater and then goes through its technical rehearsals. The stage manager is at the center of every decision and the instrument of every bit of creation at this point. For a brief period of time, it makes him or her indispensable. However, responsibilities and pressures are also at their height.

All the preparation, planning, notes, and meetings now pay off—in an incredibly short, concentrated period of time. I have often thought that if the outside world could function at the level theater people do during this stage of production, we would have a far more advanced, organized, and communicative world. It takes a great deal of concentration and cooperation from many people to pull a show together successfully. And the stage manager is at the center of it all, juggling people's time and needs, prioritizing the artistic and technical requirements to keep both elements in balance, and generally keeping everyone focused on the common goal: the successful performance of a creative and professional piece of theater.

The Load-In

The term "load-in" refers to the act of moving the set, lights, costumes, and other technical necessities into a theater and the ensuing process of setting everything up. It usually is a coordinated effort and is set for a specific day or days. In a university, stock, or resident theater, the scenic shop is often in the same building as the theater and so the load-in simply may entail moving scenic material within one building, with the lighting and sound equipment being rehung and rewired as opposed to being "loaded in." In other cases, especially when working in the commercial realm, all the technical elements must be loaded onto trucks, carted to the theater, and moved inside. But in either case, this is the time that a large crew is called to help load and set up, and a lot of work happens in a short time.

The stage manager must stay aware of the progress, continually checking to see that the set is going in as planned and that proper space is being left onstage and offstage for the actors. Problems do occur. Often the set requires bracing or masking that did not appear on any drawing and that may make a planned entrance or exit impossible. Or the sound department will suddenly appear with speaker stands and place them right where you and the wardrobe supervisor had planned a quick-change booth.

Quick compromise and adaptability is vital, and the stage manager must be the arbitrator of disputes concerning whose space requirement takes precedence. Always bring both parties together with you while you're trying to work out the solution. For example, sometimes a small speaker platform can easily be placed on top of a quick-change booth, and then both people's needs are satisfied. Better yet, you will have avoided the type of confrontation typified by comments such as, "He can't put his #@*%! change booth here if you want the show to have sound."

PREPARING FOR THE LOAD-IN

To avoid as many last-minute glitches as possible, the stage manager and the technical personnel should get together at the theater at their earliest convenience to go over space allocation and plan the schedule for the load-in. There are a number of areas that should be checked with special care as you prepare to move a show into a theater:

- *Dressing rooms.* Carefully list the size and attributes of each one. Note the distance from the stage, the number and type of electrical outlets, number of spaces for actors, the presence of mirrors, showers, or any other amenities such as rugs, furnishings, and refrigerators.
- *Wardrobe and hair areas.* Check to see if there is an area with a washer and dryer and the extra power necessary for irons, steamers, sewing machines, and so forth.

- *Wing space.* After you pace out the dimensions of your set, check that there is ample room backstage for scenery and prop storage, quick-change booths, lighting and sound equipment, and any other necessary controls (winches, special effects, for example). Often what looks ample on the ground plan turns out not to be. This may be due to peculiarities of the theater that weren't accounted for: fire doors, stairwells, various fire curtains or sprinklers, and so on. There are many creative ways to deal with cramped wing space, but decide how you will handle the situation in advance and thereby avoid bogging down the technical rehearsal process.

Some tips for dealing with cramped quarters: Quick-change booths and prop tables that are necessary only for short periods can be made to break away or may be flown. Large scenery or prop pieces that are only used once can be flown or, in some cases, taken right out the door until the next performance. One show I visited backstage had a set of prop shelves set against one wall that would fly in and collapse during the show, so as one shelf of props was used, it would stack on the floor, and the next shelf of props was used, it would stack on the floor, and the next shelf would come to preset level, until at the end of the night, a stack of shelves had piled up and could then be reset for the next show in reverse order.

- *Crossovers.* Be certain that there is ample room behind the set for the cast to cross from one side of the stage to the other. Often the ground plan may indicate space, but once all departments run their cables, place their operators, and store their offstage presets, that space may be gone or rendered impassable. Always try to make an onstage crossover possible, but if reshuffling the set storage space or the placement of operators doesn't work, then the stage manager must make the director or choreographer aware of the time it will take for crossovers to be made. The usual alternative is to make the crossover under the stage or through the basement; in this case it must be carefully laid out (perhaps with a brightly colored tape) so that a safe, easy path is kept free at all times.
- *Fly floor.* If there are flying pieces in your show, check to see if they are operated from the deck (stage level) or from a bridge above.

If they are run from the deck, be sure there is ample room allotted for the flymen to operate.

- *Stage manager's console.* The stage manager must find a place from which he or she can call the show. Optimally, a stage manager's console or desk should be near an access to the front of the house, the stage door, and the dressing rooms. If one of the backstage wing positions fits these criteria, and won't impinge on the space, sight, entrance, and exit requirements of your show, the placement of the console is easy. The key is to try to position the console where it is most central for communication with as many departments and actors as possible.

In some cases, the desk must be situated on a raised platform backstage so that scenery can come on and off without interference (the Broadway production of *Into the Woods* had so many wagons and so much scenery tracking on and off that the stage manager ran the show on a platform above the deck). Other theaters may have a booth or front-of-house position for the stage manager. However, if you are to be backstage, it is important to decide where you will be located early on so electric and sound cables can be run to your position with the proper lengths and numbers requested in the initial shop order.

- *The deck.* Be sure to check the condition of the stage floor, especially if a new show deck or floor is not part of the set. Also, check how level it is. When we arrived at the Blackstone Theater in Chicago to load in the set for the pre-Broadway production of *Death of a Salesman* starring Dustin Hoffman, we discovered that if you put a pencil down on the center line, it would roll toward the wings. Because this would severely impede the operation of the turntable and wagon that we had in the show, the load-in was extended two days so that, foot by foot, carpenters could level the stage. Meanwhile, the actors rehearsed in a hotel ballroom. We could not cancel any performances because the show had already been sold out to subscribers and the schedule precluded adding any performances at the end because of a commitment to moving the show to Washington, D.C., so we had to rush the first performance instead of having a relaxed technical and dress rehearsal period. We made it, but not without tension and frenzy that could have been avoided by one on-site inspection of the theater in advance by the designer, master carpenter, or myself. Better yet, someone on the theater's crew should have mentioned the problem in discussions prior to our arrival.

- *Sightlines and acoustics.* Be sure to spend some of your pre–load-in inspection tour in the audience so you can advise the director and actors of sightline and acoustic difficulties that could be better dealt with by adjusting the staging rather than making costly technical changes.
- *Crew and staff.* Try to meet and discuss the load-in and the production's requirements with the house or resident crew before moving into the theater. In this way they can make their plans, and you will have as few surprises as possible during the actual load-in.

SCHEDULING THE LOAD-IN

For the actual scheduling of the load-in, try to work closely with the heads of each department, getting their input and needs. Always establish the order of work so that there is little or no "battling for the stage." An old tradition has the electrician work from the front of the stage back, and the carpenter from the back of the stage forward. Sometimes it is better to schedule a separate day or days for the electrician to work over the stage before the carpenter starts settings up. This saves time because the electrician can more easily move ladders and enjoy greater access to the pipes for hanging lights. Then when the carpenters get the stage the electrician can work in the house and around the sides of the stage.

Every show will dictate different schedules and order of work, and of course touring will require a lot more simultaneous effort because the show must be set up in one day, or one and a half days at the most. Make sure the heads of all departments meet with you and schedule the work together. Otherwise, the first two days of load-in will feature endless harangues, usually directed at the stage manager, which all boil down to something like, "You tell that #@*%! to get off the stage this minute or . . ."

Of course, the most carefully prepared plans can fly out the window if various elements of the set are not ready, trucks get delayed, or any other unforeseen circumstance occurs. On the *Sugar Babies* national tour we had set the order of work that would allow us to load in and tech within the time scheduled. In Chicago, however, the second truck of four didn't show up, so we tried to keep working around what was needed from that truck until it showed up a day late. Apparently, the driver had driven straight through from Los Angeles to give himself an extra day to "celebrate." Unbeknownst to us, he had ended up at a nearby motel, and after partying on his extra day, he slept through the day he was supposed to arrive.

Needless to say, we were hard pressed to make the first performance. Everyone's patience and tolerance were sorely tested by having to interrupt the established flow of the load-in to compensate for the missing parts. Diplomatic negotiations between warring crew heads finally got the show loaded in and set up, but not before one of the carpenters had threatened the sound man with a hammer, and the electricians were forced to focus the show while the audience was coming in. This incident illustrates the importance of establishing an order or schedule of work, agreed upon by all departments, that is adhered to throughout the load-in.

It is very important for the stage manager to arrange to be at the load-in even while rehearsals are still progressing. It may seem like there is little or no actual work for the stage manager to perform, but the crew needs someone to answer questions and keep work moving along. The stage manager also provides an on-site managerial presence and can help mediate any disputes regarding overtime. It is also the stage manager's job to keep a close, quiet, supportive eye on the progress of the set going in. The stage manager should work with the production carpenter to make sure that the precious inches and feet that have been planned for in the design to make the show function smoothly are not lost to a worker's decision to cheat a set piece forward a bit or hang a drop on another line. Conversely, sometimes you can make the crew's life easier by telling them they don't have to struggle to get some piece placed exactly where it is on the ground plan because fudging a few inches won't affect the staging. However, don't forget to check any change at this point with the lighting designer, who has planned angles and lighting coverage by the original ground plan.

On tour this process speeds up, of course, and the need for adapting and changing is constant, so the stage manager has to be present. Also in tour, the stage manager usually lights the show and is therefore highly instrumental in the laying out of every load-in.

If rehearsals are continuing during the load-in, plan well in advance for your absence. Notify the director and other company members when you will be gone. Set up a contact schedule so that you and your assistant are in frequent communication. Sometimes it is possible to split time between the rehearsals and the load-in, being in each place when it is most important. Of course, this is impossible if the show is loading in in another city and the company is still rehearsing in New York. However, as long as everyone is clear about what is happening, they will help you make it work.

CREATING THE CALLBOARD

As the crew's work on the load-in progresses, take some time to organize and set up the callboard. The callboard should be as close as possible to the stage door or whatever other theater entrance the cast and crew uses. The stage manager should establish from the outset that the callboard is for schedules, the sign-in sheet, and other official company business only. It is not for restaurant notices, cabaret ads, or flyers from vocal coaches and acupuncturists. Try to establish a second board somewhere (perhaps in the greenroom—the room where actors rest and relax before, between, or after performances) for notices like the above, and keep the company callboard strictly for the business of the show.

A neat and organized callboard is a reflection of the stage manger's approach to the cast and crew, and it also keeps the necessary information clear and available, not covered up by a lot of trash. Place a nice sign on the board asking that anyone who desires to post a notice should see the stage manager first.

It is good to have the sign-in sheet and schedule always in the same place, as well as a place where any important notes or news will be posted. This can be achieved by sectioning off three areas of the board with black electrician's tape. At the top of each section write one of the following headings: SIGN IN, PLEASE; SCHEDULE; and NOTES/NEWS, ETC. Date everything you put on the board, so people will know quickly if there are any changes or new information they need to check. Just this simple amount of callboard organization will enormously improve day-to-day communication and company clarity about what is going on throughout a production's run.

ASSIGNING DRESSING ROOMS

While the crew is busy with the load-in, the stage manager can use some of the time to finalize the dressing room assignments and make signs for the doors. Dressing room assignments should be posted on the callboard, and copies should be sent to the wardrobe department, doorman, house manager, prop man, and the office. Always check what contractual arrangements have been negotiated for each cast member in regard to dressing rooms. Sometimes actors have "first choice" or "nearest to the stage" clauses in their contracts. Sometimes they negotiate to have their own dressing room, if possible.

Take all these factors into account, then work with the wardrobe and wig departments to get them intelligently situated. The object is to make the cast as comfortable and functional as possible. Try to keep people with a lot of changes and different scenes in dressing rooms closer to the stage, letting people with only one or two scenes travel farther. Keep people with wigs closer to the hair room. Attempt to make "happy" assignments, keeping people who cannot and will not get along out of the same room. It is a delicate process and one that takes a lot of thought and diplomacy. Remember that contractual obligations and production necessities, as described, are the priority. Then if you're questioned about the assignments by disgruntled company members, you can offer firm reasons for the choices you made. Only deal with special favors secondarily.

Don't forget to find a place for the stage managers. There will be many people sharing this space as home base: the company manager, crew, hair and wardrobe personnel, and all your assistants, not to mention the director and designers and their assistants during the tech and preview periods. Furthermore, you will spend far more time in the theater over the course of the show's run than any actors, so don't feel bad about taking an adequately large room, even if it means doubling a couple of actors who would rather be alone. Unless they have negotiated such requirements into their contracts, your needs come first.

Don't think these assignments can be made easily and that everyone will be happy. No theater has ever been designed that will accommodate everyone perfectly; just do the best you can with the clear knowledge that everything was done with contractual and performance priorities in mind. If anyone wants to complain, explain that you understand the problem but, due to certain show or contract necessities, you had no choice. You can suggest that if the person wants to complain further he or she should do so to the agent who did not negotiate a better deal, or to the management. The management can, of course, tell you to change someone's assignment, but hopefully they will have already approved and understood your choices and will continue to back you. There is usually nothing to be gained by being defensive or mean about any of this; just remain firm and clear and understanding. However, don't be so rigid as to dismiss an offered solution that won't make anyone more upset than they already are.

One actor in the 1989–1990 Broadway production of *The Merchant of Venice* drove everyone nuts, becoming the perfect example of why it is often hard to get management or crew to help make actors more comfortable. (Their point of view is that actors don't appreciate anything anyway, so why bother?) This actor had to have his own dressing room, but there were limited single rooms available in the theater and, as with most Shakespeare productions, a large cast to accommodate. The first time he came to the theater, we took a tour of all the possibilities and showed him various options, explaining the drawbacks of each room, giving him the choice and promising to do whatever he requested to make his selection work for him. After he settled on a dressing room, which was usually a room for two or three people, the crew went about remodeling: it was painted, carpeted, fitted out with shelves and furniture, and so on. Then, after a day in the room, he decided he would rather move a flight upstairs, which he had originally turned down and which by then had been fixed up, wired, and powered for the wig room. After much argument and misrepresentation of who had agreed to what, he was allowed to make the move. The hair department had to have electrical service run to their new room and had to move all their appliances and other possessions.

Of course, after that debacle, any actor requesting anything in terms of dressing room amenities was greeted with understandable negativity from crew and management. This actor had gotten his way at the expense of that entire cast and probably many to follow. Dustin Hoffman, on the other hand, was busy trying to make everyone as comfortable as possible. On his own he supplied the cast with refrigerators for their rooms, cots, and radio/tape players.

As the load-in progresses, and after the dressing rooms have been assigned, the stage manager should spend more and more time on the stage as well as in the wings, so that he or she becomes a familiar figure to the crew and begins to feel at home before the onslaught of technical rehearsals and the arrival of the actors. Once the designer begins to focus the lights and the cues are being set, the stage manager should be permanently on the deck or in the house, helping the lighting designer by showing him or her blocking, checking the furniture placement for focusing, getting scenery moved as needed, and handling any communication system problems. The stage manager should also watch and learn the light focus, because once the show opens, it will be the stage manager's responsibility to make sure it is maintained as the designer first set it.

Cue Sheets

Cue sheets are detailed lists that indicate what each person in each department will do backstage during the running of a show. Every cue sheet should describe the move involved, the approximate time it happens in the show, and the type of cue you as the stage manager will be giving them—whether verbal (on headset), visual (by cue light), or whatever (frantic hand signal)—and how fast or slow the cue is to be performed.

To make a cue sheet, divide a piece of paper into three columns: the left-hand column lists the type of cue, its number, and when it happens in the show; the second column indicates what the cue does; the last column denotes the speed or level at which the cue occurs. For example, one member of the running crew could get a cue sheet with the first row reading "END OF OVERTURE: FLY Q1/RED LIGHT OFF" in the first column, "GATES FLY IN" in the second, and "ON A FIVE COUNT" in the third. This means that the flyman responsible for lowering a castle's gates onto the stage will execute his or her first cue—flying the gates in—on a count of five at the end of the orchestra's overture, once the red cue light is turned off. Make the columns and boxes large enough so that the crew members can write in their own notes.

Before the first technical rehearsal, make two copies of all the cue sheets, keeping the originals for yourself. One copy should be distributed to every person who will be taking cues directly from the stage manager, and copies of all cue sheets to be executed by each department should go to that department's head.

The three department heads that should get copies of their areas' cue sheets and the personnel to whom you should give individual copies are (1) the production carpenter and all of his or her winch operators and flymen who are responsible for moving and flying scenery and/or moving curtains or travelers; (2) the production electrician and any of his or her sound and special effects operators; and (3) the production property master and any of his or her crew that must move a specific prop, fire a gunshot, or adjust props in any way.

The sound designer often provides his or her own cue sheets. If the sound operator will be listening for cues on the headset, make sure all the cues on the sound designer's cue sheets are designated by letters, instead of numbers. This system will help the sound and light operators distinguish their aural cues during a performance. In some stock and community theaters, when sound designers aren't necessarily a permanent part of the staff, the stage manager must write up sound cue sheets as well and give them to the crew member running the sound. Sometimes, the stage manager may even have to execute the sound effects—ringing doorbells, telephones, sirens, and so on—from his or her own console or desk.

Today, with the easy accessibility of word processors and computers, constant corrections aren't as much of a problem. If you set up the basic form for each department's cue sheet in a computer file or word-processing document, you can quickly and clearly update changes every day. However, if no computer is available, it is best to print all cues with plenty of room for changes to be written in during tech week by you and the crew. Then, when the cues are set, a new clean version of the cue sheets can be made. Appendix 6 has a sample cue sheet.

In the best of all possible worlds, all cues—except for those given to the light board operator—should be nonverbal—i.e., by turning off a cue light. Confusion could result if a stage manager called "Q1 . . . go" during a performance, and three different people moved into action when only one was supposed to. Limiting verbal cues to the light board operator (and perhaps the sound operator) will make the running of a show smoother. An example of how to set up a cue-light board, write out the appropriate cue sheets, and then transcribe the cues into a script may be found in Appendix 9.

The Cueing Script

As discussed in the rehearsal section, it is a good idea to keep two scripts: a cueing/running script, in which all the cues necessary to call the show are written, and the blocking/rehearsal script, which contains all acting, staging, and interpretative notes. This allows your assistant to have the blocking script in rehearsal as you work on the cueing script. Try to pre-write as much of the cueing script as possible before the technical rehearsals begin.

Several different types of cues must be included in the running script: light cues, sound cues, actor warnings and cues for entrances, and all the cues from the cue sheets. The most abundant usually are the light cues. Meet with the lighting designer and he or she will tell you where the light cues are to be placed in the script. Number each cue consecutively from the beginning of the play to the end. The most common shorthand for writing a lighting cue is "LQ" followed by the number. For example, the third lighting cue of a play may be a scene-ending blackout; it would be written "LQ3." If a new cue is added between LQ2 and LQ3, number it LQ2.5. An example of this appears later, in Figure 7-2, where you'll notice the first lighting cue for *Speed-the-Plow* is numbered LQ.7.

When entering the lighting designer's cues in the script, pay particular attention to the sequencing of the production's opening. The stage manager and the lighting designer must carefully coordinate the extinguishing of the house lights and presets. As the designer and stage manager go over the cues prior to a technical rehearsal, their relationship is at its most collaborative. They are basically trying to set the rhythm and appearance of the lights—before the director and actors arrive—in an effort to stay ahead of schedule, anticipating how the director will want the lights to look.

The next step in preparing the book is to go to the sound designer and get his or her cue sheets, as mentioned above, and transcribe them into the running script, numbering them by letter. Next, get your cue sheets, copies of which you have handed out to the sound, special effects, winch, wagon, and fly operators, and make sure you have all these same cues in their correct places in the running script.

Check that you have written warnings—whether verbal warnings to the light board operator or the visual warning of turning on the appropriate cue light—for each cue in the script, allowing plenty of time between the warning and the cue's point of execution. Always begin by giving warnings far in advance and then shorten them as the show begins to get finalized.

Everything written in the running script should be in pencil! Nothing changes faster than cues, and the only way to keep up is with a good eraser and a lot of sharp pencils. I always keep a large supply of unlined three-hole paper handy so I can write out cueing sections on pages separate from the script and then insert them facing the page with the appropriate dialogue. A sample page from my cueing script would then look something like Figure 7-1.

Once the technical cues are all written, go back through the script and make sure that all warnings for actors to take their places are written in. Include a note indicating who is to check each actor. At the start of an act, always list everyone who has to be ready, in every position, and check them visually or by communicating with an assistant on the headset. The opening page of a show's cueing script might look something like Figure 7-2.

As you can see, there is a lot to check before starting the opening sequence: every crew member and performer's presence, as well as the position of key prop and set pieces. There is nothing worse than taking house lights down to half and then having to bring them back up because you realize you have to wait for an actor or crew person to show up. If the script is prepared to this extent, the tech will go much faster and smoother. Do not ever try to start a tech and write cues as you go.

Scheduling Technical Rehearsals

By the time the stage manager has spent a load-in period with a crew and seen all the pieces and elements in person, a meeting can be held to draw up

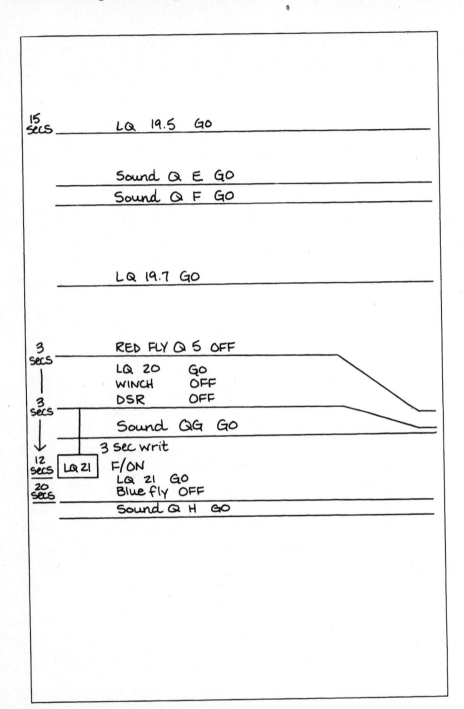

FIGURE 7-1 *Sample Pages from Final Cueing Script*

Act 2 Scene 6   **THE MERCHANT OF VENICE**

And fair she is, if that mine eyes be true;

And true she is, as she hath proved herself;   55

And therefore like herself, wise, fair, and|true,|

Shall she be placèd in my constant soul.

    Enter Jessica below

What,|art|thou come? On, gentlemen, away.

Our masquing mates by this time|for|us stay.

                       Exit with Jessica and Salerio

    Enter Antonio

ANTONIO

 Who's there?

GRAZIANO |Signor Antonio?   60

ANTONIO

Fie, fie, Graziano, where are all the rest?

'Tis nine o'clock. Our friends all stay for you.

No masque tonight. The wind is come about.

Bassanio presently will go aboard.

I have sent twenty out to seek for you   65

GRAZIANO

I am glad on't. I de|si|re no more delight

Than to be|un|der sail and gone|to|night.   *Exeunt*

   [Flourish of cornetts.] *Enter Portia with Morocco and*   2.7

   both their trains

PORTIA

Go, draw aside the cur|tains|and discover

The several caskets to this|no|ble prince:

   The curtains are drawn aside, revealing three caskets

(*To Morocco*) Now make your choice.

MOROCCO

This first of gold, who this inscription bears:

'Who chooseth me shall gain what many men desire.'   5

SPEED-THE-PLOW   June 1989
Kennedy Center

Opening Sequence

As audience enters, the stage is open with the first act set draped in drop cloths. (See preset diagrams)

AT THE PLACES CALL:

1. Actor playing Gould SR with one red script
2. Actor playing Fox SL with Filo Fax
3. 2 prop men SR, 2 prop men SL
4. All worklights and running lights out
5. Electrician ready for board and houselights
6. Monitors on (Show program and TV)

ALL READY: HOUSE TO HALF

                              House at Half: HOUSE OUT
                                             LQ.7

IN BLACKOUT, PROP MEN STRIKE THE COVERS FROM THE DESK SR AND THE COFFEE TABLE SL, AND GOULD SITS AT DESK

                              Gould sits: LQ 1

FIGURE 7-2 *Sample Opening Page from Cueing Script*

a realistic tech-week schedule, based on what is achievable each day. Some directors will avoid this like the plague, desperately afraid that they will either be pushed to keep on a schedule that is too fast or that if they get ahead they will have nothing to do. The director needs gentle guidance through this period, and the stage manager can be a great ally by showing the director clearly what needs to be achieved on a daily basis to make the first public performance with as many run-throughs and dress rehearsals as possible.

The schedule at this point should be realistic and inclusive, so that every department will know exactly when their deadlines are. There may be rehearsals with partial costumes, rehearsals with full costume and makeup, and so on. All such rehearsals must be carefully thought out and clearly planned. If the director thinks actors are going to be in costume, but the wardrobe people have taken costumes to be fixed or altered, you will have a problem. If the director wants to concentrate on acting, but the designers are all over the stage trying to look at lights and different sets, friction can mount. As the stage manager, be sure to double-check that you and the director are clear about each step, then clearly outline and schedule those wishes and expectations for the cast, crew, and designers. The tech-week schedule that is included in Appendix 8 should give some idea of the complexities involved in its creation; it also makes clear the necessary information the schedule must contain.

In the professional commercial theater, there are three basic unions whose overtime and break requirements have to be factored into the creation of a schedule: Actors' Equity Association (actors and stage managers) American Federation of Musicians (orchestra members on a musical), and International Association of Theatrical Stage Employees (stagehands). In Appendix 10, I have included AEA's work rules concerning rehearsal hours, which include those for technical rehearsals. All the performing unions have different work rules for the periods before and after the opening or first paid public performance of a show. Basically, these rules outline the hours that can be worked without incurring overtime, both on a daily and weekly basis, and they are wildly divergent from one union to another. Of course, in a college or community theater production, the only restrictions are the time and energy of the show's participants.

During technical rehearsals, Actors' Equity Association members are allowed to work a seventy-hour week before going into overtime, as long as they only work ten out of twelve consecutive hours in a day and are given an hour-and-a-half break at the end of five hours. The stagehands, however, enter overtime scale after forty hours in a week and eight hours in a day, so they do very well in the tech week (or weeks) in which they work the same hours as the actors mounting the show. A careful perusal of the sections on rehearsal hours shown in Appendix 10 will give the reader an appreciation of the complexity of trying to mount a show under union contracts. This is further complicated when touring, because every city has different rules, and a schedule that was fast, cheap, and efficient in one city may be financially ruinous in the next.

I always try to keep working in five-hour chunks, so if the crew has been working in the morning, I schedule their hour break while the actors are getting into costumes and makeup or having notes. This can often make a half hour of otherwise wasted time productive. Similarly, at the end of the afternoon, the crew will have a half hour of time without the actors to fix, correct, or run things. Better yet, if all is well, they will have an extra half hour to rest.

Breaks are the hardest element to keep unified during tech week, especially because the unions have varying requirements. If you can remember to give the orchestra an official five-minute break whenever you know the technical department is going to take at least that long to reset or fix something, then the ten-minute break every one and a half hours required for actors should take care of the crew's union requirements as well. Why the musicians' union believes their members' bladders cannot stand up to the same time limitations as an actor's is a mystery, but it's one you have to deal with or have your rehearsal suddenly interrupted. So always give them five when you can.

Technical Rehearsals

Technical rehearsals are the rehearsals during which the physical production and the actors mesh and the full show is realized. Often, before actors get on the stage, the crew and stage managers try to "dry tech" as much of the show as possible, setting basic light and sound cues and getting the scenery and drops moving in the right way. There is more about this subject later in the chapter.

By far the hardest thing about a tech is getting it started. Everyone seems to have last-minute problems. I have found that calling out the time before the tech rehearsal is to start—at half hour, fifteen minutes, and five minutes before—greatly enhances everyone's belief that the tech will indeed begin. Sometimes, the director will want to address everyone first, and if so, it is a good time to introduce the crew to the cast, something that cannot be done enough in the first few days. The stage manager and assistants, as the liaisons between the actors and crew, should introduce the production's personnel whenever they can. It is important to try to break down the barriers as fast as possible between company members who will work incredibly hard together, under a lot of pressure and in very close quarters, and who in the end will have to depend on each other completely for success.

DRY TECHS

In the best of all possible worlds, you will have some time scheduled for a dry tech. This is a purely technical rehearsal that gives the stage managers and the crew a chance to work out scene changes, the movement of set pieces, and light sequences. In the commercial theater, producers rarely want to pay for this extra rehearsal, so you should try to practice some of the more complex scenic moves and changes as soon as everything is loaded in and set up.

On large, complicated shows it is essential that you run some of the fly and deck moves with the crew members before adding the actors, especially with the complex computer-controlled moves that must be programmed in advance. However, even the simplest show will benefit enormously from a dry tech. It gives the crew and the stage managers a chance to iron out any glitches before the actors and director are running around going crazy.

THE FIRST TECH

Armed with schedules, cue sheets, and a cueing script, the stage manager now takes on the challenge of finally pulling it all together. You and your assistants should arrive early and be ready on the first days in the theater to serve as "tour guides," helping the cast find their dressing rooms, the wardrobe and wig rooms, and their quick-change and crossover areas if they need them.

One assistant should be responsible for collecting valuables from dressing rooms for safekeeping in the stage manager's desk. This service should be available and offered every time actors rehearse in the theater. The best tool to accomplish this is the "valuable bag." These can be strong zip-lock bags or fine mesh laundry bags made by the wardrobe department. Each actor should find a bag with his or her name on it in the correct dressing room every time he or she comes into the theater. These are collected during the half hour, or actors can bring them to the stage manager's desk themselves at "places." When the valuables are reclaimed by the actors after the rehearsal or performance, the bags are returned to their rooms, ready for their next use or need.

Each assistant should also have a preliminary cue and checklist, detailing what actors he or she will be responsible for getting onstage and offstage and what technical events and changes each will be checking or supervising. This list will grow rapidly as the technical rehearsals continue. By the opening preview, it should eventually resemble the wonderfully complete tracking description of ASM cues in Appendix 7, prepared by Charles Kindl, one of the best assistants I have ever worked with. You'll notice that he has even diagrammed a desk top so that every prop's position is clearly mapped. In the opera prop running sheets in Appendix 7, you will see an example of more of a cue-sheet-type form that would be given to the crew.

Some shows, particularly those that are very simple technically, lend themselves to going "cue-to-cue," which means taking each cue or technical event and working it before going on to the next one. This means that often large sections of the show are skipped as everyone moves from one cue to another. However, it is my experience that trying to jump ahead by a page or several lines only wastes time as everyone tries to figure out where they are. Unless there is a five- or six-page section in which no new character, prop, set piece, or lighting cue is introduced, it is better to go straight through the play once. This will give everyone time to see the lights, set, and costumes and learn their entrances and exits.

If the show is one where the only real "tech" occurs during scene changes and at the beginning and end of each act, then it may be wise to go cue-to-cue. You can get every cue written and rehearsed once technically before letting the actors and director refocus on the performing as the lighting adjustments continue around them. In any case, be sure everyone knows in advance how you will be proceeding. When I stage managed *Death of a Salesman,* we had a cue-to-cue technical rehearsal for which I drew up an outline (see Appendix 8). The one I drew up for the show is a very good example of a schedule that should answer every department's questions about what is and isn't included in the tech. It also gives all the actors exact information on what lines and scenes will be run, so they don't have to guess whether they will be working through their scenes or skipping them. The schedule, approved by the director, should be given to everyone involved: cast, crew, designers, wardrobe, and stage management personnel, with a copy to the manager or producer's office.

Another problem with cue-to-cue techs is that crew members won't get a sense of how much time they have between cues. Other than starting a technical rehearsal, the most difficult part of techs is persuading the director to let the crew run sections of a play all the way through so that they will get a clear idea of how fast their cues come. Often each element of a sequence is run and discussed and fixed, and then, due to time pressure, the director will insist on moving on to the next cue. Therefore, the crew ends up with a bunch of cues written but has no idea if they can execute them in "real time." Then along comes the dress rehearsal or first preview, and everyone's timing is way off. The stage manager must use good judgment and rely on the crew to tell him or her when it is and isn't necessary to rerun a section. If it is necessary to repeat a cue, the stage manager must insist on it even if it means temporarily incurring the wrath of the director. It is better than having a fiasco or a dangerous situation occur later, perhaps during a performance.

An example of this problem occurred during the techs of *Accomplice.* There was an electrocution sequence near the end of the play with many elements—sound, light, trap doors opening, smoke, and explosions. This cue was run endlessly to try to perfect its execution. After we ran the sequence, there would always be endless discussion about how to perfect it, and then we would have to skip through to the end of the play. Therefore, no one on the crew ever realized how little time there was between the explosions and the final curtain and sound and light sequences. Sure enough, at the first preview, which was the first time we were ever allowed to go through to the end of the play without being stopped, I cued the final curtain and it didn't come in. I figured it was not going to come in at all, and I started the curtain call music and lights. All of a sudden the curtain flew in, trapping one actor in front of it and the rest of the cast in back.

The problem was that the curtain people never realized that the time between the explosion and the final curtain was so short, and they were only on their way to their position when the cue was given. So they untied and brought the curtain in as fast as possible, but by then I had gone on without them. All this could have been avoided by my insisting the ending be run just once all the way through, from the beginning of the effects sequence through the curtain calls. But in the heat of trying to perfect the cues in the complex special effects section, I had mistakenly decided the final cues were routine and didn't need the same amount of time and work.

COMMUNICATIONS SYSTEMS AND CUEING

Before starting the tech, the stage manager should be sure the communications and cueing systems are functioning perfectly. At the stage manager's desk or console should be a headset/microphone attachment that can talk selectively to every position where cues take place and to every position from which there may be an entrance or exit of actors or scenery.

The best headset system is one that allows up to five channels to be separately or collectively programmed to talk and/or listen to the stage manager. This means that the stage manager can assign one channel to lights, another to the fly floor, another to winches, another to ASM's, and one to the designers and director at the "tech table" in the house. All those stations can hear the stage manager without hearing each other, so if the lighting designer is using one channel to set cues with the light board operator, no one but the stage manger will be able to hear. However, everyone will hear everything the stage manager says unless the stage manager turns them off at the console. This system allows the director to talk to crew members or the stage manager privately and without shouting.

CUE LIGHTS

Because the stage manager must remain at the desk to cue the lights and sound effects through the headset, a second mode of cueing has developed. Basically, a cue light is a dark-colored light bulb of low wattage that is turned on by a switch at the stage manager's console, serving as a warning to the crew or to a performer that a move or entrance is about to happen. When the stage manger turns off the cue light, the crew person or performer executes the cue. Simply, the concept of the cue light is this: ON = WARN; OFF = GO. In the case of the fly floor, it is often necessary to have several different colored bulbs, so that several drops or pieces can simultaneously be warned to move but then cued to move separately a few beats or words apart.

Cue lights are used at all operator positions and entrances and exits; basically, once the show is set, all cues other than lighting (and sometimes sound) cues are given by cue lights. This avoids confusion because the electrician or light board operator will know all verbal cues he or she hears are for lights and does not have to distinguish all night the light cues from the set cues, and so forth. Cue lights should always have two bulbs at the cueing position, so if one burns out the other is still lit. I've included some cue sheets and examples of the way the cues are written in the stage manager's book in Appendix 9.

At the desk or console, the stage manager should have a cue-light panel with each switch carefully defined and marked. When the light is switched on, an indicator light should light up on that switch. The "name" of each cue light should be the same as the name in the cueing script.

Often actors will tell you they don't want a cue light or don't need one. But the lights are especially necessary if actors cannot see what is happening onstage just before they open a door, or if they can't hear their cue line clearly in the wings. The cue light serves as a safety against their walking in and seeing a piece of action they aren't supposed to see or overhearing dialogue or facts they should only discover later.

THE STAGE MANAGER'S CONSOLE

In addition to the cue-light panel, the stage manager's console should be equipped with two microphones: one to talk to the dressing rooms and one to talk into the stage and house speaker system. During techs, it is important to make all announcements (half-hour calls, breaks, places) on both mikes. The house speaker system is also useful to tell everyone when the tech is ready to resume and what cue line to start from. It is also vital in emergencies, both before and after the show is running. This mic also becomes the "audience announce" microphone—sometimes a stage manager will be required to remind audiences that smoking and flash photography is prohibited. The dressing room or paging mic allows the stage manager to call and make announcements to the cast and backstage crew before and during the tech or performance.

It is important that the stage manager be able to turn up the volume of the paging system to the dressing rooms if there is an emergency or an important announcement that will have to cut through the backstage and dressing room din. It is equally important to remember to turn off the show monitor in the dressing rooms when there is no rehearsal or performance in progress. Especially during technical rehearsals, this allows conversations to take place onstage or in the front rows of the audience that are not broadcast to the whole building and prevents any hammering or sawing occurring onstage to go pounding into the ears of everyone backstage.

The stage manager's desk may have to be equipped with sound and video monitors. This is necessary because often the position of the desk does not allow for an unobstructed view of the stage, and the stage manager often will not be able to hear the dialogue clearly enough "live" to call cues.

Calling Cues

There are very few exceptions to the way a stage manager calls cues in the theater. For every cue, a stage manager should give a warning, about thirty seconds in advance, and then a "stand-by" warning, one or two lines in advance. The cue itself is then called by giving the title or number of the cue a few words or beats ahead, before saying "go," one beat in advance of the desired moment of execution. The beat allows the crew member to hear and respond, and it must be consistent and clear. This same beat must be built into the cueing of any production element on a cue light, because the operator or actor must register that the light has gone out before doing his or her cue.

After you have given a warning, a stand-by, or a cue number, avoid ever saying anything on a headset other than the cue itself. Once, during the run of the Broadway musical *The Wiz*, we were having a technical rehearsal for the new actress who was taking over the role of Dorothy. Just as we were getting ready to do the tornado sequence that involved Aunt Em's house twirling across the stage, lightning and thunder, and the entrance of a chorus of dancers, all taken off the "go" for the lights, a chorus girl asked me if she could be excused early and skip the curtain call. I emphatically responded "no," and you can imagine what happened next as lights blacked out, sound cues started, and wagons rolled. It was a disaster. If only I had said "yes"!

During a tech rehearsal, the stage manager initially should verbally give warnings for a lot of the cues that will eventually be done by cue lights. This will ensure that everyone is doing the same cue and understands how and when to execute it. Once the cues have been practiced in techs, the cues can be warned by the cue light.

As the tech begins, the stage manager should make sure that chatter is kept to an absolute minimum on the headsets and that only cues and checks or questions are going back and forth. Make sure *everyone* is ready to perform a cue or sequence before you start it, because the wasted time and energy of running a cue over and over is a serious drain on everyone's nerves and energy. The most frequently used words by the stage manager during tech week are "thank you" and "quiet!"

Keep the actors aware of what is going on while setting up for a cue. A simple announcement stating, for example, that you are going back to a certain point to run the lights and sound again, and it will take a couple of minutes, so please relax, will gain much respect and goodwill. Then give the company a stand-by warning and clearly and loudly request a line of dialogue as a starting point. Choose a line three or four lines before the cue and ask them to please take it from that line when they are ready. The tech continues this way through the end of the day.

Techs can be frustrating and tedious for a lot of people, especially the actors and crew members who are standing around doing nothing for large amounts of time while small technical adjustments are made. But for stage managers techs are the period of time when all their work and preparation pay off. The stage manager must always be alert, anticipating the next step, while clearly communicating to everyone exactly what is going on and who will be needed to do something next.

The tone of the stage manager begins to control the mood of a tech very quickly. Try to be clear and commanding without being officious, frazzled, or rude. It is also the time to employ a full understanding of the great rule of theater taught me by my mentor Bob Currie: *"All things are not of equal importance."* Basically, this rule is a constant reminder that, as every day in a theater progresses, priorities will emerge that the stage manager must keep straight, even as other company members maintain that their problems or needs should be the number-one priority. It is also a gentle reminder that we are not doing brain surgery or nuclear fission experiments but an adult version of "dress up." I print this rule in clear letters and hang it somewhere near the stage manager's console. Sometimes in the heat of trying to keep a tech flowing, with egos colliding and fatigue putting an edge to everyone's work, reflecting on this dictum may help you get through the moment.

Furthermore, the stage manager must fully accept that during the tech week he or she is perceived as being responsible for everything. Actors will complain about the food at a local restaurant as if it were you who ordered them to go there. Every schedule you post will anger at least half the people who read it, and they will think you are responsible for their early calls. (It's never the designer who needs them for the fitting or the director who wants to go over a scene once more.) People will tell you to tell other company members things that you must use your common sense to ignore, as in, "You tell that so-and-so that if he thinks I am coming in at ten to run her scene . . ."

Think of techs as Tommy Tune has described them—as the chance to reenact our childhood fantasy of "putting on a show" in the garage or living room—and it will make it all a lot more fun. Maintain a positive and pleasant tone and keep what you are doing in perspective. Once during a particularly trying technical rehearsal, Glynis Johns was raving on and on at the designer about the costumes and how the jelly madrilène bowls were wrong and how she couldn't be expected to perform a lady of class in this mess. I happened to look over at the headline of the paper, and it said, "Nuclear Disarmament Talks to Start Today." It put things in a healthier perspective.

Remember that all shows do eventually get off the ground. One mental exercise that has always helped me during techs and periods of stress has been to picture myself on the other side of the event happy and feeling that all has gone well, then looking back and seeing what steps it took to get me there. Somehow the journey to completion seems easier from that vantage point than from the beginning.

At every break, go over the tech's progress and priorities with the director and designers. Schedule discussions often occur as people are rushing out the door to dinner; be sure to be available and involved so that there are no surprises later on. Basically, anything is possible as long as there is time to plan and prepare for it. If there are to be any changes, try to update the schedules and get them posted as quickly as possible.

The stage management crew should try to meet and go over notes and problems every chance they get. The assistant stage managers are invaluable sources of information, and often they hear and see things during the course of a tech that can forestall or eliminate problems before they occur: actors not getting along with their dressers, or safety problems that can be fixed with a little additional glow tape or foam padding on a sharp corner. Sometimes, the assistants can give a more realistic appraisal of whether a certain costume or set change will get faster or smoother or if additional help is needed. All their input should be discussed, and then the stage manager must decide which problems can be dealt with and which ones must be taken to a higher court for a decision.

The running of technical rehearsals is a totally absorbing time for the stage manager. Sometimes, even though I live in New York, I find it better to check into a hotel to block out the demands of family and regular life. In that way I can better focus on the job at hand. No one in the normal world can conceive of how much we in the theater world achieve in a short period of time by the combination of fierce concentration, creative energy, and a large dose of preplanning by the stage manager. Keep communication with all departments and creative personnel fluid and constant. Keep an eye on priorities and the clock. And the show will go on. It always does.

8

PREVIEWS AND OPENING NIGHT

Once you have guided your show through all the technical and dress rehearsals, it is time to add that unknown element—the audience. The first preview or public performance often creeps up suddenly. This is especially true when you've had a dress rehearsal or final tech that afternoon—it is always a shock to come back from dinner and find the house full of strangers.

The stage manager must be a firm and supportive part of the transition between private and public performances because everyone else's nerves will be on edge, and the more the stage manager can treat the event as business as usual, the better. Try to complete all checks and preparations early so you can be ready to deal with last-minute needs of others—a forgotten makeup kit, first-aid needs, wardrobe or prop problems, and a hundred other unforeseen possibilities. The stage manager should try to quell any frenzy produced by actors as they confront what seem to them like insurmountable problems with a calm statement like, "Don't worry, we'll take care of it; you just worry about getting ready for the show."

Opening the House

The first preview is also the time to solidify with the house manager the plan for opening the house (allowing the audience into the theater), starting the show, and late seating. Well before the first performance it is a good idea to approach the director and discuss the late-seating policy so you can clearly translate the information to the house manager. As the stage manager, try to initiate this discussion by telling the manager what time you will start the show unless the house has a reason for starting it at a different time. That solves a lot of guesswork on both sides and gives the house management the responsibility of getting the audience seated and ready on time.

If you have a curtain, the best way to signal that you are ready for the house to be opened is to close the curtain. Otherwise, show the house personnel the preset (the "pretty lights," as I like to call them) and tell them that as soon as they see those light up instead of the work lights they may open the house at their leisure. Then make very sure the electrician knows never to turn on the preset until you call for it.

LATE SEATING

Seating ticket buyers after a show has started is one policy that often raises animosity between the house management staff and the production personnel. The ushers and house manager are faced with a horde of angry, obnoxious people (only angry, obnoxious people arrive late for the theater), and the staff wants to get them seated as soon as possible. On the other hand, you and the director are trying to protect the rights of the people who have arrived on time. Early in a play, important dialogue must be clearly established and the mood of the evening set. This is made difficult when an audience's suspension of disbelief is suddenly interrupted by late-arriving theatergoers being led into the theater by flashlight-swinging ushers.

Everyone tries to find a place where the action is pedestrian—a scene shift or a long procession—but invariably the interruption overlaps into the next scene, and actors get distracted and upset. Try to be the instrument of the policy; let the producer and director argue the concept of timing with the house manager. Stage managers should only have to work out a way to give a clear cue warning the ushers and house manager that the seating interval is imminent. Then go over very clearly what they must see or hear before they start the people down the aisle.

Because there is no controlled late seating after the intermission, it is important to make sure that the audience is back in before starting. Otherwise the first scene or number in the second act may be ruined. At the first preview of *Orpheus Descending*, Sir Peter Hall became so distraught at the way in which the returning hordes of people were destroying the opening moments of Act 2 that he shouted from the back of the house,

"SIT DOWN!" at which point Tammy Grimes, who was onstage at the time, promptly sat on the stage floor. The best way to handle latecomers after intermission is to make sure that at least the front of the orchestra section is filled.

Musicals often afford stage managers the luxury of an overture and an entr'acte, which greatly alleviates the problem of late seating. Nothing moves audience members to their seats (or actors to places, by the way) faster than the orchestra starting to play.

The First Preview

The first preview is often a technical nightmare for the stage manager because all those cues that were set without audience reactions now must be executed in and around laughter and applause. Furthermore, the audience responses occur in totally unexpected places. When the musical *A Day in Hollywood/A Night in the Ukraine* had its last out-of-town tryout, the staid old Baltimore subscribers gave it hardly a chuckle. Certain songs were met with no applause or response at the end. The audience reception was so bad that the producer reportedly was trying to sell the show to the highest bidder before it got to New York, but there were no takers.

Led by the charismatic and inspirational tone that Tommy Tune creates when he works, the cast stepped onto the stage of the Golden Theater on Broadway undaunted, believing in themselves and the show. The first night of previews the house came down—there were ovations after the musical numbers and show-stopping laughter throughout the second act, which was a Marx Brothers movie put to music. Of course, all the cues had been timed for the type of response we received in Baltimore. During that first performance in New York there were times when at the end of a number the lights would cross-fade into the next cue, while the actors waited in near darkness for the applause to subside. Some numbers ended in poses that became physically difficult to maintain, because the cast had never had to hold them for any length of time in Baltimore. That first night in New York, a couple of performers either fell over or lost their balance trying to remain still long enough for the applause to ebb. It was a thrilling, surprising night. The show became a big hit and ran for two years.

Often, the performers themselves will throw a lot of curves at the stage manager during the first performance in front of an audience. Actors have a tendency either to speed up or go slower, or to speak louder or softer, than in rehearsals. This can wreak havoc with the timing of your cueing between warnings and "go" cues, but usually it seems worse to the stage manager than to the audience.

The crew may also have trouble hearing cues because of laughter and applause and may consequently miss cues. The stage manager must be especially alert during the first performance and check everything and everybody more than at any other time.

During the preview period, a show is often still rehearsing and changes are being made. The stage manager is the central clearinghouse of information, ascertaining what the desired changes are, advising the director on how much time will be needed to achieve the changes, and then scheduling the work and rehearsal times needed to implement these changes. At the same time, the stage manager must protect the company's ability to do a clean and safe show for the public. There is a delicate balance he or she must maintain between the pressure and desire to look at fixes and make changes and the cast's and crew's ability to perform them.

I always try to explain that it is sometimes better to wait one more day before inserting revised material or a new effect than to rush it into the show and see the result half realized. Often the creators don't care, and the result is that the show is really doing rehearsal work in front of an audience, a practice that often generates the dreaded bad word of mouth that can sink a show. Mainly, the stage manager must remember he or she is in a service position at this time. Try to give the creators, who may be embroiled in a fight for their professional lives, as much support as is humanly possible.

I have had no better experience of this creative process than on *A Day in Hollywood/A Night in the Ukraine*, thanks to director Tommy Tune's ability to understand the show's problems, and work them out, while sharing his creative impulses with everyone involved. Although the show had developed well in rehearsal, major changes were clearly called for. However, because the opening in Baltimore was so close, it was decided to freeze the show until after the first performance so the company could get through technical rehearsals without simultaneously dealing with new material. After the opening weekend, the schedule called for two full days and nights off and the day off before that evening's performance. All changes would be implemented during this period.

For two days the whole creative staff gathered in Tommy's hotel room and slowly worked through the show, making revisions. Each time there was a change, we would collectively go back through the show with the musical director, singing through the music, while I called the cues. We discovered where there were problems and where new music or dialogue or scenic or lighting cues had to be created. The writers then were called in and given their assignments, and slowly over the two days a new first act emerged.

The ensuing rehearsals to implement the changes were exciting and fruitful, because everyone had shared the experience of creating the new material and nothing was being tried that was impossible or irrational. As I said, this kind of experience is a rare one in the theater; I have never been so closely involved in the evolution of a successful show. Stage managers are often looked upon as mere minions who execute the dictums of the creative people. However, while working with Tommy Tune I could feel and see my own input having a direct effect on the total outcome, and that is a thrill like no other in theater.

Opening Night

Opening night is similar to the first performance of a preview period, except that the show has hopefully become a little more routine. Stage managers should arrive long before curtain time on opening night to handle any last-minute emergencies and also to help deal with flowers and gifts. At the opening of *Sugar Babies*, we discovered early in the afternoon that, if we didn't do something with Ann Miller's flowers, the halls would become impassable, and we would be unable to do the show. We had to order a van to come and cart the flowers back to where she was staying.

The advent of computer-operated light boards has done much to add to the sophistication and art of stage lighting, but in my experience they have seemed as jittery as any human performer on an opening night. On the opening nights of both *A Day in Hollywood/A Night in the Ukraine* and

Sugar Babies there were problems with the light board. On *Hollywood/ Ukraine*, everything was calm—everyone expected the best after the tumultuous response during previews—and while there was excitement backstage, there was no panic. The audience was arriving, and I made one last check of the stage before calling the actors to places. As I stepped onstage, every light in the theater suddenly came up to its fullest reading. I thought maybe the electrician was playing a trick on me or maybe making one last full check of the lights before returning to the preset. Basically, I didn't really think anything of it until I walked off the stage and into the alley outside the stage door and saw the electrician standing there. "How come all the lights are full?" I asked. "[Expletives deleted]!" he replied and ran back into the theater. After a few worrisome minutes, he brought all the lights down manually and reprogrammed the board; the proper preset came up, and the show ran smoothly. We guessed that there may have been a surge in the power lines that affected the light board's sensitive computer controls. Perhaps the reason for the surge was that our early opening-night starting time coincided with the approximate time that the other Broadway theater electricians came in and turned on their power. Since then, surge regulators have been developed to prevent such an occurrence.

On *Sugar Babies*, the reverse happened. About halfway through the show, Mickey Rooney was doing a long monologue in a spotlight with very dim blue light washing the remainder of the stage. I was enjoying Mickey's routine and the audience response when I noticed the blue lights very slowly fading out. Since we had no cues for about five minutes during this monologue, the electrician was off-headset relaxing. I flashed him by flicking his cue light on and off. (Even though the light cues are given verbally, it is a good idea to have a cue light run into the light booth in case the headset system goes dead or an emergency like this one occurs.) He got on the headset, and I asked him if there was a reason that all the stage lights had just gone out. For a second he thought I was joking, then he realized it was absolutely true. After considering various options, he decided that the only possibility was to turn off the board, turn it back on and reprogram it, then punch in the cue that was supposed to be up and see what happened. By now there were a lot of people on the headset asking where the pretty blue lights had gone. We all held our breaths and, as if he were an astro-naut and we were in Houston control, the electrician talked us through each step: "I am now turning off the board, removing the old disc, putting in the new disc, turning on the board, calling up the cue . . ." His litany progressed, and we all watched the blue lights as they came back to a nice low glow. I'm sure the collective sigh of relief made the audience think the air-conditioning had come on. Fortunately, the show continued without a hitch. No one ever really knew why it happened, just that it did. The board may have had a power surge or drop. Luckily, the new line voltage regulators seem to have stopped these problems from happening.

BACKSTAGE SUPERSTITIONS

Opening nights intensify many of the superstitions and traditions that most theater cast and crew members believe in very strongly. Among the more universal of these are:

1. Never wish an actor or singer "good luck." Instead, the accepted backstage version of good wishes is "break a leg." Singers use the expression "voco lupe" (Italian for "voice of the wolf") to wish good luck to each other. French performers offer each other the expletive "merde," politely translated as "crap."
2. Never whistle backstage or in dressing rooms. This has a very practical origin: Cues for the fly floor used to be given by whistles, so an inadvertent whistle could result in scenery falling on someone's head.
3. Never mention the character or play *Macbeth* in the theater.
4. Never say the last line of a play except during performance.

9

MAINTAINING AND RUNNING A SHOW

After opening night, there is an exodus of the creative personnel. The artistic director and designers move on to their next projects, and when the dust settles, it is the stage manager who is responsible for maintaining the artistic quality of the show. Obviously, in a community or university theater situation where the show only runs a weekend or two, the stage manager's responsibility for maintaining the show's quality will be slight compared to a run of several weeks in a regional theater or a commercial run or tour that may last months or years. Here are some steps that are taken as a matter of course when setting in for a long run; they will be valuable to understand and follow to whatever extent they are applicable to your particular situation.

Training Stage Managers

As soon as possible after opening night, all assistant stage managers should learn to call the show and run each other's deck cues. This means the stage-right assistant should learn what the stage-left assistant does, and all assistants should be trained by the stage manager to call cues for the show. The PSM should know everyone's position and then be free to go out front and watch a performance. As soon as it's practical, every assistant stage manager should watch the show from the front, especially before calling the show, so that he or she has a concept of what happens when a cue is called.

Training an assistant stage manager to call a show progresses at a different pace with everyone. There are several steps involved and, depending on the complexity of the show, they will take varying amounts of time. First, the person learning the show should see it from the front, so he or she will understand each cue better as it is taught. I like to go over the cueing and how all the cues are written and what all my symbols mean before having someone watch with me as I call the show. This step of allowing the assistant to watch me call the show is best done at the desk or console, so the person becomes familiar with the cue-light positions, the TV monitors, the paging system, and so on.

During the show, I try to talk through each sequence before it is run, then execute it while the assistant watches and answer any follow-up questions. It is often very helpful to make a recording at the desk with the show's dialogue and music recorded from the monitors. This results in a tape of the show with the lyrics, music, and words in the background and the stage manager's spoken cues louder on top of all the rest. It provides the stage-manager-in-training with an audio record of the exact placement of the cues, along with any instructions or questions that might have arisen while the assistant was watching the cueing taking place.

Note that Actors' Equity has very strong rules about taping the performances of any of its members, whether on video or audio. The union is attempting to protect against pirate tapes that can be reproduced and sold without any compensation to the performers. Clearly no one is going to be interested in paying for a cassette tape of a show with the poor audio quality one gets from the stage manager's monitors, especially when it includes two stage managers reciting cues and talking over most of the show. However, in any situation that may be at odds with the union, it is best to tell the Equity deputy and the stagehands what it is you're doing to avoid any problems.

After recording the show as it is called, the new stage manager can then take the tape and work on getting the exact timing of the cues. These tapes are invaluable tools for learning to accurately and safely call the cues for a show. Obviously, a videotape of the show that the training stage manager could take home to study would make this process even easier and far safer for the performers, whose lives sometimes depend on the accurate move-ment of set pieces or firing of effects. However, the union continues to refuse to allow videotape as a rehearsal tool. Perhaps the time has come for the union to understand how videotape can be used to enhance the creativity of the rehearsal period and promote the safety and quality of the performances after opening night.

Most often, it is the Actors' Equity members themselves who suffer most from not being able to use videotape. For instance, if choreographers creating dance pieces could go home at night and review their work for the day, they could then eliminate the tedium of starting each new rehearsal reviewing the work of the day before, most of which they will cut or change anyway. How much more exciting and enjoyable it would be for the performers to start each day with new material instead of rehashing the old. In the Tony Award—winning musical *City of Angels*, there is a magnificent fight sequence that is a spoof on old Hollywood movies. Each punch is accompanied by a sound effect—a "biff" or a "bam"—and there are crashes, glass tinkling, and so on. The sound operator had to learn this sequence by heart so he could time his sound effects perfectly. To do this, he told the company that he either had to have the actors come in and run the sequence over and over again, or they would have to provide him with a simple three-minute videotape of the sequence. The union insisted the actors be called.

Learning stage managers should make a number of "dry runs" at the desk or console, simulating the cueing and training their fingers and speech to coordinate and execute the written cues successfully before trying them in performance. It is often helpful for people learning a show to write their own books, so the cues are in their handwriting and the little notes or reminders are in symbols or phrases they understand. The PSM must be sure to go over such rewritten books to make sure no warning or cue has been left out. The placement of the warnings and pause between the time the number of a cue is spoken and the "go" should always remain the same. For instance, if the lighting man is accustomed to hearing "Lights 25," a pause that lasts a measure of a song, and then the word "go," and someone new only waits a single beat before the "go," the board operator will be late until he or she adjusts to the new stage manager. The rhythm of calling a show should remain constant, both from night to night, and from stage manager to stage manager, as new people take over the responsibility.

As soon as possible I try to let the training stage manager call uncomplicated segments of the show (internal light cues in a scene, for example), which allows the crew to get used to the new stage manager and the stage manager to grow comfortable with the task. The faster, more difficult sections take longer, and often I try to have each new assistant stand with me and tap my shoulder at the point when he or she would give the cues, until the taps and my cues are simultaneous. I then turn over the headset and cueing to the assistant, remaining by his or her side for two or three shows as a safety net, until there are no mistakes and the assistant is comfortable with the entire show.

Understudies and Replacements

UNDERSTUDIES

If your production looks like it is going to run for a while, hopefully there are understudies who were hired during the rehearsal process and who have watched and learned the show along with the cast. Understudies should have attended every rehearsal that involved the actors that they are covering, taking down blocking and interpretive notes from the director. If this is the case, the stage manager's job is simplified greatly. If not, the stage manager must start from scratch with each understudy.

Read through all your notes on the discussions of character that took place during auditions, rehearsals, and previews, and explain them as best as you can to the understudy. Then sit somewhere with your blocking/rehearsal script and have him or her take down all the blocking and stage business notes. Afterward, the real work of getting a performance ready can be developed. It is very important to remember that the primary responsibility of the stage manager's work with an understudy is to get the actor ready to go on at a moment's notice. To reach this emergency state of readiness, many of the niceties of the creative process have to be sacrificed.

At first, understudies should watch every performance, and once they know their roles, they should return once or twice a week to keep up with the little changes and nuances that both the persons they cover and the people they will be playing with develop. The stage manager's task is to help each understudy develop a performance that can be fit into the show, often without the benefit of rehearsal with the whole cast, as seamlessly as possible.

Of course, the actor and the stage manager may be tempted to "improve" the role and make it fit better on the understudy. But that is not the job. It is a far more difficult and creative challenge to develop a truthful performance within the boundaries of another actor's interpretation than to start with no bounds and give free rein to interpretation and character development.

Understudy performances are always charged with excitement the first time they happen. Often the infusion of a new performer creates a different direction or pace that is a needed contrast to the uniformity of a long-running production's performance. The rest of the company usually rallies and is very supportive for an understudy's first show.

The subsequent performances are more difficult, because the other actors will give the stage manager—or worse, the understudy—a lot of notes, usually only from their own acting points of view. It is a delicate and diplomatic time for the stage manager, who must try to keep the cast happy while not undermining the understudy's ability to give a decent performance. Once understudies become paranoid or lose the confidence of the rest of the cast, their performances fade into some obscure realm of "defensive acting," as though they are performing to avoid getting a note. To prevent this situation, try to get an understudy having problems to work onstage, before the curtain, with the regular cast member on whatever moments are giving him or her trouble. It is often the only time an understudy gets to rehearse with the actor with whom he or she is playing. This small amount of rehearsal often boosts the confidence of both actors and helps eliminate any negative feelings.

Once during the run of *Hollywood/Ukraine*, the actor playing Groucho was on vacation, and the understudy who was supposed to play for the week did not show up at the theater for the matinee. We called his home, tried his agent, friends, family, and so on. No one knew where he was. I remembered, however, that David Garrison, who had been nominated for a Tony Award when he originated the role, was rehearsing a new play nearby. I called his rehearsal hall and got him on the phone; after a moment of disbelief, he agreed to do the show, even though he had been out of the cast for about six months. We held the curtain fifteen minutes, but the audience didn't mind when I switched the microphone to "public address" and told them the reason for the delay. They were delighted that they were going to see the original instead of the replacement's understudy.

David was unbelievably good. I have never seen a performer pull off anything like he did that afternoon; it was an inspired performance. And of course the audience and the rest of the cast were 100 percent behind him. When he did falter or forget for a moment, it just made the performance better. Fortunately, as Groucho, he was able to get away with a lot of wild ad-libbing and improvisation. It was by far the most successful emergency I have ever been through.

Normally, understudy rehearsals are held once or twice a week. As soon as the actors know their parts, it is best to run the show straight through and not spend a lot of time working on scenes, because understudies must keep up their stamina, honing their ability to play their roles from beginning to end. This process is much like keeping an athlete in shape.

Occasionally, if an understudy is going to be on for any extended period of time, the regular cast will join the rehearsals and run scenes and work out any special business or fights. Furthermore, a tech/dress is usually scheduled the afternoon the substitute goes in.

REPLACEMENTS

Cast replacements are usually handled in a slightly different manner than understudies. Often the director is more involved with the replacement process and will mold the new actor's performance to fit within the original interpretation. The director may work with the full cast to help them play certain moments or scenes with a new attack.

It is a fascinating process to watch a show evolve with different actors playing the same roles and yet bringing whole new meanings and emotions to scenes and moments. The play *I'm Not Rappaport* was particularly affected by the replacement casts. Over the course of a two-and-a-half-year run the two male leads changed from Judd Hirsch and Cleavon Little to Hal Linden and Ossie Davis to Jack Klugman and Ossie Davis and then back to Judd and Cleavon. The running time of the show changed by over twenty minutes during the course of this run, with different casts taking it faster and slower. The balance of strength between the characters changed totally from one cast to the other, and yet the play remained the same. It was the emotional content of the evening that was in constant flux.

Technical Maintenance

It is the responsibility of the stage manager to see that the physical quality of the show remains at a high level. This requires a watchful eye from the front for any technical problems: fading color quality in the lights, worn-out set pieces, costumes that are fraying.

It is important to balance the cost and effect of each fix. A costume that might cost thousands of dollars to replace may appear on its last legs backstage, but because it is only worn for one dance number or during a fleeting crossover, it may not need to be replaced. On the other hand, a suit that looks all right in the dim backstage light may show threadbare and worn under the stage lights, and a new one should be ordered.

Always try to coordinate any maintenance work calls so that the crews come in all at once and the cost is held down and more work can be done. Often, only the lights need attention, and the stage manager must make a separate call to change gel colors and fix the focus.

Every technical element that involves the safety of the cast or crew should have a regular maintenance schedule. Do not wait until these items show wear or tear to fix them. Every moving and working piece should be tested before every performance for function and safety. Because almost all special effects must be rigged and/or charged before every show, this attention serves as a constant check. Railings, ropes, and steps should be inspected constantly for sturdiness and wear.

The crew and stage managers should usually get to the theater at least an hour before curtain time for these checks. Sometimes with more complicated productions or shows without a curtain, this call could be extended to an hour and a half before curtain. This must all be worked out carefully as it may involve overtime payment to crew members.

Of course, no matter how well a stage manager maintains and inspects a show, there will always be mishaps. Every stage manager will collect a number of anecdotes about unforeseen emergencies that occurred during a performance. One of the most frightening experiences I've had was the time I had to put out a fire onstage. Some wigs were stored behind a piece of scenery, and they blazed up when hit by sparks from a flash-pot effect. I had my assistant hold back the entering cast members while I leapt up on the piece of scenery with a blanket to smother the flames and was met by one of the electricians with a fire extinguisher. In less time than it has taken you to read this, the fire was out, and the show was continuing, interrupted only by the audience's applause.

During the run of *Othello*, I was watching from the back of the house as the transition into the climactic bedroom scene began, where Desdemona (Dianne Wiest) is murdered by the jealous and enraged Othello (James Earl Jones). As blocked, Desdemona would cross the stage to her bedroom in dim light, accompanied by a hauntingly beautiful piece of viola music, and her maid would enter to help her prepare for sleep just as the bed, driven onstage by a motorized winch, would appear. I was always bothered by the noise that the winch made during this transition and had been working with the carpenter to muffle its sound. Simultaneously, I had been working with the sound man to find a level for the viola music that would drown out the winch's hum but not be so loud as to alter the mood of the scene.

At this particular performance, I thought we had finally found the perfect sound level, but then to my horror I realized no bed was appearing. The music drew to its final measures, and now a constant strained whining hum could be heard. I ran as fast as I could backstage and saw the crew trying to fix the winch but having no success. I grabbed the ASM, who also played a servant in this scene, and together we pulled the mattress off the bed and dragged it as ceremoniously as we could on to the stage and dumped it in front of a startled and slightly terrified Dianne Wiest, indicating to her to get onto it as if she were in an early Venetian hippie pad. We exited, the lights came up, and we all breathed a sigh of relief . . . until we realized that the dagger James Earl Jones used in the scene was preset on the headboard of the bed that lay worthlessly in the wings. James also realized this and spent a great deal of one of Shakespeare's most famous soliloquies making eye contact with us backstage while maneuvering himself to a doorway where he could stand with his back in the arch and grab the dagger, which we had waiting for him.

Unfortunately, there is no way to teach someone "successful reactions to stage emergencies." You'll find that most theater workers have a built-in instinct for quick reactions to such situations, and as the examples from my experience demonstrate, everyone works together to ensure that the show goes on. Don't be overzealous about continuing a performance, however. The safety of the performers and audience is the top priority. If someone is seriously injured onstage or a fire breaks out that can't simply be smothered by a blanket or doused by a fire extinguisher, don't be afraid to stop the show completely to deal with the situation.

Performance Logs

It is vital to keep accurate logs of every performance, just as it was necessary to keep reports of rehearsals. The performance logs are a resource that possibly may be used to arbitrate all payroll and insurance disputes. They also serve as a way for the stage manager to air grievances to the producer, manager, and, often, the director. Any artistic feelings or needs voiced by the cast should be written down in the log. These daily report forms are also useful as a place to note any growing technical, artistic, or temperament problems that may eventually affect the ongoing operation of the show. Figure 9-1 is an example of a form that I use for my daily performance logs. All the boxes for notes should be self-explanatory, but I have also included an example of a filled-in form in Appendix 11.

Giving Actors Notes

Giving actors notes on their performances and calling and running brush-up rehearsals are perhaps the most delicate and important part of the stage manager's maintenance work on a show. Very few performers are of the mind-set of Dustin Hoffman. After a performance, he would take me by the arm and plead, "Give me some notes," and mean it. However, few actors have Dustin Hoffman's ongoing dedication to perfecting the craft of acting. Most often, a stage manager's acting notes are met with a hostile and negative response. Don't let this stop you.

Confronted by a stage manager giving them a note, most actors will give notes back, usually concerning someone else's performance. (It is amazing how few problems are ever solved by one note.) If possible, therefore, get everyone together for a note session that will allow small sections and problems to be worked out on their feet. With the whole cast present, no one feels cornered or attacked or singled out, and much more can be achieved.

There are ways to go about offering notes as a stage manager that are different from that of the director. I will often enlist the help and advice of one or two of the actors in a scene, asking them how we can get back to the original pace, intensity of emotion, or whatever. Share the problem with the cast, asking them how, as a company, everyone can get the show back to the level at which it was originally performed. Don't demand the result you want or give notes in a punitive fashion.

Giving acting notes to performers is the most delicate and hard-to-teach function of stage managing. The best way to learn is by doing it. If you are enrolled in a university theater program, be sure to take acting and directing classes. They will help make you aware of the complexity of the task. However, the main thing a stage manager must remember is that he or she is a maintenance director, not an interpretive director. The role of the stage

```
          T H E   M E R C H A N T   O F   V E N I C E
STAGE MANAGER REPORT                    46TH STREET THEATER

DAY:               DATE:              PERFORMANCE #

ACT I  Up        :              WEATHER/AUDIENCE/FOH

ACT I  Down      :

  Running Time:  Hr.  Mins.

Intermission:    Mins.


ACT II  Up       :
                                ABSENT, ILL, ACCIDENT
ACT II  Down     :

  Running Time:  Hr.  Mins.

Total Running Time:    :

Total Elapsed Time:    :


    REHEARSAL, WORK CALLS, P.R.        NOTICES, OFFICE NOTES




           PERFORMANCE & TECHNICAL NOTES












                            STAGE MANAGER:  Tom Kelly
```

FIGURE 9-1 *Sample Performance Report Form*

manager is to fulfill the director's vision and keep the level of performance as close to the original as possible.

There are a number of acting problems that a stage manager must watch for carefully, to which I now turn.

PACING

As actors get to know a play by performing it over and over, they often start to speed up the pace of the show. Actors' tongues start to move faster than the thought behind the lines, because they no longer have to remember the words or consider their meaning. This results in a mechanical, one-level performance. Getting actors out of this habit can be achieved by gentle reminders or requests to go back to the text and reacquaint themselves with the subtext and the meaning of their lines.

An occasional brush-up rehearsal may be necessary when a scene or section has become rushed or superficial. In this manner, the play can be broken down again and worked on without an audience. During these rehearsals strive to get the performers' creative juices flowing again.

The opposite pacing problem also occurs. Usually, a slower pace is caused by actors falling in love with certain lines or sections and becoming indulgent with them, basking in the laughter or emotional response of the audience, milking every moment. Eventually, especially in a dramatic play, an actor's emotional indulgence can numb and stupefy an audience and distort the meaning by giving a moment or a scene portentous weight. In such cases, tactful notes and some brush-up rehearsals are necessary, as well as the cooperation of all the actors in a scene. It doesn't help if the actor portraying Hamlet, for instance, is cooking along, putting energy and pace back into the performance, only to have Gertrude, Ophelia, or Claudius drain the energy from every moment they have with Hamlet.

STAGE BUSINESS

Some actors employed in a long-running show get bored. This usually leads to the creation or expansion of "stage business." Simple actions, discovered by an actor at one performance, may get a big reaction from that audience. Thereafter, the business will find its way into the play. If a fly appeared onstage during one performance, and the actors' attempts to swat it away drew loud laughs, soon the shooing of the fly will become a permanent bit. The folding of a handkerchief or the balancing of a coffee cup on a tray may become whole one-act plays in themselves. The stage manager must be ruthless in holding this down, or the play will become overrun with such "bits."

The danger is that stage managers are also human and become bored watching the same show, and sometimes the business or bit seems so inspired it is tempting to let it stay in. Remember that all such stage business is only the director's prerogative. As directors are fond of reminding stage managers, it is their name out front and in the program following the phrase "Directed by." They are not interested in having casts and stage managers become associates.

AD-LIBBING AND AUDIBILITY

A big tendency in a long run is for ad-libs to become part of the play. If actors have trouble with certain lines or phrases, they will often find suitable (to them) alternatives that convey the same meaning or emotion. However, the rhythms and word choices are the playwright's and must be changed only by him or her.

Some actors have a habit that is annoying to other actors and drives playwrights to distraction: They add little "uh-huhs" or "rights" or "phews" to the dialogue. Sometimes this gets to the point where there are literally hundreds of additional words in a play. These insertions interrupt the play's rhythms and get in the way of the flow of dialogue as envisioned by the writer; they must be policed by the stage manager.

A constant audience complaint in the theater is "I can't hear." This is partially caused by the amplification of electronic media; because they bombard our ears and supply handy volume controls, movies and television have reduced listening skills to lost attributes. However, the actors and stage manager must also remember the audience is hearing the play for the first time, and although the performers know it by heart, certain key phrases or meanings must be underscored vocally and with pace.

Otherwise, it is difficult for an audience to stay with the narrative flow and understand what is happening on the stage.

Morale and Company Spirit

There is a certain talent to stage managing a long-running show that is hard to describe and that all stage managers should possess in their own fashion: promoting company get-togethers that help engender a positive working atmosphere. Sometimes there are company members who take on this responsibility, but often it is left to the stage manager. Almost everyone will respond to softball games, a trip to a bowling alley, or other sporting activities. In New York there are show business leagues in both these sports, and if the show has a team it can be fun to attend or play in the games. Birthdays are another excuse to get together for cake and a small celebration after the show. Don't feel shy about going around to the company members and asking for their birth dates.

On matinee days sometimes it is fun to do "potluck" dinners in the theater between the two shows. Once in a while on Broadway, companies will take turns hosting each other; you might have two or three shows taking turns being the potluck host.

Contests are another company morale booster. All sorts of possibilities exist, from the standard betting pools on sporting events such as the Super Bowl, the World Series, and so on, to pastimes such as baby-picture contests where everyone brings in his or her own baby picture and posts it on a board, and then everyone tries to guess who is who. Other contests include postcard contests (with categories for the prettiest, funniest, and tackiest) or holiday decoration contests with similar categories. All these are simple to organize, and they bring the company together for something other than "doing the job."

Holidays shouldn't go uncelebrated either. A "secret Santa" party at Christmas, where everyone gets one other person a gift, is fun. Easter egg hunts in the theater, Halloween pumpkin-carving contests—it all makes for a happier and more involved company.

As important as special days and events are, it is also important to keep a generally positive, genial side to the day-to-day operation of stage management. Try to make the theater a pleasant place for people to come to work. This can have many dividends, including people staying with the show longer, which will hold down the number of extra replacement rehearsals needed.

Accidents and Medical Emergencies

No matter how careful people are, there will be emergencies. Injuries and accidents happen, and the stage manager should be well prepared to handle them. All stage managers should take a first-aid or CPR course so they know the basics of emergency treatment.

There should be a clear system of handling emergencies worked out among the stage management personnel as well. The system must designate who keeps the show running, who calls for the ambulance, and who helps the person with whatever first aid is required.

The backstage first-aid kit should be equipped with adequate bandages for major cuts, smelling salts, hydrogen peroxide, ice packs, and a small oxygen tank and mask. These are basic requirements—the well-equipped first-aid kit should go well beyond this. There should be treatments available for every part of the body—from a headache to a corn on the little toe—so anything that might prevent a performer from going on doesn't. (Check the list of first-aid supplies in chapter 3.)

Maintaining a show is a little like caring for a family. Everyone's health and happiness are of direct consequence to the successful operation of the whole, and it is the stage manager who must constantly remind people of the importance of rest and good health as well as keep tabs on the performance of their jobs. As the stage manager of a running show, it is important to set up a schedule so that you watch the show and call it on a regular basis, because if left to chance, the quality of the show, in some way, will slide because of your lack of attention.

10

CLOSING A SHOW AND TOURING

The end of a show is a time when most of the cast involved with a production is getting ready for a break and some rest, while the stage manager and crew have to get it together one more time to cleanly close the show, strike the scenery, take inventory, and move out of the theater. Sometimes a show will tour after closing, which creates separate problems. (Sometimes the financial situation is so bad that the producer cannot even afford to get the show out of the theater, but these are rare occurrences.) It is important for a stage manager to know the basic responsibilities involved with striking a closing show, as well as striking a production that will then tour.

When the general manager and producer have decided to close a show, they notify the stage manager and crew to start planning for it. In regional and stock theater, this date is usually preestablished by the season schedule, but the same planning and care must be taken.

Immediately following the final performance of a show, in the midst of all the emotion and farewells, the stage manager must secure the production's property and pack his or her own supplies and equipment. I always try to do as much of this in advance as possible, moving any of the producer's equipment or supplies to his or her office and letting the first-aid kit and other supplies run down to the bare necessities. To further ease the workload on a closing night, I try to make sure any extraneous personal possessions of mine have been taken home before that final curtain.

All shows and theaters are different. On tour the show usually loads out directly after the last performance; in New York or a regional theater, the load-out might wait until the next day. If it is immediate, the stage manager and his or her assistants should pack up their things as quickly as possible to be out of the crew's way and be available for emergencies and to supervise the proceedings. Always save packing the first-aid kit as long as possible; many accidents happen during load-outs, because everyone is moving fast and a lot is happening at once.

Load-Out

The first step to a successful and smooth load-out is to have an advance production meeting with the heads of all departments to discuss their time and labor requirements. Prior to this meeting the stage manager has to find out certain key facts from the producer:

1. Will the show tour, and if so, will the same set be used?
2. What belongs to the producer or theater in the way of props and set pieces, and what is borrowed or rented?
3. Which set pieces, costumes, and props will be saved and which will be destroyed?
4. What kind of arrangements or truck rentals will you have to make to dispose of props and costumes? Many theaters and some active commercial producers keep warehouse space for storing set pieces, costumes, and props for future shows. Other theaters and producers prefer to sell their stock at the end of a production or to donate it to schools or not-for-profit theater organizations for a tax deduction.

Once the above questions are answered, the crew and stage managers can carefully schedule the load-out in terms of the necessary manpower and trucking. As with the load-in, the process will be simplified by advance planning that will ensure that no one is impeding anyone else's progress because the stage is full of one department's equipment or scenery at the same time another department needs to have space. Careful ordering of trucks combined with timing for each department's work will keep the process flowing. In Appendix 12 there is a fairly detailed schedule outlining the move of *I'm Not Rappaport* from the American Place Theater, a small Off-Broadway venue, three blocks west to the Booth Theater, a Broadway house. It should give a clear example of the complexity of moving what was a pretty simple show.

THE LAST PERFORMANCE

At the final performance, it is very important for the stage manager to stay calm amid the emotion and general craziness that sometimes surrounds the event. For instance, actors often have a brilliantly funny joke they want to play on someone in the cast during the performance. These brilliantly funny jokes are usually funny only to the jokesters who do them, and they invariably go over horribly onstage. Discourage any change from the normal performance of the show; try to maintain the integrity of the production as fully as possible.

Also, in conjunction with the department heads, it is the stage manager's responsibility to ensure a minimal amount of "souvenir procurement" by the cast. Clearly you have the right to give away items that are otherwise going to be thrown out, but you must help protect those costumes and props that certain cast members may have been eyeing for months but that have been sold, that have been given away elsewhere, or that the producer expects to see in his or her office or home.

The first area of responsibility for the stage manager should be the dressing rooms. If the strike is not going to immediately follow the final curtain, try to remain at the theater on closing night until all the actors have left. Go through the dressing rooms after they have gone and check on what may have been left behind. Remove immediately any company property—phones, fans, heaters, or refrigerators, for example—and lock them all up in the stage manager's office so they are not lying around when the load-out crew arrives to strike. Speaking of the crew, the last performance can be ruined by excessive backstage noise as some of the workers begin packing and the extra stagehands start arriving during the show. This is especially true on tour. Try to have a word about last-night noise with everyone backstage before the show. A stage manager's loyalties are torn, because you want the crew to get as much done as possible, but not at the expense of the show.

During the actual load-out, keep a close eye on the progress, and be available for any questions of "to save or not to save." Sometimes on a "tryout" tour, you must decide if you can leave behind any scenery or furniture that has been cut from a scene or that was in a scene that was cut. Be wary of leaving anything behind, because the director may want the scene back or the designer might find use for the set piece in some new and different scene. Only leave behind something that itself was cut, not something that was part of a scene or song that was cut.

Touring

On tours, the stage manager sometimes "calls the load" or tells the loading crew what goes on the truck and in what order. This is vital because often there is only one way the entire physical production will fit into the truck or trucks allotted to it. You don't want to let others start loading and then end up with a bunch of full trucks and part of the show still sitting on the loading dock. This will usually be worked out with your carpenter and prop person, but on tour they sometimes prefer the stage manager to be at the truck so he or she can be onstage moving the local crew along.

One terrible night in Chicago, Leo Herbert, the prop man of *Sugar Babies*, a legendary and brilliant man with over a hundred Broadway shows to his credit, came to me enraged and demanded I come look at the truck. Previously, the wardrobe cartons had successfully fit into the front third of a 45-foot truck. Now they had filled half the truck and were still coming. It seems a new wardrobe mistress had gotten the brilliant notion of packing every cast member's costume in a separate box, thinking this would facilitate unpacking on the other end while cutting down on the wrinkling due to packing many costumes tightly in one box. Needless to say, this had doubled the number of costume boxes and, therefore, the space that wardrobe had taken on the truck. A stage manager should be constantly on the lookout for this kind of incident.

On tour, it is vital that the stage manager know in advance what the next theater is like. Before you arrive in the next town or city, contact that theater's house crew and go over all the needs and requirements of your show and try to iron out any potential problems with load-in. For example, some theaters have raised load-in docks that require forklifts. Often these must be ordered to get the show off the truck and into the theater. This is an example of something you must take care of in advance.

Be sure you have a clear picture of the dressing room layout and the rooms available for wigs and wardrobe. Then once you arrive, go through the dressing rooms and make sure the assignments you've made in advance make sense. Sometimes a dressing room described on the phone will bear little resemblance to reality, so be prepared to change and adapt your company's room assignments real fast.

On tour you are moving quickly, and so much changes for the performers from week to week that anything the stage manager can do to keep things similar the better. If it is possible, try to keep actors on the same side of each new theater in terms of dressing rooms so their traffic patterns stay the same. Carry the same name cards or signs for their dressing room doors, and make the callboard as uniform as possible from city to city.

Backstage in the wings, things should be exactly the same to the greatest possible extent. This means that prop tables and dressing booths should travel with you and be in the same places whenever possible. All signs and tape marks on the steps and floor offstage should be exactly the same.

On the road, the theater becomes the "family home" for a large group of people, so try to let the environment reflect that. Try to always have a "greenroom" area where the company can gather, have coffee, and read or play games.

During the load-in on tour, the stage manager is often responsible for focusing lights and must be totally familiar with the light plot and design concept. In this way, during the hanging of the lights, you can make decisions about light positions and instruments that can or can't be cut if there is not ample space. The lighting designer should arm the stage manager with lots of paperwork, including all the information on the basic focus. This is basically a written description of where the stage manager should stand so that the "hot spot," or brightest part of the lights, may be focused on him or her. Then the designer indicates how the lighting should be cut off, or shuttered off, certain pieces of scenery or furniture, or how high up the backdrop or wall the lights are to play. The stage manager should be with the lighting designer the first time the lights are focused to learn all the intricacies of the plot, and then he or she must translate that from theater to theater.

One constantly changing element in theaters is the distance from the stage to the front of the balcony where lights are hung. It is sometimes necessary to carry two sets of lights for that position. Then you can change instruments depending on the length of the throw required.

Another fascinating and terrifying wrinkle to touring is the constantly changing crew. In New York or at a regional or stock theater, the crew with whom you train and learn the show is the crew you basically have every night, but on the road, you are constantly training and teaching the show to new crews. Depending on the size and complexity of the production, various numbers of stagehands will travel with the show. For instance, there is always a "road" carpenter and usually an electrician and prop person. Increasingly, producers will attempt to hold down on the number of road crew because of the cost of their travel and housing. Always try to convince the producers to err on the side of paying for too many at first and then cutting back if they're not necessary, rather than going out on the road shorthanded with their promise that skilled crew members will be added later (read: It will never happen).

If you have a good road crew, they will train and watch the local crew, and you will be free to supervise and run the cues in the more difficult sections. Make sure the local crew is clear about the terminology and cueing system that you are using. The crew probably deals with a lot of different shows and all manner of stage managers, and they are not always seasoned stagehands used to any one style of cueing. There are theater crews that may not automatically know to wait for the stage manager's "go" or that may read a cue light turning on as the signal to execute the cue instead of taking it as a warning.

Never take anything for granted. House lights are often operated on a strange system that requires you to call on an intercom or paging device; be sure to check out how they are run. Also check the ventilation system. If you have drops and curtains, be sure to run them with whatever blowers or air-conditioning systems will be circulating during performance. Frequently, if left untested, curtains or drops may billow or blow back on the stage, which is distracting at best and at worst may knock over furniture or people.

Always try to have a sound check and some rehearsal with the cast onstage before the first show in a new theater (although you and the cast should realize this sometimes may be impossible). A sound check is vital because acoustics vary tremendously from theater to theater. Every microphone and speaker needs to be adjusted and balanced differently, and the cast has to understand that their audibility will vary from house to house. In one theater the cast may feel like they are shouting to be heard in the balcony, and the next week they may find they hardly have to project. But if the sound person is going to help with the audibility of the show, he or she must have a chance to hear the cast onstage.

Unfortunately, sometimes schedules are so tight that there is no time for sound checks with the cast. Once with *Sugar Babies* in Detroit, the load-in was so far behind schedule that we had half of the set outside at the start of the show and had to keep bringing in pieces as we needed them during the performance. Occasionally this would mean that a backstage crossover passage that had been clear for dancers before their number was blocked by the time they finished. With a few hair-breadth arrivals and costume changes we made it through, but it was harrowing for the performers.

Throughout the trials and tribulations of that pre-Broadway tour, the spirit and good humor of Mickey Rooney was a godsend and a great example to all of us. Once, the computer light board was going haywire, running cues on its own, and bringing up strange combinations of lights for other cues. (Early computer boards were a lot like the early days of the space program: well-meaning but often a total disaster.) Mickey stepped to the edge of the stage and proceeded to give an impromptu lecture on the evils of modern technology and compared working with these computer-board-operated lights to being inside a pinball machine gone wild. He was always willing to cover when we had problems, even working some of the glitches into the show permanently.

There was a scene with a telephone in it that I once accidentally rang at the wrong time, and from that night on, Mickey and I had a scene together where I would purposely ring a phone at the wrong time or fail to ring it at all. He would get exasperated by its ringing or not ringing at the proper time and then build and build his reaction to hilarious proportions. He also had a fake fight with Ann Miller during one performance in which his wig got knocked off, and he replaced it backwards on his head. This one-time mistake also grew into a major comedic moment in the show. His comic instincts were incredible; he always knew just how far to go with those moments so that they remained funny and didn't become stupid or mean-spirited. Most important, it was a great lesson in making the best out of a bad situation. Unfortunately, it is a lesson stage managers must learn well.

Basically, a touring stage manager is always on his or her toes, adapting to and dealing with a lot of different situations and personalities, but somehow making the show work every night. It is never boring, and it can be a lot of fun. It is vital to keep the cast active and together on tour, and the stage manager and company manager can work together to arrange sightseeing jaunts, parties, and tours—anything to keep people together and into the show.

Maintaining the artistic quality of a show on the road is quite a challenge, not only in terms of finding time for rehearsals and accomplishing all the technical tasks but in dealing with the vast differences in audience reactions from one section of the country to another. What may play well and get huge laughs in one city will die in the next, and a local reference or inside joke can cast a whole new light on a scene.

The stage manager must keep accurate contact sheets on the road. Convince everyone that it is essential for them to report any changes in their hotels or living accommodations immediately to the stage manager.

Travel days are far from days off for stage managers. Stage managers should help move the company by assisting in baggage pickup and handling, organizing and scheduling but pickups, signing people in, and, in general, shepherding the company from one city to the other.

A tour stage manager must use the same skills and attributes necessary for successfully stage managing a stationary production: a combination of the ability to handle a lot of detail and organizational work with hands-on care for and attention to the well-being and spirit of the company and crew.

11

STAGE MANAGING OPERA

For several years now, I have been involved in the stage management of opera. Contrary to opinion, it is not boring, difficult, or weird, but it is different in some ways from traditional theater stage management. My experiences with the New York City Opera Company for six seasons called upon every facet of stage management already covered in this book and added some refreshing new ones.

Inherent in much of opera stage management responsibility is a grasp of the same details and philosophies discussed in other sections of this book on the care and handling of rehearsal and performance in theater. Many operas, however, are huge productions and require a lot more organization and performance cueing and oversight, certainly more than any straight play. The numbers can be daunting: sometimes over a hundred people onstage, running crews of thirty or more, and anywhere from three to twenty scene changes and fast costume changes. Stage managers must be constantly aware of what's going on and be ready to assist an injured performer, have crew and wardrobe personnel ready for changes, and be able to deal with myriad emergencies. He or she needs to always know when things are clear, safe, and ready.

Underscoring everything, literally and figuratively, is the *music*. The orchestra will continue to play until a halt is called because the maestro sees utter calamity onstage or the fact a set has not been changed and the singers are not onstage. But that is so rare that I never saw it in performance, even though there were many close calls. It takes an enormous amount of teamwork, cooperation, and extreme efficiency from every department to make a smooth performance, and it is a shared exhilaration that grips everyone when it is exceptional.

Music being the driving force, it is important that stage managers identify its place in every facet of their work with that focus. Whereas in theater it might be plot or scenery or character, in opera, the music will be in control of all other elements of production and given priority in terms of space, rehearsal, and environment. Many stage managers approaching opera will worry about being able to "read music." However, if you can count to ten, learn some basic principles of notation as simple as blocking notation, and have ever tapped your foot along with a song, then you can master the basics of calling an opera from a score.

Opera singers are mainly an incredibly professional, workmanlike group. The demands on their voice make them very careful about their health, and they know the importance of rest, so you seldom have the "party hearty" kind of company and problems sometimes associated with other performers. It takes an incredible amount of work and training to be an opera singer, and they will arrive at the first rehearsal pretty much solid in their role, knowing their vocal parts close to perfectly. They are booked or hired to sing roles sometimes two or three years in advance, and they will have been studying it and working with their own coaches for a long time before rehearsals begin. This also tends to make rehearsals more of a working atmosphere than the long discovery and developmental rehearsals in theater as actors create their character and learn roles simultaneously.

Our primary function with them is care and safety. Lozenges will disappear at an alarming rate. Fresh, pure water is a necessity wherever they perform. This water should not be "iced," as cold water tends to shrink their vocal cords—just room temperature is fine. As they are justifiably acutely aware of the spreading of germs, you must be sure that all water bottles get marked with which singer is using them, likewise cups and goblets onstage. It is also good to keep bottles of hand sanitizer on your desk in rehearsal and readily available backstage as opera staging often involves a lot of physical contact and also the handling of many props. Singers cannot be exposed to or breathe heavy perfumes or aftershaves. This should always be explained tactfully to people new to the opera world and with a politely worded sign in rehearsal rooms. On a concert tour with some of the members of NYCO, during the dinner break, a local florist brought in a beautiful, huge arrangement of gardenias for the piano onstage. I hated to put them out in the back alley but had no choice, as the smell of gardenias is especially famous for closing the throat.

One of the most frequently used first-aid provisions is the ice pack. You should purchase these by the case, both the large and small ones.

Opera scenery is notoriously sharp cornered and consists of many levels, steps, and other obstacles. As the singers never take their eyes off the conductor, they do tend to do things like slam into furniture and edges of walls and miss steps a lot. Quickly applying ice to these simple bruises and twists can keep a performer going. Of course, it should be examined if swelling and pain persist. Another use of these ice packs is to quickly revive the overheated performer. Often costumed in heavy, bulky, and many-layered costumes, singers are then staged to run, fight, and dance, all bathed in hideously hot lights. You should have ice packs backstage to quickly break and put on their wrists and back of their necks. This is the best way to bring someone back from minor heatstroke, as it cools the blood as it pumps through the wrists and neck closest to the surface skin.

Temperature control in dressing rooms, rehearsal areas, and the stage can never suit everyone, but singers prefer too warm to too cold. I have spent many a break putting cardboard over dressing room blowers and working with the house engineers to keep the stage warm enough without decomposing the audience.

Singers expect to be called to the stage comfortably before their entrances. This allows them to warm up, listen to the orchestra for pitch, and compose themselves. They then need to be cued on their entrances as they only know their vocal cue, and often the staging calls for them to begin an entrance long before they sing. This will be worked out first in rehearsal and then during early stage rehearsals so that the deck stage managers will always know the exact beat to send them on to arrive at the perfect moment vocally and staging-wise. This is one of the places where it is vital to follow the score, and here is some of what you will need to know to do so.

Every piece of sheet music of full score will have certain similarities which you must attune yourself to in order to cue from music instead of text. Here are some of the terms and examples which will help as you approach musical notation.

1. *System*: This describes and refers to the number of large sections of musical lines on a page of a score. Each system contains a musical line and vocal lines for as many singers as are involved; so the number of systems to a page is directly reflective of the number of people singing. Once you have five or six soloists and a chorus

of men and women singing at once, the pages will only contain one system, and following the score involves fast reflexes and turning of pages to keep up. In a solo or duet, where you have only one or two singers, the page may have six to eight systems.

2. *Bar* or *Measure*: Used interchangeably, these are the spaces on each musical or vocal line that are delineated by vertical lines (or bars). Each measure or bar will have separate notes in it. When following the score, you will be counting the number of beats in a measure or bar, not trying to land on every note.

3. *Time Signature*: At the beginning of every new piece of music and whenever the time signature changes, you will see what looks like a fraction at the start of the first measure. The top number will be the number of *beats*, or counts, in a measure. The bottom number indicates the type of note that will be given one count. The number of counts each note contains will add up to the number in the signature. *Whole notes* will represent all the counts in a measure, half notes half the counts, and so on. If you tried to count every note you would become incredibly lost and crazy, so stage managers usually count along the bottom line in each system using the tempo and number of beats set by the time signature and the conductor's tempo. Tempos are also reflected in the score, and here is a list of basics and what they mean to help you:

BRIEF GLOSSARY OF COMMON MUSICAL TERMS USED IN OPERA SCORES AND REHEARSALS

(The numbers refer to metronome settings, signified by bpm, or beats per minute)

Tempo—refers to the speed of the main rhythmic pulse in a piece of music
Lento or *Largo*—40–66 bpm; very slow
Adagio—66–76 bpm; slow, but with a flowing feel
Andante—76–108 bpm; walking pace, unhurried
Moderato—108–120 bpm; walking with a purpose

Allegro—120–168 bpm; light, happy, brisk pulse
Vivace or *Presto*—168–200 bpm; very fast, often taken in one pulse per measure
Prestissimo—200+ bpm; as fast as possible

Other markings that may be referred to in a rehearsal or musical score:

Più mosso—a little faster than what came just before
Meno mosso—a little slower than what came just before
Ritardando (rit.)—a slight slowing down of the pulse, often used at the end of a phrase or section
Rallentando (rall.)—a slowing down of the pulse over two or more measures
A tempo—a return to the previous section's tempo
Tempo primo—a return to the first tempo of the section
Accelerando—gradually getting faster
Subito—suddenly, as in "subito piano," suddenly soft.
Change of key—denoted by one or more "natural marks," followed by one or more sharps or flats in the staff lines

Once you have figured out how to count the bars, you are ready to cue from a score. One very helpful tool is making your own marks in a score. I usually use a highlighter to mark all the systems on a page so as I turn it or look ahead, I am ready to adjust the line I am following and counting. Another valuable set of marks are the names of the singers' roles so that if you get lost while the soprano is singing, you can just pick up again when the tenor enters. Other notes I make are the very high notes in the soprano or tenor lines, as they tend to stand out, and any silences or clearly sung wording like a series of laughs (ha ha ha ha, for example) or screams or one word repeated many times. Orchestral markings are also helpful—for instance, trumpet calls, cymbal crashes, loud drumbeats or rolls; all these will stand out as you listen and can provide a landmark to get you back onto measure-by-measure following of the score. Depending on where the cue you need to call is located, you can mark your score to follow intently measure by measure or just keep on the "right page."

A good way to start learning is to get a musical score or sheet music to something with which you are familiar, then put some cues into the music, and practice while listening to your selection. Progress then to an opera, perhaps a familiar one like *Carmen*, and again follow with a performance CD and see if your counting comes out the same as the singers and orchestra you are listening to.

In an opera score, you will see numbers in squares throughout the work. They generally occur in bold print between lines. These are what are called "rehearsal numbers." They are places that are easy to find musically and at which to pick up rehearsing if you have stopped. Quite often in a tech or dress, the director or conductor will announce picking it up at rehearsal five, or three before or after five, which will mean the number of bars before or after. Sometimes you will need to request that the conductor starts at a certain rehearsal number or just before or after in order to get your warns and cues in, so it is good to be familiar with this concept.

To successfully call an opera, you *must* have a conductor monitor on your desk so you can follow his beats, cutoffs, and down beats. You can only get the tempo exact for counting by watching him as he directs the orchestra and singers. Also, he will always be the one who gives cutoffs and entrances, and so often those are where you need to call cues.

Stage managers in opera function in very specific areas of preproduction: rehearsal and performance. There are marked differences from theater, and this chapter will address those differences. The single most important responsibility of a stage manager, anywhere, is *clear, concise, and correct* communication, be it written or spoken over headset or paging microphone.

Stage managers must always concentrate on safety issues. Anything that arises from preproduction on through the final performance that seems at all dangerous should be brought to the attention of people responsible who can fix it. This can be a bit tricky, as directors and designers sometimes have different priorities than performers in this regard, and sometimes the economic ramifications of fixing a safety problem can be huge, requiring work calls, additional crew, and the like. Often effects such as guns, fire explosions, and strobes are called for by the artistic staff; it is vital that stage managers supervise and control all these elements not only in terms of cueing them but their placement onstage in relation to singers.

Open flame is another hazard we often encounter in opera. Torches, candelabras, candles, and lanterns always seem to find their way into performances. First, try and convince people to use the new "flicker" candles, which look almost more real that candle flame. However, if real flame is used, costumes—as well as curtains, bedding, tablecloths, etc.—anywhere near it must be fireproofed. Also beware of the staging. In rehearsal, once you know a flame will be live, watch to be sure no one is in a position to knock it over, sit on it, or get their hair, veil, or skirt singed by it.

At first rehearsals, always remind the performers that we welcome and need their input as to anything they see or feel may be dangerous. Before every first stage rehearsal, stage managers should inspect all steps, railings, running lights, and light booms in the path of exits to make sure that every step is taken in advance to avert dangerous conditions for performers entering or exiting the stage.

Stage managing opera, like stage management anywhere, should focus on the creation of an environment in which the creative process can proceed with as little external impediment as possible. Although the exact means of doing that may vary from company to company and theater to opera, the principle remains that stage managers are there to facilitate rehearsal and performance as their first priority.

If you are working in a unionized opera company, you will be represented by AGMA (the American Guild of Musical Artists). AGMA also represents soloists, singers, chorus, dancers, and assistant directors. The crew/stagehands and wardrobe department often belong to IATSE (the International Association of Technical Stage Employees), and the musicians often belong to the AFM (the American Federation of Musicians). Every opera company has different union affiliations and rules. You will have to clarify in advance the exact nature of the unions and their rules in the company with whom you work.

Many opera companies work with similar basic production department setups that will include stage management. There is usually a production manager or director of production who is responsible for all elements of production from a management point of view, and he or she will usually also be the stage manager's direct supervisor. Large opera companies, and especially those that work in repertory, will often also employ a production stage manager who will run the department under the direction and supervision of the director of production.

There will almost always be a technical director and assistants who are responsible for the running of the crew and the development and handling of all scenic elements. Any questions, requests, needs, complications, and complaints of any kind should be channeled through them. Stage managers' communication with the crew should always take the form of information and clear and concise cue and running sheets pertaining to the running and handling of the show and its moves. Any discussion of how many people it will take or what department will or won't handle something is usually worked out between the technical director and the IATSE crew heads.

In theater, the stage manager is often responsible for the maintenance of the lighting of the show, working out calls to fix focus and color with the head electrician, but most opera companies have a lighting supervisor and staff who handle all lighting issues and do the initial focus and all changeover focusing. Stage managers must keep them aware of all issues regarding lighting in rehearsal and performance.

Preproduction for opera is very similar to theater, and most of the work and thinking outlined in chapter 2 functions in opera as well. Opera stage managing will include a lot more reproduction of existing operas, and companies with a large stock also usually have a very good set of documentation and files, including calling scores and cue sheets.

Obtain from the technical director ground plans and all the information he has about such things as hanging plots, shifts, and deck moves. Draw from his info and supply what you need for taping the floor and setting up your preset and deck cue sheets. Also, get whatever you can from existing files: drawings, renderings, costume sketches, etc. for display in the rehearsal room. The more visual aids we provide, the less time is wasted in the valuable but limited time onstage with "I never knew it would look like this, or that we would have a step up here" and the like. If the opera has an archival video of their production (unlike Actors Equity, opera unions do allow archival tapings of dress rehearsals), get it and watch it, ideally as a team with calling and deck stage managers. The funny thing about these "archival tapes" is that since they are quite often of dress rehearsals, there may have been subtle changes in the production following the taping. These changes are often in the area of costumes and wigs, but sometimes scene changes and show furniture will have been changed to accommodate singers' moves or costume changes. One of the inherent values in the dress rehearsal tapes is you get to see as a stage manager where the rehearsal stopped or broke down technically and foresee the problems inherent at that point in the production and prepare to avoid them this time.

On many theatrical shows, whether musical or dramatic, the stage manager will be expected to do the restaging of the production. This is never the case in opera. Stage managers are not included in the directorial, creative team either on new productions or revivals. There are assistant directors on any opera company staff who fulfill all the directorial functions considered part of the stage manager's duties in theater, and stage managers restrict themselves to the technical aspects and the orderly running of rehearsals and performances as well as the calling of breaks. This includes the training of covers and replacements, as well as the recreation of productions. One responsibility the opera stage manager must be aware of is the discipline of recreating productions; one cannot allow the assistant director restaging the opera to make major changes in blocking and stage business and the like, because the opera has been designed and cued before, and all set, prop, and costume changes have been laid out before, so there is less time scheduled for stage rehearsals of a repertory piece. Some strange things like singers wandering out of lights or the whole chorus looking stage left for a singer changed to enter from stage right can happen without stage-managerial vigilance. One time in *Madama Butterfly*, in which about thirty chorus women enter from one side of the stage, the director restaging thought it would look better from the other side. However, as we thought through what this would mean in terms of the whole opera, it would have meant changing every entrance and exit, because the "offstage world" would have to be reversed so the inside of the house and the outside entrance could be totally reversed. Clearly what seemed like a simple change became completely out of the question.

Preparing for rehearsal, the stage manager should lay out the set plan on the floor in the rehearsal rooms as well as a set of dance numbers downstage. As in theater, the stage manager should then work with the director or assistant director's input to ensure that the technical staff delivers necessary props, furniture, and rehearsal costume pieces. The stage managers should then meet as a team to discuss assignments and responsibilities in terms of deck assignments, calls, responsibility for wardrobe, and prop communication and checking. To fully prepare a room for opera rehearsal, the stage manager must be sure the piano is tuned and in place as requested by the maestro. The maestro must also have a podium stand and large music stand for rehearsal, and the pianist must have a clear view of the maestro. When rehearsals are held in a rehearsal space outside the theater or opera company's home, they must be carefully planned.

Figure 11-1 is a schedule for the rehearsal hall load-in of *Candide* for NYCO. As the New York State Theater does not have sufficient rehearsal space for the ballet and opera, we need to rehearse elsewhere, and it needs to be planned and laid out like an invasion. This schedule also serves as a memo to all departments of what is expected to be loaded into the studio and the theater so as to maximize the use and value of the crew call and trucking for the day.

ASSISTANT DIRECTOR AND STAGE MANAGER PAPERWORK

Here is a basic list of the paperwork responsibilities for stage management and assistant directors. Various companies and individuals will divide the responsibilities differently:

1. *Who/What/Where*: This is basically the same as a production analysis as explained for theater. The difference is that everything is set to timings and also with what is called "placement." This refers to three numbers: the page number in the score, the *system* on the page, and the *measure* in which the cue or entrance happens. (See example in Appendix 13.)

2. *Staging Book*: A full and detailed record of all entrances, exits, and movements of singers, chorus, supers, onstage banda, and dancers. A full description of the set for every scene and its props and furniture. A full record of all stage business, fights, gestures, and emotional content for each scene. The directing or staging book should also include the rehearsal plan, any musical cuts, and a title-screen script.

3. *Calling Score*: A complete record of the cueing for every opera. It will include some blocking required to call cues but also the separate cue sheets as follows:

NEW YORK CITY OPERA

MEMORANDUM

THOMAS A. KELLY, PSM

NEW YORK CITY OPERA REHEARSAL LOADING SCHEDULE

TO: ALL PRODUCTION PERSONNEL

FROM: THOMAS A. KELLY

RE: **CANDIDE TO 42ND STREET STUDIOS**:

MON. FEB. 7th: CANDIDE FIRST REHEARSAL @ 42ND STREET STUDIO 9A

> **8AM:** Stage Managers set up room. Rental chairs from 42nd St. Studios (60) and tables (6) delivered.
> Between 8+10: (30) Music stands delivered as arranged by Michael Lonergan with Van rentals.
> **9AM:** Production Mtg./Participants called as per Jim D'Asaro.
> **10AM:** Meet and Greet, etc. followed by Music rehearsal as called
> Taping of floors in 9A and 9B continues through day.

TUES. FEB. 8: CANDIDE LOAD-IN to 42ND STREET STUDIOS

> **8AM**: Work Call at **NYCO**:
> Bring to loading dock:
> Stage Managers Road Box
> Stage Manager's Rolling Racks to be used as Walls
> All Wardrobe Racks to be transported w/ Rehearsal Costumes
> 2 Carmen Rehearsal Tables w/ castered rolling frames
> 1 Rolling Rehearsal Ladder
> 1 Plain 2 sided ladder/10'
> Rolls of Muslin, Brown Paper from SM Office
> 6   4' x 8' risers/stackable to assimilate DSR and DSL platform areas.
> 3   2' step x 2' step units
> 3   3' step x 4' step units

> **8AM @ Warehouse**:
> Load truck with rehearsal props and furniture as per Karin and Theresa
> This includes all rehearsal furniture for *Candide*, hampers, and rehearsal furniture

> **9AM**: Begin loading **Walton** truck at NYCO
> **9:30**: **Center Line Truck:** Deliver to NYCO. Cross load onto Walton:
>   Rehearsal Deck platforms
>   2 Props hampers and some loose props (banners, etc.)
> **9:45**: **Warehouse Truck** Cross Load to Walton
> **10 AM**: **Walton Truck** to 42nd STREET STUDIOS
> DELIVER: Props, Furniture, Wardrobe, Rehearsal Deck and hampers and
>   NYCO CREW called to help load in and assemble rehearsal deck

> **2PM**: Rehearsal on Rehearsal Set/Full Cast

FIGURE 11-1 Candide *Load-In Form*

a. *Fly Floor*: See appendixes. Detailed listing of the preset and position of each flown piece and its moves.

b. *Props*: See Appendix 13 for examples. Both presets and moves are clearly laid out for the prop crew. Examples are from *Il Matrimonio Segreto*.

c. *Costume Breakdown* and *Running Sheets*: See Appendixes 18 and 19. For each character, a costume plot of what they wear, in which scene, and what changes they make into additional costumes or pieces like aprons, a coat, or hat. The running sheets are for the performance crew and lay out the costume changes as to the where and when. Examples of both of these are in Appendix 13, from *Il Matrimonio Segreto*. Note again that the timings of all these are marked as to how far into the running time of the act they occur. They are also marked at the first entrance timings and location of each entrance so that dressers and hair crew can plan out their schedule both before and during the show to have every principal ready for entrances.

d. *Deck*: Running sheets and cues are shown for props and carpenters and are required for each move of scenery both within the act and at intermissions.

e. *Electric* and *Lighting*: Stage managers should get fully documented lighting cues and plots from the designers and also follow spot cues, which will be in the score where called, but a separate sheet should detail the cue with descriptions as well as color and other details. Another electric cue sheet would be for the placement and moving in the wings of any effects, conductor monitors, lights on stands and lighting for backstage musicians, work lights, and cue lights.

f. *Schedules*: All production scores should include both the daily and weekly schedules as shown by the examples in the appendixes. These are usually created on a weekly basis by the director and rehearsal department or supervisor and then amended on a daily basis by the assistant director.

g. A *Contact Sheet* and any production photos.

4. **Rehearsal and Performance Reports**: Every day in rehearsal and after every performance, a report must be filed. This is very similar

in style and content to the theater versions, and examples can be found in the appendixes.

As room rehearsals progress, it can be invaluable to have a few things on hand. A roll of muslin can quickly become a shawl, an apron, a hanky, a napkin, a skirt, or sling. It can save so much time and hassle to be able just to create something when a director wants it. A roll of heavy brown paper can cover mirrors, wrap around a wardrobe rack to make a screen or wall, or be cut out in the shape of a column, wagon, or platform that needs to change from scene to scene. A dolly is very helpful if you have clunky furniture to set and reset in different scenes. An assortment of half-inch dowels can quickly become canes, swords, or other implements. The quicker something in rehearsal can be tried, the better, because if it works, it can be ordered from the costume or prop shop, but if rejected, the shop has not wasted time and money getting you something.

The stage manager should call breaks and call the cast back from breaks. Here are descriptions of the various types of rehearsals at the New York City Opera, followed by a guide to the types of breaks required for each. Notice that every type of rehearsal has different requirements for breaks, and the presence of the orchestra changes all the break structures.

Stage Piano Rehearsals are basically technical/spacing and staging rehearsals as the director, choreographer, and musical staff adjust to the stage and the set. Sometimes limited costume pieces are used, but the concentration is on scenery, lighting, and performer positioning. *Piano Dress Rehearsals* add the element of costumes and costume changes to the stage piano. This is the time to work out all quick-change/ set-change coordination backstage and provides the chance to see if all video and audio monitors are placed as needed. Hair and makeup are also introduced at this rehearsal, and their needs in terms of setup and performance of changes are also addressed. It is important that all technical needs in terms of set, lights, costume, hair and makeup, sound, and visual be addressed in the piano rehearsals, as it is impossible to stop when the full orchestra is in the pit, except for musical needs.

Stage Orchestra Rehearsals: Basically a walkthrough with all scenic and tech moves but concentrating on the addition of the orchestra and balancing it with the singers. This is the maestro's rehearsal, so seldom are costumes worn or any stops made for staging, technical cues, or the like. *Orchestra Dress Rehearsals* are often the final rehearsal, and the attempt is to be run as a performance. There are sometimes guests invited, and this rehearsal is sometimes referred to as the "general" rehearsal.

THE BREAK RULES—A REFRESHER

1. Break requirements for all Principals, Chorus, and Assistant Conductors:
   - A two **(2) hour rehearsal** must contain at least **10 minutes** of break time.
   - A three **(3) hour rehearsal** must contain at least **20 minutes** of break time.
   - A four **(4) hour rehearsal** must contain at least **30 minutes** of break time.
2. **Stage Managers** must receive **15 minutes break** within each three (3) hour period.
3. **Room Rehearsals**
   - After discussion and mutual agreement between the AD and the SM, **breaks are called by the Stage Manager.**
   - The **Assistant Directors** will call breaks when no Stage Mangers are able to be present.
   - The **Assistant Directors** will assist in calling the performers to return as necessary after the break has ended.
   - **Music Rehearsals** must have a **10-minute break after 50 minutes.**
   - **Staging Rehearsals** must have a **10-minute break after 60 minutes.**
4. **Stage Rehearsals**
   - **Stage Piano Rehearsals** must have a **10-minute break after 90 minutes.**
5. **Stage Orchestra Rehearsals**
   - **Stage Orchestra Rehearsals** must have a break for the orchestra after **no more than 70 minutes of rehearsal.**

- There is no minimum break length for the orchestra, but 10 minutes is the norm on short breaks.

Rehearsal Length	Total Break Time
2 hours	20 minutes
2½ hours	25 minutes
3 hours	30 minutes
3¼ hours	33 minutes
3½ hours	35 minutes

6. **Orchestra Dress Rehearsals**
   - Breaks are taken concurrent with the Act breaks as though in performance. If more time remains the orchestra may elect to receive notes before the break, up to one hour of combined playing and notes. Orchestra must break at the curtain for the Dress rehearsal.
   - If there are notes given prior to the actual start with the stage, the rehearsal proper must begin within ten (10) minutes or a break is required.

7. **Performances**

Prior to Performance
   - Orchestra may be buzzed to the pit at Posted Curtain Time.
   - Orchestra clock starts five (5) minutes after the Posted Curtain Time.
   - Tuning will start at Stage Manager's discretion.

Intermission
   - Thirteen (13) minute minimum before signal to pit after previous Act Curtain.
   - May tune at minimum of five (5) minutes after signal to the pit.

In performance, the stage manager maintains the same responsibilities as in theater in terms of calling the show, keeping track of all timings and changes, technical problems, audiences reactions or problems, and injuries, sickness, and complaints. A sample performance report and schedule for an opera is presented in Appendix 13. This report reflects the need for precise reporting and calculations of the performance's running times. The stage manager's performance report is the detailing of time that will decide any overtime for singers, orchestra, or crew. Tone and a clear explanation of events are vital in reports.

Guests backstage can be a big problem in opera—as singers are often called for makeup and costumes and warm-ups hours before performance, the habit of having family, friends, coaches, managers, and others in their dressing rooms can get out of hand. Although the stage manager is not responsible directly for these areas, it can have a serious effect on the running of the show, the mood of the singers, and so on, so we must always be alert when offstage problems are happening.

During performance, the stage management team should be in constant contact through headsets, checking on the presence of singers, crew, and wardrobe and making sure all is well backstage. Stage managers should be a visible and permanent presence for the security of everyone involved, knowing they can have problems solved immediately in any crisis or emergency.

Thus we see opera is not wildly different from theater stage management; it has different components, but the whole is still the same: The goal is a smooth-running, safe, and artistically cohesive production, and the control of its elements must be firmly but sympathetically in the hands of the stage management. One singer told me our presence was "like a cool river in a thirsty land." I can think of no finer compliment or clearer goal.

12

CAREER INFORMATION

Most frequently, stage managers find jobs through word of mouth. The more a stage manager works, the more his or her work will be known, and the more he or she will be recommended to friends and associates.

It is vital to remember one thing: Every hour a stage manager spends in a theater is valuable, no matter what the job. Stage managers must feel completely at ease and at home in the theater and backstage environment so that they can in turn make their production's company feel relaxed. The more time you spend working on any facet of theater, the better.

Any backstage technical work is valuable for two main reasons. First, the contacts you make may lead to jobs in the future. For example, the lighting designer that you help hang lights one day may remember you are really a stage manager the next time he or she is asked for a recommendation. But perhaps more important, every technical job you take will add to your understanding of your role as stage manager, a position that requires a working knowledge of many theater skills and their impact on a theater production.

As a young stage manager combing trade papers, advertisements, job hotlines, or websites for job listings, look out for notices seeking production assistants. These are often non-Equity assistant stage manager positions that involve running errands, buying rehearsal props, sweeping the rehearsal room, and so on, but they are a great way to meet working stage managers and directors. Or try to get on a show as a director's assistant, taking notes and facilitating his or her instructions. In any such position, you will learn a lot about the theater and will meet people who will get to know your talents in a working environment rather than hear you talk about them in an interview situation.

As I mentioned in the introduction, my own career has evolved into more production management and less theatrical stage management, but I use stage management tools every day. In our scenery shop, I program and schedule the work process much the same as a show, establishing priorities, figuring out space and crew responsibilities and time, and looking at the finished product being done in time for the production team to see it and make adjustments as necessary.

Recently, we had a show, *Ivanov*, in which there was a large back wall of doors that had to fly in and out. The doors were all closed on the way in, but when they had to fly, people had just fled through them, and one actor was lying dead across one doorway. Fortunately, the stage manager saw this problem looming early in the discussions of the design for the show and called us about it. This resulted in our developing a very special hinge that has since been incorporated into the designs of several other shows. Basically, the weight of the flown piece landing releases the tension on a bungee closer so the doors can work normally while they are on the deck, but when the weight is removed as the piece is flown, the bungee tightens again and closes the door automatically. This was a great example of a stage manager helping us by being knowledgeable and alert enough to foresee a problem while there was still time to be inventive about a solution, so that we did not have to restage or change blocking in the theater itself.

Production management is a natural step in career development for stage managers, especially with the training and experience in communication and organization that inevitably become part of a stage manager's makeup.

In the nineties, I had the pleasure of working in New York City for the Lincoln Center Festival productions in Damrosch Park, and some of the logistical problems there were examples of what to look for and sort out when doing a live outdoor production. They included the very obvious element of the weather. One show I did there, Merce Cunningham's creation called *Ocean*, called for 112 musicians spread out over four platforms directly behind the audience seating risers. Obviously, music, instruments, and musicians were exposed to the elements, and we had to evolve very clear agreements and procedures for the musicians' "evacuation" from the platforms in case of bad weather and the protection of their instruments and music with tarps, as well as the lowering of a large lighting rig from above the stage to protect it and those on it from rain and wind damage. Everything was discussed and worked out in advance, and the one night that the performance did have to be interrupted because of bad weather, the process was smooth, swift, and safe because there had been preplanning of exactly what to do: Every musician, crew member, and performer knew exactly what to do and where to go. This avoided confusion, and the audience was cooperative and easily guided, because there was no air of panic among the performers and crew. Panic, chaos, and confusion are contagious, but so is a steady calm in the face of emergency. Often it is up to the stage/production manager to plan ahead so as to be able to effectively maintain calm and safety in emergency situations.

Earlier, I spoke of communication as being so vital to every element of production, and at the Lincoln Center Festival, there were two wonderful examples of it.

The first had to do with scheduling. There is a problem in scheduling at Lincoln Center in the summer, because the plaza by the fountain is the location of a dance series called Midsummer Swing. Bands play live dance music of all types from salsa to rock and roll, and people come to dance. Meanwhile, a hundred yards away, theater or dance that relies on quiet and other kinds of music is happening, and it can be a real problem for an artist performing a death scene or dancer trying to embody the rhythms of classical environmental music to be fighting the cucarachas of a salsa band in the background. Both summers that I was at Lincoln Center, those managing the live dance music series and I worked together to try to schedule their musician breaks or starting times to best avoid conflict. During performances, I would keep in constant touch with their stage manager via walkie-talkie about sound levels and where we were in terms of his ability to tell the live band to play up-tempo or slower tunes, as well as about coordinating breaks. It was not only the technical communication afforded by the walkie-talkie that eased this potentially disastrous cacophonic conflict but the basic communication that people who work in production tend to share, which is the "there must be a way we can work this out" attitude. By the two production managers working together to find a solution, we were both able to deal with our productions better than if territorial battles and power plays had evolved into antagonism.

I should also mention a different kind of "scheduling" problem that arose in this instance: Just when I had relaxed, thinking the problem of noise for the performers in Damrosch Park was dealt with, a Mr. Softee truck with the loudest musical bell I've ever heard playing over a crackling microphone drove up to service the kids in the apartment complex across the street, and that involved another kind of communication: a favorite New York outdoor tradition called bribery, or "If you won't play that bell, I will come over every night, buy an ice cream, and make up for the missed sales you might experience."

The second example of the uses of communication had to do with translators: At Lincoln Center I had to deal with foreign companies: the Vietnamese Water Puppet company and the Rumanian National Theater troupe. In such cases, one has to check and double-check that the interpreter really understands what you are saying, otherwise very wrong information and directives can be the result. For example, one hot day, when my crew and I were waiting for the Vietnamese crew to come work with us to show us how to put up their set, they arrived thinking they were going for a day of sightseeing due to a confusion over a few words or expressions. But my favorite communication mix-up with this group was their name for me, which was "Imetom." This evolved because on the first day, through the interpreter, I introduced myself by saying "I'm Tom" and pointing at myself. The interpreter then told them my name was Imetom, which they proceeded to use every day thereafter to greet me, along with big smiles.

In Appendixes 14, 15, 16, and 17, I have included some basic checklists for various outdoor jobs and schedules for other productions and events that show some of the differing priorities and problems of productions outside of theater.

Career- and Job-Oriented Organizations and Publications

There are many organizations and publications that will aid you in your search for work as a stage manager. Don't forget, however, that in the end, your contacts and previous employers are your most important source of theater jobs. But to start out, here are some of the more useful publications and organizations for a budding (or an experienced but unemployed) stage manager.

Today there are a myriad of websites, chat groups, and technical job sites available on the Internet. If you search for the terms *stage manager* or *stage management*, you will open a world of knowledge about jobs, techniques, and networking opportunities. Here are some of the organizations, publications, and websites I employ both for my own interest and for job information.

ARTSEARCH

ArtSearch is subtitled the "National Employment Service Bulletin for the Arts" and is published by the Theatre Communications Group, a not-for-profit organization serving the country's theaters. *ArtSearch* is a bulletin that is issued twice a month, listing information about stage management, design, teaching, and other theater-related job opportunities in many nonprofit resident and university institutions around the country. TCG publishes twenty-three issues a year. To subscribe, write *ArtSearch*, c/o TCG, 355 Lexington Ave., New York, NY 10017, or call (212) 697-5230 for more information. Also available online through a TCG subscription (www.tcg.org/artsearch).

TCG also prints many other useful publications, including *American Theatre* magazine, annual and biennial theater directories, plays, and other theater-related books. They will keep you better informed of what is going on in theater in the United States, which will help you know where to look to find work. You can write, call, or visit TCG's website and ask for a publications catalog.

THE ALLIANCE OF RESIDENT THEATRES/NEW YORK

The Alliance (ART/New York, for short) is a trade and service organization for more than 130 not-for-profit theaters in New York City. Their office maintains two "books" that may be of interest to an unemployed young stage manager, especially one new to the town. The "Job Book" is a collection of job descriptions of employment opportunities at ART/New York's member theaters. The "Resume Book" is a file that the organization maintains, consisting of resumes from stage managers and other technical personnel.

A prospective stage manager coming to New York should write the Alliance for more information: The Alliance of Resident Theatres/New York, 131 Varick St., Room 904, New York, NY 10013, or call (212) 989-5257 (www.offbroadwayonline.com).

THEATRICAL INDEX

Published weekly by Price Berkley, *Theatrical Index* lists the staffing information for almost every show currently running in New York theater, both on Broadway and off. The names of all production stage managers are listed, and it is an excellent way to get their names and the theater addresses to which you can send a letter and resume seeking an interview as an assistant or future replacement.

Also, every week *Theatrical Index* has a section describing shows that are planned for the future. This allows you to send letters and resumes in advance to those managers and producers with whom you think you would like to work. It can be subscribed to weekly, twice monthly, or monthly by writing *Theatrical Index*, 888 Eighth Ave., New York, NY 10019, or calling (212) 586-6343 (www.theatricalindex.com).

THE STAGE MANAGER'S ASSOCIATION

This organization was started in 1982 as a professional association founded by and for stage managers. It seeks to create and develop an ongoing network through which stage managers can share their problems, exchange ideas and information, and educate themselves and those for whom they work about stage management issues. The organization has meetings regularly in New York and around the country and sponsors insightful forums on many topics relating to stage management as well. They publish a newsletter and have a program called "Operation Observation," which allows members to join stage managers as they run their shows, observing the workings of a Broadway or regional theater firsthand. For information on membership or publications write: The Stage Manager's Association, P.O. Box 275, Times Square Station,

New York, NY 10108-2020; telephone: (212) 543-9567; or send email to: info@stagemanagers.org (www.stagemanagers.org).

BACK STAGE, SHOW BUSINESS, AND VARIETY

There are three trade weeklies that stage managers can peruse in New York for listings of job opportunities and theater news: *Back Stage, Show Business,* and *Variety.* All three publications also feature informational articles and up-to-date news items concerning theater production.

Resource and Research Suggestions

There are many ways to go about gaining additional information about a career in stage managing, and there are many resource publications that help the stage manager begin to amass the information needed to start feeling truly qualified to take on the responsibilities of a major production.

WWW.BACKSTAGEJOBS.COM

A source of every kind of technical job across the country and also across the various forms of technical and production type. A very valuable tool.

ENTERTAINMENT DESIGN (ED) (FORMERLY THEATRE CRAFTS INTERNATIONAL)

Published ten times a year, *ED* has articles about every facet of theater technology and design written by many of the best people doing it. There are also many advertisements in the magazine for a myriad of technical devices, aids, and shops. Contacting these companies for brochures and information is the best way to keep up with advances in lighting and sound technology, as well as new scenic, prop, and costume techniques and materials. Once a year *ED* publishes a directory that is the most complete listing I have ever found of theatrical supply shops and services, many of which you may have an opportunity to work with during your stage managing career. For subscription inquires write to entertainmentdesignmag.com or *ED*, 32 W. 18th St., New York, NY 10011; telephone: (212) 242-3425.

THE NEW YORK THEATRICAL SOURCEBOOK

The Association of Theatrical Artists and Crafts People compile and edit an annual directory called *The Entertaining Sourcebook*. It is a spiral-bound specialty guide (sort of a theatrical Yellow Pages) to everything you need to know about companies that provide theatrical products and services, organizations that set safety and health standards, firms that sell and manufacture personal protective equipment, organizations that offer support services to theaters and the arts, and a listing of New York theater and dance rehearsal spaces, sound shops, and stages. Whether you need fake blood or bleached-blond wigs, it is a wonderful resource for the working stage manager. It also serves as an eye-opening learning experience for anyone wanting to know more about how technical theater crafts people find the basic (and often exotic) materials that go into most theater productions. This sourcebook may be ordered from Sourcebook Press, Inc., 163 Amsterdam Ave., #131, New York, New York 10023; telephone: (212) 496-1310; fax: (212) 496-7549; email: sourcebook@theatre.com.

OPERA AMERICA

This is the production resource group for all of the opera companies in America. It lists the companies in its directory with all their production personnel with addresses and emails so you can reach out with resumes or for further information. It also has a website full of information. For more info: 330 Seventh Ave. 16th Fl., New York, NY 10001. Phone: 212-796-8620. Email: Frontdesk@operaamerica.org. Website: www.operaamerica.org

PLAYBILL

Just enter playbill.com and learn about all sorts of entertainment, theatrical, classical, dance, and opera news as well as new about jobs and future plans. A really good website no matter what you want to find out.

THE STAGE MANAGER'S NETWORK

A great website for communicating with fellow stage managers. Questions and answers, forums, formal and informal chat rooms, and a job-listing service are all available free of charge. Just go to smnetwork.org.

CONCLUSION

Writing this book has been a revelation to me. At the beginning I thought it would be a relatively simple task, because actually doing the job seems easy after all these years, especially compared to, say, raising a teenage daughter or understanding the workings of Congress. However, trying to explain endless details and responsibilities without losing sight of stage management's more lofty purpose in the general scheme of creative collaboration, from which all successful theater grows, has proven a difficult and complex task.

When I started writing this book I resolved to attempt to make it more fun to read than a straightforward textbook. But as you've undoubtedly noticed, there is an overwhelming amount of information and basic knowledge that a young stage manager must absorb in order to perform well in the position. I believe that this book should simplify the process of stage managing a show for those who are trying it for the first time, while offering useful alternative methods and suggestions to those who have already begun their careers.

Throughout the book, I have tried to stress the human aspects of the position over the increasingly overwhelming technical side of today's theater, because I believe that the working relationships one must establish and maintain are the top priority. What makes live theater one of the most exciting arts is the joint collaboration of so many artists and craftspeople, all working together to make a show happen on a nightly basis. As theater begins to rely more and more heavily on the computer chip and synthesized sound, theater may overwhelm and amaze audiences with the spectacle of technological innovation, but it runs the risk of not involving an audience emotionally, or not making them care.

When I first became involved in the theater, it was a very different world backstage, one that involved a lot of human beings and not so many different machines and motors and computers. I used to get a thrill every night during the runs of *The Wiz* and *Sugar Babies* because to make these shows successful over a hundred people were required to work together in whatever harmony and structure the stage managers provided. Now, all too often, the show is completely programmed and the only excitement backstage is overcoming a "glitch" in the system. Fortunately, in many arenas—community theater, some college and university programs, and in smaller theater companies everywhere—the theater remains a live, vibrant, and very human art. It is to the people who want to learn, practice, and experience that art that this book is addressed.

Obviously, these ideas are an indication of how I feel about stage managing, and my own approach to stage management is reflected throughout the book. However, I hasten to remind any budding stage managers that there is no one way of doing this job, any more than there is one method of acting or directing. And as actors must in the end perform, stage managers must in the end support and facilitate that performance to the utmost of their abilities. While there are many ways of accomplishing this, every stage manager should have the same goal: a smooth-running show and a happy, satisfied company.

I believe experience is the best teacher. Hopefully, some of my experiences described in this book will help the learning stage manager. However, one's own experiences, in any endeavor, serve as the ultimate graduate course.

Stage managing is not a dull profession; often it is too exciting. The stress and pressures that befall stage managers can often be the job's greatest drawback. The position offers little glamour, but then, for many of us, that is part of its appeal.

Many things that help make stage managing easier or more successful are also invaluable in life, and that has been one of its joys for me. As I matured and learned to take life one day at a time, I saw immediately the value of doing so in my work. Conversely, stage managing has taught me the ability to prioritize, and that talent has made a big difference in my personal life.

Most of all, in both my life and my work, I have learned the value of fully knowing and appreciating that *all things are not of equal importance.* And so I will end with that thought and the hope that, however you translate it into your own work, it will prove as valuable a tool as the eraser and the three-hole punch.

APPENDIXES

1. Definitions of a Stage Manager

The following is the Actors' Equity Association definition of a stage manager's duties.

Definition of the Duties and Obligations of a Stage Manager
A Stage Manager under Actors' Equity Contract is, or shall be obligated to perform at least the following duties for the Production to which he is engaged, and by performing them is hereby defined as the Stage Manager:

1. He shall be responsible for the calling of all rehearsals, whether before or after opening.
2. He shall assemble and maintain the Prompt Book, which is defined as the accurate playing text and stage business, together with such cue sheets, plots, daily records, etc. as are necessary for the actual technical and artistic operation of the production.
3. He shall work with the Director and the heads of all other departments, during rehearsal and after opening, schedule rehearsal and outside calls in accordance with Equity's regulations.
4. Assume active responsibility for the form and discipline of rehearsal and performance, and be the executive instrument in the technical running of <u>each</u> performance.
5. Maintain the artistic intentions of the Director and the Producer after opening, to the best of his ability, including calling correctional rehearsals of the company when necessary, and preparation of the Understudies, Replacements, Extras and Supers, when and if the Director and/or the Producer declines this prerogative. Therefore, if an Actor finds him/herself unable to satisfactorily work out an artistic difference of opinion with the Stage Manager regarding the intentions of the Director and Producer, the Actor has the option of seeking clarification from the Director or Producer.
6. Keep such records as are necessary to advise the Producer on matters of attendance, time, welfare benefits, or other matters

relating to the rights of Equity members. <u>The Stage Manager and Assistant Stage Managers are prohibited from the making of payrolls or any distribution of salaries.</u>

7. Maintain discipline, as provided in the Equity Constitution, By-Laws and Rules where required, appealable in every case to Equity.

8. Stage Manager duties do not include shifting scenery, running lights, operating the box office, etc.

9. The Council shall have the power from time to time to define the meaning of the words "Stage Manager" and may alter, change or modify the meaning of Stage Manager as herein above defined.

10. The Stage Manager and Assistant Stage Managers are prohibited from handling contracts, having riders signed or initialed, or any other function which normally comes under the duties of the General Manager or Company Manager.

11. The Stage Manager and Assistant Stage Managers are prohibited from participating in the ordering of food for the company.

12. The Stage Manager and Assistant Stage Managers are prohibited from signing the closing notice of the company or the individual notice of any Actor's termination.

EXCERPTS FROM VARIOUS OTHER AEA CONTRACTS

The following excerpts define additional duties and obligations—and the limits of those obligations—of a professional stage manager. They are extracted from the Actors' Equity Association COST (Council of Stock Theaters), Dinner Theater, Industrial, LORT (League of Resident Theaters), and Off-Broadway contracts.

Definition of the Duties and Obligations of the Producer and a Stage Manager

- Because of the responsibilities of the Stage Manager for the success of the production and safety of the Actors, the Producer agrees that producer will use Producer's best efforts to employ a person who is experienced in theatrical stage management. (Industrial) (Dinner Theater)

- In every company in which an Equity member is employed, all Stage Managers, Assistant Stage Managers and Advance Stage Managers shall be and continue to be members of Equity in good standing, and shall be signed to the appropriate contract. Because the duties of the Advance and Resident Stage Manager include a comprehension of the technical and artistic aspects of a production, these positions should not be considered entry-level positions, but should be filled by individuals with stage managerial experience. The Stage Manager has the right to consult with the Producer in the selection of an Assistant Stage Manager(s). (COST)
- Whenever a Stage Manager or Assistant Manager does work related to the production, which shall include but not be limited to attending meetings, doing administrative work, scheduling and contracting cast, crew and liaisons, said work shall be regarded as part of the permitted work week. (Industrial)
- It is agreed that it is the duty of the Stage Manager to assemble and maintain the production script required for the actual technical and artistic operation of the production and that production script remains the property of the Theater. (LORT)
- The Stage Manager or the Assistant Stage Manager must be present in the rehearsal area and during all performances and must keep a prompt book which includes technical cues, blocking, business, direction, plots and daily records. No Stage Manager's or Assistant Stage Manager's duties shall be performed by anyone other than a Stage Manager or Assistant Stage Manager respectively under an Equity contract. (Dinner Theater)
- No member of the Stage Managerial staff will be required to prepare any additional production script or book for publication or archival purposes or for use in any other production of the play or musical. (LORT)
- A member of the Stage Managerial staff shall be present in the rehearsal area and during all performances except in an emergency. The Stage Manager's Assistant Stage Manager's duties shall not be performed by anyone other than a Stage Manager or Assistant Stage Manager respectively, under an Equity contract. (Off-Broadway)
- A Stage Manager or Assistant Stage Manager must be present on the deck or in communication from the booth with all backstage areas

during all performances, run-throughs, technical rehearsals, and dress rehearsals. Under no circumstances shall anyone other than the Equity Stage Manager or Assistant Stage Manager be on book calling the cues of a production. (LORT)

STAGE MANAGER'S DUTIES *DO NOT* INCLUDE THE FOLLOWING:

- [The Stage Managerial staff shall not be required to] arrange for living accommodations for the company, but may act as the means of communication between the Actor and the Producer. (COST)
- Members of the Stage Managerial staff are prohibited from doing janitorial, custodial or building maintenance work as part of their Stage Managerial duties. (COST)
- Members of the Stage Managerial staff are not required to design, build, hang, shop for lights, sound, scenery, props, wardrobe, etc. as part of their Stage Managerial duties; and they are prohibited from doing janitorial, custodial, building maintenance or restaurant work as part of their Stage Managerial duties. (Dinner Theater)
- It is agreed that the Stage Manager will not be assigned responsibility for the preparation of payroll, reservation of accommodations (except prior to commencement of rehearsal), preparation of contracts, provision of transportation (except in an emergency on the road), procurement of food, and that the Stage Manager shall not function as Director or Choreographer. It is further agreed the personnel assigned duties of a Stage Manager or Assistant Stage Manager shall be signed to an Equity contract. (Industrial)
- The Stage Manager or Assistant Stage Manager shall not be required to design, build, shop for, or hang scenery, props, lights, or costumes. Further, the operation of lights and the design and operation of sound is not a basic Stage Managerial duty but may be agreed to on an individual basis. (LORT)
- It is not the function of the Stage Manager or the Assistant Stage Manager to transport any employees of the Theater, including, but not limited to, Actors, Directors, and Designers, to appointments, performances, or rehearsals. (LORT)

A GENERAL MANAGER'S DEFINITION
OF AN IDEAL STAGE MANAGER

Jose Vega, a retired general manager on Broadway (*The Wiz*, *Ain't Misbehavin'*), shared his ideas on the duties of a stage manager at a round-table discussion sponsored by the Stage Managers' Association.

Could You Describe the Ideal Stage Manager?

"That's simple . . . someone with a good working knowledge of all technical aspects. Someone who can act as a director but who doesn't want to be one, who just likes maintaining the show. Someone who, on the road, can be a parent figure for all the actors, keep them together, keep them as happy as you can possibly keep actors.

"So when a general manager looks around for a stage manager, what does he get? If you have a show that is not technically difficult, you look for someone who can direct and maintain shows. If it's technically difficult, you look for one person who can do the technical part and one who can work with actors. One thing you don't want is any personality problem with the stage manager whatsoever. [A GM] has enough other problems without the one person you've got to keep problems away from you creating personality problems of his or her own."

How Do You Define the Duties of a Stage Manager?

"I think the stage manager should know everything that goes on on that stage. One thing stage managers [forego] a lot of the time is working with the crew. No matter how good a crew you have, they all have their departments, and their departments are the most important. You, hopefully, are objective. If you see the carpenter's set is going to get up but the lights are not going to get hung, you should be able to go to the carpenter and say 'Look, he's way behind, let him on the stage,' or, 'You start with your back pipe, and let the property man (who never gets a chance to do anything) come onstage now.' I see that happening less and less. Without a lot of experience you can get your head knocked in because they [the crew] are not going to take it unless you know what you're doing."

Describe the Division of Duties Between a Stage Manager and a Company Manager.

"I think [an] SM, from the curtain line back, is responsible for everything that happens. The company manager is there for the day-to-day business, to make decisions the SM can't, from the apron out. It differs—some company managers have 'their' crews. I'm against that. I think the crew should go to the SM. You are not co-managers, which is something you have to live with and use as productively as possible. Yes, there are CM's who interfere with everything back there and they shouldn't. But your job is to please the people you work for, and if your CM thinks it's his job to come backstage, well, that's the person you're working for, and there's nothing you can do. If there is a decision to be made, the CM is going to make it and the SM is going to have to live with it."

2. Sample Production Schedule

The production schedule to follow would be structured in a similar fashion in opera or theater. There are three columns: The left column is for the day and month; the middle column is for the exact time, or as exact as possible when the schedule is drawn up; and the right column, for which the most room should be left, is for the description of what happens during each time slot. These types of schedules provide an overall view and are not to be confused with or substituted for a rehearsal schedule.

Some reminders when preparing a production schedule:

1. When work is happening simultaneously at shops, in rehearsal rooms, and/or at the theater, note the location of each call or event.
2. Always date each revision because production schedules change frequently.
3. Remember that these schedules, as opposed to rehearsal schedules, should focus on the technical aspects of the show.
4. Don't be afraid to use the abbreviation TBA (to be announced) if a date is open or subject to change.
5. Don't be rigid about the form of the schedule; circumstances will dictate whether changes or improvements are advisable.

PRE-BROADWAY TOUR: *PECCADILLO*

Garson Kanin's drawing-room comedy *Peccadillo* starred Christopher Plummer, Glynis Johns, and Kelly McGillis. Unfortunately, the show never did make it to Broadway, although Florida audiences responded enthusiastically. The following production schedule is a good example of the complexities of rehearsing a play in a different city than that in which it will open. Notice, for instance, that as production stage manager, I was required to be in Florida before the rest of the company to supervise the focus.

PECCADILLO PRODUCTION SCHEDULE

Important phone numbers for any emergencies regarding schedule:
```
     Tom Kelly              XXX-XXXX
     Chuck Kindl            XXX-XXXX
     Production Office  XXX-XXXX
     Garson Office      XXX-XXXX
```

Mon. Jan. 28	2:00 - 10:00	First Rehearsal	**MANHATTAN CENTER** XXX West XXth St. (XXX) XXX-XXXX 7th Floor Stage XXX-XXXX
Tues. Jan. 29	12:30 - 8:30	Rehearsal	
Wed. Jan. 30	12:30 - 8:30	Rehearsal	Interviews set-up with St. Petersburg Critic, Tom Sibullus NYC Cinnamon
Thurs. Jan. 31	12:30 - 8:30	Rehearsal	1) By end of week, final- ize all costume/hair designs & complete first fittings
Fri. Feb. 1	12:30 - 8:30	Rehearsal	2) Light plot complete & bid in shop
Sat. Feb. 2	12:30 - 8:30	Rehearsal	3) Sound plot complete & set recording session for week ending Feb 9 - Set who & how to record "Fledermouse" audition song
Sun. Feb. 3	DAY OFF		**DURING WEEK**
Mon. Feb. 4	11:30	Production Meeting	1) Record session CP, GJ, CK and AUDITION SONG
Tues. Feb. 5	12:30 - 8:30	Rehearsal	2) Finalize all props, furniture, etc. Begin delivery of any actual
Wed. Feb. 6	12:30 - 8:30	Rehearsal	props, furniture, etc. to 311 W. 34 for use
Thurs. Feb. 7	12:30 - 8:30	Rehearsal	in reh. 3) Finish show tape for
Fri. Feb. 8	12:30 - 8:30	Rehearsal	use in reh. 4) Costume & wig fittings
Sat. Feb. 9	12:30 - 8:30	Rehearsal	5) Finalize all travel & hotel plans for
Sun. Feb. 10	DAY OFF		Florida 6) Order all trucks for Florida

Rev. January 28, 1985   2.

PECCADILLO PRODUCTION SCHEDULE

Mon. Feb. 11	11:30	Production Meeting	**DURING WEEK**
	12:30 - 8:30	Rehearsal	1) Confirm Fla. baby grand piano
Tues. Feb. 12	12:30 - 8:30	Rehearsal	2) Final fittings MON & TUES
Wed. Feb. 13	12:30 - 8:30	Rehearsal	1) Local truck pick up props from reh. hall, etc. & deliver to scenery shop - also work boxes etc.
Thurs. Feb. 14	12:30 - 8:30	Rehearsal	2) Load-out props, set, cost, sound, elec.
Fri. Feb. 15	12:30 - 8:30	Rehearsal	
Sat. Feb. 16	12:30 - 8:30	Rehearsal	3) Pre-hang elex in St. Petersburg
Sun. Feb. 17	DAY OFF		4) T. Kelly & Crew to St. Petersburg
Mon. Feb. 18	12:30 - 8:30	Rehearsal	FLA. 8:00-Midnight load-in, hang, etc. focus in St. Pete

Tues. Feb. 19   12:30 TRAVEL CALL at 311 W. 34th Street

3:00 (Approx) Co. Flight to Fla.

In Fla.   8:00 - 12:00 (Midnite) Continue load-in, hang, focus
& set cues in Fla.

Wed. Feb. 20	8:00 - 12 Noon	1) Piano tuned
		2) Finish cue setting, clean-up & pre-set props & costumes & quick-change rooms
		3) Dry tech all scene changes w/out actors
	1:00 - 6:00	Begin TECH/DRESS with actors
	7:30 - 12:00	Continue TECH/DRESS with actors
Thurs. Feb. 21	8:00 - 12 Noon	TECH work as needed
	1:00 - 6:00	Finish TECH/DRESS with actors
	7:30	Half Hour
	8:00	FULL DRESS REHEARSAL
Fri. Feb. 22	8:00 - 12 Noon	Tech work as necessary
	1:00	Full Company, Notes & Scene work
	2:30	Half Hour
	3:00	DRESS REHEARSAL

Rev. January 28, 1985   3

PECCADILLO PRODUCTION SCHEDULE

Fri. Feb. 22   6:00   D i n n e r
                     7:30   Half Hour
                     8:00   **PERFORMANCE**

Sat. Feb. 23   12:30 Noon   Notes
                     1:30   Half Hour
                     2:00   **MATINEE**
                     7:30   Half Hour
                     8:00   **EVENING PERFORMANCE**

Sun. Feb. 24   1:30   Half Hour   1) Pre-hang Elex
                                                             in Palm Beach
                     2:00   **MATINEE**
                     6:30   Half Hour
                     7:00   **EVENING PERFORMANCE** 2) Load-out &
                                                             truck to PB

Mon. Feb. 25   COMPANY DAY OFF - COMPANY TRAVEL TO PALM BEACH
                    8:00 a.m. - Midnight Load-in, hang & focus Palm Beach

Tues. Feb. 26   8:00 - 12 Noon   Finish hang, focus, etc.
                     1:00   Pre-set & dry tech
                     3:00   TECH with Actors
                     6:00   Break
                     8:00   Half Hour
                     8:30   **OPEN PALM BEACH**

3. Production Meeting Notes

The following are minutes (or notes) of a preproduction meeting for *The Merchant of Venice*. Stage managers should take careful notes during all such meetings and, at the first opportunity, type them up and distribute them to all participants. The most important features to include when typing minutes are (1) the date, (2) the names of all attendees, and (3) the major headings that were discussed, which can be taken right from the agenda.

```
THE MERCHANT OF VENICE

Notes of Production Meeting 10/11/89

In attendance: Tom Kelly
               Barbara Forbes
               Kathleen Gallagher
               Scott Anderson
               Joe Harris, Jr.
               Duke Durfee
               Jeremiah Harris
               Donna Drake
               Chuck Kindl
               Peter Kulok
               Kathleen Griffin

Truss
1. A request has been made from the designers for both a
   lighting truss and a sound truss. There is however not
   enough steel in the ceiling for a truss to be hung. Due to
   the fact that the theatre is landmarked we would have to go
   through the ceiling and tie to the steel in the roof. This
   is a very costly operation and is being considered by the
   powers that be. More later.

Sound
1. Scott Anderson has just received the shop order from Paul
   and will now proceed to amend and flesh out the list before
   it goes to Sound Associates. He will also be adding
   communication equipment for the Stage Managers.
2. Scott has requested that the portals which are being built
   to match the existing house portals be made at least
   partially of acoustic cloth so that speakers can be placed
   at strategic points.

   This is a potentially expensive proposition since the cloth
   will have to be dyed to match the existing theatre color.
```

page 2

The position of these speakers will be dependent upon the possible installation of a sound truss.

3. Sound position will eliminate eight seats at house left. Four seats will be pulled from the last two rows.

4. The three "musicians" will be wearing body mics. This should not necessarily force us to hire a backstage sound op since they wear the mics throughout, and wardrobe is used to dealing with them.

5. For teching the show, the communication and cueing system will be duplicated in front of house and backstage so Tom can initially cue and run techs and first dress from house.

Lights

1. We are waiting on additional information from Mark Henderson and Cass so that the final shop order can be put together. It is becoming increasingly important that Neil receive this information as soon as possible.

2. The preliminary bids have been returned and Jeremiah is going over them. More later.

Schedule

1. The containers are due to arrive at the dock on October 18. They will be transported from there to East Coast Theatre Supply by the 23rd where they will be broken down, customs inspected, and the necessary work undertaken.

2. Load-in will begin at the theatre on the 30th to be completed by the 4th. Once the focus is finished we will break to minimum crew until the beginning of Tech rehearsals or need.

3. The schedule needs to be finalized to reflect the proper playing schedule for Christmas week.

4. Everyone seems to be comfortable with the progress to this point. Although there is some concern that the new costume designs and remainder of the light order arrive very soon.

Pyro

1. There are kerosene torches carried in the show which will have to be cleared with the fire marshall here. A licensed pyro tech may also have to be on staff. Jeremiah and Joe Jr. will be dealing with this.

2. It is possible some fireproofing may need to be done to costumes worn by torch carriers. Also, wardrobe voiced their concern over the blackening of hands and costumes due to dripping of kerosene.

Wardrobe

1. Barbara is going to discuss budget with Peter so that she can begin the process of finding a shop or shops which can handle the necessary work.

2. Once the costumes are broken out of the containers at East Coast they will be sent to the 46th Street Theatre for a

page 3

    wardrobe call. Barbara and Kathleen will then start fittings and determine what work needs to be done.

3. Are the costumes in wooden crates, cardboard boxes, or loose racks?

4. It is very important that Barbara have the new costume designs as soon as possible as all shops are very busy at this point and the longer we wait the more expensive this will become.

5. Barbara also voiced her concern over the lateness of the final casting and how this may affect the cost and readiness of costumes.

Seats
1. There is a possibility that we will gain a few seats on the pit. This will be known once the deck is installed.

4. Rehearsal Schedules and Scene Breakdowns

Rehearsal schedules come in many forms and may change frequently. At the beginning of a production, it is possible to create a rough schedule for the entire rehearsal period. This can be done in a linear fashion, like the production schedules. However, it may be better to provide the company with a calendar-style schedule.

As the rehearsal period progresses, it will be possible to draw up weekly schedules that detail what scenes and acts will be rehearsed at a given time. Using the rehearsal scene breakdown that can easily be created from the stage manager's initial production analysis, he or she can list every actor needed for each scene. However, in a large-cast play or musical, the stage manager can save him- or herself work by providing the company with a rehearsal scene breakdown that details what actors are necessary for each section of the play. Then the stage manager can simply write a schedule listing the scenes to be worked on each day.

Scene breakdowns and weekly schedules together give company members a clear idea when they will or will not be needed at rehearsal. Breakdowns are also helpful to other members of the production team—costume designers or press representatives, for instance—because they can determine which actors might be available for outside appointments.

All schedules, as well as a copy of the scene breakdown, should be posted on the callboard.

Several rehearsal schedules are shown. A "calendar form" schedule from *Coward in Two Keys* (giving the rough outline and parameters of the production's rehearsal period) is followed by a scene breakdown and both a weekly and a daily schedule for *Death of a Salesman*.

COWARD IN TWO KEYS
Rehearsal Calendar

July

Sunday	Monday	Tuesday	Wednesday	Thursday	Friday	Saturday
		1	2	3	4	5
6	7	8	9	10	11	12
13	14	15	16	17 Director arrives 1:00 Prod. Mtg. at Lavan Reh. Hall	18	19
20 3:00: Tape Set and Prepare for Reh. At: Lavan 1	21 10:00: M + G Read Play Design Present 2:00 Lunch 3:00 Staging 5:30: Cast Measured Prod. Mtg	22 10-2, 3-6: REH AM: Fittings Females	23 10-2, 3-6: REH AM: Fittings Men	24 10-2, 3-6: REH	25 10-2, 3-6: REH	26 10-2, 3-6: REH
27 DAY OFF	28 10-2, 3-6: REH	29 10-2, 3-6: REH	30 10-2, 3-6: REH	31 10-2, 3-6: REH		

COWARD IN TWO KEYS
Rehearsal Calendar

August

Sunday	Monday	Tuesday	Wednesday	Thursday	Friday	Saturday
					1 10-2, 3-6: REH	2 10-2, 3-6: REH
3 DAY OFF	4 10-2, 3-6: REH	5 10-2, 3-6: REH	6 10-2, 3-6: REH	7 10-2, 3-6: REH	8 10-2, 3-6: REH	9 10-2, 3-6: REH STRIKE LAVAN Final LION
10 CAST DAY OFF LOAD IN SET BEGIN FOCUS	11 AM: LITE/ SET 12-5 TECH 7-12 TECH	12 AM: Tech Notes 12: Half Hour: Dress Reh w/ Pix 5:00: Break 8:00: Prev. # 1	13 AM: Tech Notes 12-5: REH/ Notes 8:00: Prev. # 2	14 2:00: Prev. # 3 8:00: Prev. # 4	15 AM: Tech Notes AFT: Cast Notes 8:00: Perf. # 1	16 2:00: Perf. # 2 8:00: Perf. # 3
17 DAY OFF	18 8:00: Perf. # 4 *Audience Talkback*	19 8:00: Perf. # 5	20 8:00: Perf. # 6 *Student Talkback*	21 2:00: Perf. # 7 8:00: Perf. # 8	22 8:00: Perf. # 9	23 2:00: Perf. # 10 8:00: Perf.# 11
24 DAY OFF	25 8:00: Perf. # 12	26 8:00: Perf. # 13	27 8:00: Perf. # 14	28 2:00: Perf. # 15 8:00: Perf. # 16	29 8:00: Perf. # 17	30 2:00: Perf. # 18 8:00: Perf. # 19

SAMPLE REHEARSAL SCENE BREAKDOWN

Here's a rehearsal scene breakdown. Every time a new configuration of actors appears, whether through an entrance, exit, or the beginning of a new scene, number that section and continue numbering consecutively through the end of the play. Doing this for *Death of a Salesman*, I came up with forty-four scenes.

Page 2

DEATH OF A SALESMAN

Rehearsal Scene Breakdown

ACT II

Page	Scene	
1- 5	17	Willy & Linda
6	18	Linda
6-15	19	Willy & Howard
16-20	20	Willy, Ben, Linda, Bernard, Happy & Biff
20-22	21	Charley, Willy, Linda & Biff
22-23	22	Willy, Bernard & Jenny
23-27	23	Willy & Bernard
28-29	24	Bernard, Willy & Charley
29-32	25	Charley & Willy
32-34	26	Stanley & Happy
34-36	27	Stanley, Happy & Miss Forsythe
36-38	28	Biff, Happy & Miss Forsythe
38-40	29	Biff & Happy
40-45	30	Willy, Biff, Happy & Stanley
45-47	#31	Bernard, Happy, Biff, Willy & Linda
47-50	32	Biff, Willy, Happy, Operator, Page & Woman
51-52	33	Happy, Miss Forsythe, Letta, Woman, Biff, Willy
52-54	34	Letta, Miss Forsythe, Biff & Happy
54-58	35	Willy, Woman & Biff
58-60	36	Willy & Biff
60-61	37	Willy, Stanley & Waiter
62-65	38	Happy, Linda, Biff & Willy
65-68	39	Willy & Ben
68-69	40	Biff & Willy
69-75	41	Willy, Biff, Linda & Happy
75-78	42	Ben, Linda, Willy & Happy
78-79	43	Willy, Linda, Biff & Happy, Charley & Bernard
R-1- 3	44	Linda, Biff, Charley, Happy & Bernard

SAMPLE WEEKLY SCHEDULE

Once the rehearsal scene breakdown is complete, it is much easier to draw up a more specific schedule. Further, when a partial run-through is scheduled (see Tuesday, 3:30 P.M., for example), the stage manager doesn't have to list every actor included in that chunk of the script.

```
                    DEATH OF A SALESMAN

                    Rehearsal Schedule

MINSKOFF REHEARSAL STUDIO #1
1515 Broadway—3rd Floor
212-575-0725


Monday, December 12—11:00 Full Company Assemble
    12:30     Scene #1    Willy & Linda
    2:00           2      Biff & Happy
    2:30     LUNCH
    4:00     Scene #3     Biff, Happy & Willy
    4:30           4      Biff, Happy, Willy & Bernard
    5:30           5      Biff, Happy, Willy & Linda


Tuesday, December 13
    10:00     Scene #6    Willy, and Woman from Boston
    10:45          7      Linda, Willy, Bernard (Woman—Off Stage)
    11:30          8      Happy, Willy & Charley
    12:15          9      Uncle Ben, Willy & Charley
    1:00      LUNCH
    2:30      Scene #10   Uncle Ben, Willy, Linda, Biff & Happy
    3:00           11     Charley, Linda, Willy, Ben & Bernard
    3:30      RUN-Scene #1-11
    4:30      Scene #12   Linda & Willy
    5:00           13     Biff, Linda & Happy


Wednesday, December 14
    10:00     Scene #13   Biff, Linda & Happy
    10:30          14     Willy, Biff, Linda & Happy
    11:30          15     Linda, Biff & Happy
    12:00          16     Linda, Willy, Happy & Biff
    1:00      LUNCH
    2:30      Scene # 17  Willy & Linda
    3:15           FULL COMPANY—Equity Business
    3:30      RUN-Scene #11-17
    4:30      Scene #18   Linda
    5:00           19     Willy & Howard
```

Page 2

DEATH OF A SALESMAN

Rehearsal Schedule Continued

Thursday, December 15

10:00	Scene #19	Willy & Howard
11:00	20	Willy, Ben, Linda, Bernard, Happy & Biff
12:15	21	Charley, Willy, Linda & Biff
1:00	LUNCH	
2:30	Scene #22	Willy, Bernard & Jenny
3:00	23	Willy & Bernard
3:45	24	Bernard, Willy & Charley
4:15	25	Charley & Willy
5:30	26	Stanley & Happy

Friday, December 16

10:00	Scene #26	Stanley & Happy
10:30	27	Stanley, Happy & Miss Forsythe
11:00	28	Biff, Happy & Miss Forsythe
11:30	29	Biff & Happy
12:15	30	Willy, Biff, Happy & Stanley
1:00	LUNCH	
2:30	Scene #30	Willy, Biff, Happy & Stanley
3:00	31	Bernard, Happy, Biff, Willy & Linda
3:30	32	Biff, Willy, Happy, Operator, Page & Woman
4:30	33	Happy, Miss Forsythe, Letta, Woman, Biff & Willy
5:00	34	Letta, Miss Forsythe, Biff & Happy

Saturday, December 17

10:00	RUN-Scene #19-34	
11:30	Scene #35	Willy, Woman & Biff
12:00	36	Willy & Biff
12:30	37	Willy, Stanley & Waiter
1:00	LUNCH	
2:30	Scene #38	Happy, Linda, Biff & Willy
3:30	39	Willy & Ben
4:15	40	Biff & Willy
4:45	41	Willy, Biff, Linda & Happy

Sunday, December 18   D A Y   O F F

PLEASE NOTE:

This schedule is clearly subject to change, and you will also
be called individually for costumes, hair and make-up. So
PLEASE make no commitments you cannot easily break during
rehearsal hours. We will endeavor to schedule as far in advance
as possible, but last minute flexibility is essential.

Thank you.

Tom Kelly   Chuck Kindl
xxx-xxxx   xxx-xxxx

SAMPLE DAILY SCHEDULE

Stage managers should try to post a daily schedule on the callboard or in some other prominent place so everyone in the theater or rehearsal room knows what is happening and when. The following schedule from *The Merchant of Venice* is a good example.

THE MERCHANT OF VENICE

SCHEDULE/ MON. NOV. 13

NEDERLANDER THEATRE
XXX West XXst St.
XXX-XXXX

10:00	Act III-1
	Salerio, Solanio,
	Shylock
	Tubal, Antonio's Man
12:00	Act III-3
	Antonio, Solanio,
	Shylock
	Jailer, Courtiers
12:00	Julia Swift to
	Wigs @ 46th St.
1:00	LUNCH
1:00	Dustin Hoffman to
	Wigs @ 46th St.
2:00	Act I-2
	Portia, Nerissa,
	Balthasar
2:00	Francesca Buller to
	Wigs
3:00	Act II-8
	Salerio, Solanio
3:00	Geraldine James to
	Wigs
3:30	Act I-1
	Antonio, Bassanio,
	Graziano
	Salerio, Solanio,
	Lorenzo
	Beggar, Innkeeper
4:00	Verse with Sir Peter
	Hall
	All new company
	members and any
	old company who care
	to renew.
6:00	Conclude

46TH STREET THEATRE
XXX W. XXth Street
XXX-XXXX

8:00 a.m.	FULL CREW
	Work call & Hang &
	Focus & Truss
6:00 p.m.	Conclude

CARROLL MUSIC
XXX W. XXst St.
XXX-XXXX

10:00	Robert Lockhart
	w/ Wilbur Pauley
	Margery Daley
	Elisabeth Engan
	Christina Sunnerstam
3:00	Conclude

5. Rehearsal Report Form

The following rehearsal report form is one that I completed during work on *The Merchant of Venice*. It gives examples of the kind of notes that should be written in the rehearsal log. The importance of this form is discussed in chapter 5.

THE MERCHANT OF VENICE		
REHEARSAL REPORT		46TH STREET THEATRE
DAY: Wed.	**DATE:** Nov. 8, 1989	4, 10

SCHEDULE	FITTINGS OR APPOINTMENTS
10:00 — 1st Reh. Beckwith, Ben-Ari, Browder, Buller, Karter, Hugo-Daly, Dickey, Holmes, James, Lawson, Rayppy, Swift, Thomas, Whitlock, Wojda 11:30–1 — Portia & Nerissa 2–6 — Portia & Nerissa scenes with all others Excellent work!	11:30 — Thomas 1:00 — Ben-Ari 2:30 — Wojda 4:00 — Dickey 　　　　 Pauley **ABSENT, LATE OR OFFICE NOTES** ① Late/Denis Holmes Confusion about call ② Discuss Alex Hardy capacity ③ Browder now to understudy Lorenzo & Stephano not Graziano

PROP NOTES	SET
① Prop crew standing by and very helpful - drew raves from Thelma, Sara & PH ② Thelma & PH would like front row out ASAP!	DRY TECH for Thelma to be run Tues. AM Truss to be hung Mon. — Reh. at Brooks if habitable

COSTUME NOTES	LIGHTS & SOUND
① Wig man: Jeff Franks to meet Frida tomorrow ② B. Forbes mtg. w/Dustin Fri. at 9:45 re costumes	① Carroll Music small room booked for reh. Mon., Wed., Th., Fri. 10-3 / hold on Sat. 10-6

COMMENTS & NOTES:
① Set-up TV shoot for Dustin w/Thomas TV- in front of stage / Fri. @ 9:00. ② Barbara Toye & Joe Harris Jr. met about DH dressing rm. ③ Great day - getting going - company coming together easily - Sara a big help with blocking, etc. ③ Peter Hall seems pleased - But: 　　① NOISE (fans, blowers, etc.) } Big 　　② LATECOMERS — LATE CURTAIN } things with him　　Stage Manager: Tom Kelly

6. Sample Cue Sheet

The following turntable cue (or "Q") sheet for *Death of a Salesman* follows the fairly standard three-column format: the cue's name and number come first; then the description of the move; and finally the speed of the move. The document was initially devised for the turntable operator, who would revolve the turntable that was built into the main unit set. This is the type of move that has been greatly defined by automation, but it is wise to know how to cue it when run by a single motor and operator as well.

For more examples of cue sheets and how to set them up with cue lights, check Appendix 9.

TURNTABLE OPERATOR'S Q SHEET

TURNTABLE Q'S—SALESMAN ACT II		
Q	MOVE	DIRECTION/SPEED
PRESET ACTS I & II	KITCHEN DS HOWARD'S US	PRESET
(5 MINUTES INTO ACT) Q1	REVOLVE TO HOWARD DS KITCHEN US (UNIT STAYS DS)	COUNTER/CLOCK MED.-FAST
10 MINUTES Q2	REV. TO KITCHEN DS HOWARD US (UNIT MOVES US DURING REVOLVE) (HOWARD CHANGE TO CHARLEY US)	COUNTER/CLOCK MED.-FAST
4 MINUTES Q3	REV. TO CHARLEY DS KITCHEN US (UNIT MOVES DS DURING REVOLVE) (CHARLEY CHANGE TO RESTAURANT US)	COUNTER/CLOCK MED.
10 MINUTES Q4	REV. TO RESTAURANT DS CHARLEY US (UNIT MOVES US DURING REVOLVE) (CHARLEY CHANGE TO KITCHEN US)	CLOCKWISE/MED.
- 20 MINUTES - Q5	REV. TO KITCHEN DS RESTAURANT US (UNIT MOVES DS DURING REVOLVE) END OF TURNTABLE	CLOCKWISE/MED.

7. Tracking Sheet and Prop List

As a show becomes set, it is vital that all assistant stage managers prepare a tracking sheet, detailing what each of them does during the running of a performance. This is one of an ASM's more important responsibilities. The sample tracking sheet included here was prepared in meticulous detail by Chuck Kindl for the Broadway replacement cast of *Speed-the-Plow*. (Bob, David, and Flicka refer to Bob Balaban, Davis Rasche, and Felicity Huffman, the actors playing Fox, Gould, and Karen.) If every ASM prepares such a tracking sheet, an unexpected absence shouldn't cause any undue trauma backstage.

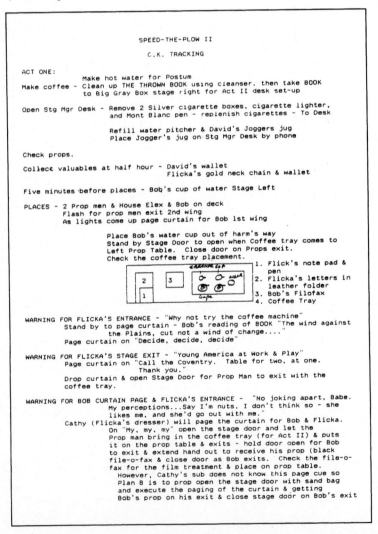

TRACKING SHEET (CONT.)

SPEED-THE-PLOW II - C.K. TRACKING

Page 2

WARNING FOR SCENE CHANGE - "Give me a platform to do good, and I'll do good"
Cue for change - "and tell him that he owes me $500 bucks."
Follow 2 prop men to curtain man - curtain comes in head-high.
When Props start to pull carpet with coffee table upstage tap
the curtain man's shoulder which cues him to bring in the
curtain.

Enter stage and work lights will come on - put LS end of carpet
up on coffee table - place chair upstage (sofa high) out of way
Then put RS end of carpet on coffee table.

As Coffee table is being taken to stage right indicate with toe
SL mark, then cross in front of sofa giving it a look as to
neatness & Book - give SR sofa end carpet a sweep away from
front of sofa. Take 2 glasses from bar and cross behind sofa.
Give Flicka empty glass & David glass with water and as you
exit Stage Right 2, give the drape a flip so it swags properly.

Ready desk for Act II
Prop men remove all scripts.
Strike the Flicka leather letter folder to gray box.
Strike leather pad holder & pen to gray box.
PLACE - THE BOOK (II) on desk from gray box.
Set cigarette box, opened appointment book & lighter
Pick out 3 throwable scripts & 3 scripts for coffee table
    3 throwable scripts with THE BOOK on top - Chair area
    3 coffee table scripts - desk end

Take leather pad holder & pen to Stg Mgr desk & relieve Tom
from script - Tear out written sheet from Leather pad & throw
out & take the Jogger's cup to gray box. Clip pen to closing
tab. Neaten up the phone messages trying to keep out any
creases and paper clip to left-hand flap.

Keep track of book for Light cue #8.5

END OF ACT ONE - Tom relieves you from book - Clean out ash tray with a
kleenex and put in a couple of drops of water.

Flash off Flicka & David.

When curtain comes in for intermissin change - retrieve Flicka's shoes
and 2 glasses. Glasses to green bar - shoes to dresser. Carpet biz.

Check props - Give a look in bar for brandy & 2 glasses
Place arm chair. Check desk top. As props places coffee cup,
saucer & spoon, give him the 3 coffee table scripts. Desk chair
should be turned downstage. (8 items)

ON COFFEE TABLE	1. Ash tray
3 scripts	2. Coffee cup
Cig. box	3. 3 scripts
Cig. lighter	BOOK on top
Tray with coffee etc.	4. Cigarettes
Ash tray	5. Lighter
	6. Appt book
	7. Telephone

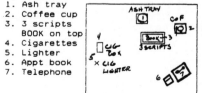

```
                    SPEED-THE-PLOW II - C.K. TRACKING
                                                        Page 3
END OF ACT ONE (Continued)
          Coffee table - Add: Coffee tray with 1 cup & pot, creamer etc.
                        3 scripts
                        Cigarette box, lighter, ash tray & phone

          Take Leather correspondence folder from gray box to Prod Office

          Give Bob fresh water
          Go to Quick change table for THE BOOK (Act I) & Flicka's note pad
          Note pad with pen on SL Prop table with Bob's filofax
          Take THE BOOK (Act I) to Prod. Office

          C.K. unplugs hot water & empties.  Throws out both coffee grinds.
          Unplugs Decaf.

ACT ·II· PLACES - Standby to page Curtain for Bob's entrance at top of Act.

          Put Bob's water out of harm's way.
          Take THE BOOK (Act I) & diet soda to Stage Right.
          T. Kelly gets soda & THE BOOK placed on gray box with phone
          messages inside.

          Relieve Tom from the script.

          When Bob reads from THE BOOK after David's "wait" turn on the
          phone buzzer.

          Tom takes over script, then go to Stage Left.  Tuck up the
          door blacks and wait for the thrown BOOK.  Put BOOK in Prod.
          office and go stage right for curtain calls.

          Return the valuables.

          Turn off the phone buzzer.

          When Tom takes out the pre-set - Take Flicka's note pad & pen
          and Bob's Filofax to Production Office sand bagging the SL
          door open so props can return coffee tray to Prod. office.
          Then get 2 silver cigarette boxes, lighter & Mont Blanc pen
          and place in Stage Manager's desk drawer to be locked.
          Look for any buttons on stage.

          Pull plugs on coffee etc.

          Put phone away. Secure stage managers desk.

          Reports.

          Go home.
```

PROP RUNNING SHEETS

Here are examples of prop running sheets that give the clear picture of the preset for each act and the moves and use of the props during the act. These sheets are for a small chamber opera, *Il Matrimonio Segreto*, at the Brooklyn Academy Opera Company. The paperwork that follows was used when the production was directed by Jonathan Miller.

 May 2008 Director: Jonathan Miller	Il Matrimonio Segreto Props Run Sheet	ASM: Francesca DeRenzi SM: Tom Kelly June 4, 2008 Page 1 of 3 Final Version

TOP OF SHOW PROPS PRESET

STAGE RIGHT	ONSTAGE	STAGE LEFT
• Tiny Book (CONTE) • Pill Tin (CONTE) • Wedding Ring (PAOLINO)	ALL DOORS SHUT • Chaise, set USC • Silver/Green Arm Chair set SR • Silver/Green Side Chair set SR • Silver/Green Side Chair set SL • Mirror, set in UL corner • 2 Brown Side Chairs, set outside UR Doors	• Letter (PAOLINO) • Napkin (GERONIMO) • Chicken Leg – *consumable* (GERONIMO) • Sandwich – *consumable* (MALE SERVANT) • Letter (GERONIMO) **In Ms. Brillembourg's Dressing Room:** • Small Book (FIDALMA) • Glasses (FIDALMA)

Act I Diagram
(<u>Please Note</u>: This drawing is not to scale)

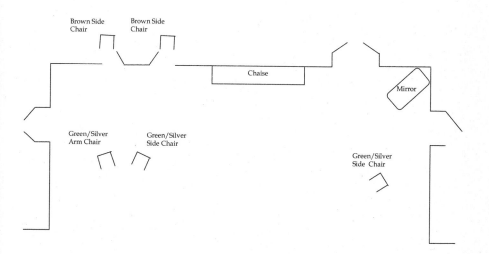

	ASM: Francesca DeRenzi
Il Matrimonio Segreto	SM: Tom Kelly

May 2008

Il Matrimonio Segreto
Props Run Sheet

Director: Jonathan Miller

ASM: Francesca DeRenzi
SM: Tom Kelly
June 4, 2008
Page 2 of 3
Final Version

ACT I PROPS PRESET
Running Time: 73:00

STAGE RIGHT	ONSTAGE	STAGE LEFT
• Tiny Book (CONTE)	**ALL DOORS SHUT** • Chaise, set USC • Silver/Green Arm Chair set SR • Silver/Green Side Chair set SR • Silver/Green Side Chair set SL • Mirror, set in UL corner • 2 Brown Side Chairs, set outside UR Doors	• Letter (PAOLINO) • Napkin (GERONIMO) • Chicken Leg – *consumable* (GERONIMO) **In Ms. Brillembourg's Dressing Room:** • Small Book (FIDALMA) • Glasses (FIDALMA)

Intermission (20:00) –
- Strike Small Book and Glasses from Chaise
- Check stage floor for chicken pieces

Act II Diagram
(Please Note: Furniture placement remains the same – there is no intermission shift!)
(Please Note: This drawing is not to scale)

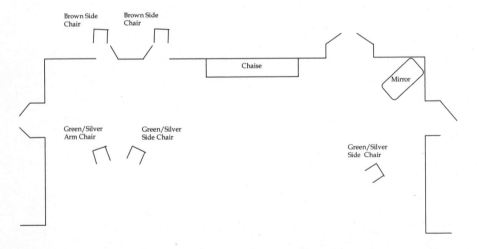

Il Matrimonio Segreto
Props Run Sheet

ACT II PROPS PRESET
Running Time: 63:00

STAGE RIGHT	ONSTAGE	STAGE LEFT
• Tiny Book (CONTE) • Pill Tin (CONTE) • Wedding Ring (PAOLINO)	ALL DOORS SHUT • Chaise, set USC • Silver/Green Arm Chair set SR • Silver/Green Side Chair set SR • Silver/Green Side Chair set SL • Mirror, set in UL corner • 2 Brown Side Chairs, set outside UR Doors	• Letter (GERONIMO) • Sandwich – *consumable* (MALE SERVANT)

8. Technical Rehearsal Schedules

Technical rehearsals can take many forms, as discussed in chapter 7, and include a wide variety of information. Two schedules are presented here as examples. The first tech schedule is very specific, detailing the work planned for one day; the other is a general overview, much like the production schedule in Appendix 2.

CUE-TO-CUE SCHEDULE

The following schedule was created for one technical rehearsal for *Death of a Salesman* to keep the cast and crew apprised of the sections that would be worked on that day. It begins by offering general technical guidelines for the actors before listing the sections of the script that will be rehearsed, specifying all costume changes and technical cues that are to be worked through.

CUE-TO-CUE SCHEDULE

DEATH OF A SALESMAN   1.

WEDNESDAY REHEARSAL OUTLINE

1. No wigs necessary.
2. Costumes for Linda, Biff, Happy, Bernard & Charley only
    (Fast changes only)

ACT I

Run - stopping as necessary

From 1-1   Opening
Stop 1-4   LINDA: Take an aspirin.

Cut to 1-8 WILLY: How can they whip cheese?
Stop 1-14 BIFF: Hap, I've had 20 or 30 different jobs

                (Linda can make her change even with cuts.
                Should be plenty of time for change)

Cut to 1-17 BIFF: Remember, Bill Oliver.

                Run with costume change, set change
                        light & sound cues

                Includes: Bernard's entrance
                           Linda's wash entrance
                           Hap has time to change to PJ's
Stop at 1-28 LINDA: It's got the biggest ads.

Cut to 1-30 WILLY: I'm small.
                Includes: Woman from Boston & Bernard & Linda
Stop at 1-35 Charley's entrance

Cut to 1-38 WILLY: Did you see the ceiling I put up in the living room.

                Includes: Hap has time to change to young boy
                           Ben's entrance
                           Linda & boys sword fight
                           Boys quick change to PJ's
                           Charley's change
Stop at 1-49 BIFF: What is he doing out there?

        Walk thru moves to 1-57 - Linda & Boys - Attention must be paid

---

Start 1-57 LINDA: Biff, I swear to God! Biff, his life is in your hands.
Stop at 1-59 WILLY: Go to Filene's.....

        Walk thru moves to 1-63 - WILLY: Don't be so modest.

Start 1-63 WILLY: Don't be so modest.
Thru end of Act One 1-68.

CUE-TO-CUE SCHEDULE (CONT.)

```
                                                                  2.
           DEATH OF A SALESMAN - WEDNESDAY REHEARSAL OUTLINE

                              ACT II

From II-1  Top of Act

                  Includes:  Coffee scene
                             Linda's phone call
                             Revolve into Howard's Office
                             Linda's change - Set Charley's Office
Stop II-9  End of tape in Howard scene
                  Howard:  That was my wife.
```

```
Cut to II-13  Howard:  YOu'll have to excuse me, Willy, I gotta see some
                                                              people.

                  Includes:  Ben - Linda thru Ebbetts Field
                             Bernard & Charley
                             Bernard's quick change
                             Revolve into Charley's Office
                             Charley's quick change
                             Set Cafe juke box

Stop II-27  Charley's entrance - Charley:  Hey, you're goin' miss that train.
```

```
Cut to II-31  Charley:  You been jealous of me all your life, you damned fool.

                  Includes:  Revolve into cafe
                             Set kitchen
                             Stanley & Happy & Miss Forsythe
Stop II-36  Biff entrance - Biff:  Hello, kid, sorry I'm late.
```

```
Cut to II-40  Willy's entrance - Happy:  You leave the house tomorrow......

Stop II-41  Willy:  Well, what happened, boy?
```

```
CUT TO II-45  Willy:  Famous for the way he listens.

                  Includes:  Mrs. Loman, Mrs. Loman - Bernard & Linda
                             Standish arms
                             Woman from Boston
                             Miss Forsythe
                             Letta

Stop II-55  Biff enter in Boston - Biff:  Why didn't you answer.
```

```
            Walk moves thru Woman exit
```

3.

<u>DEATH OF A SALESMAN - WEDNESDAY REHEARSAL OUTLINE</u>

ACT II (Continued)

Start II-60 Biff exit - Biff: You fake.

                  Includes: Biff quick change
                             Revolve into kitchen
                             Linda, Happy & Biff roses

Stop II-62 Linda knocks flowers to floor

Cut to II-65 Biff: Scum of the earth and you're looking at him.

Stop II-69 Biff: People ask where I am ....

                  Includes: Willy seeds
                             Ben

           Walk thru moves for lights to II-75 Biff: I'll go in the
                                              morning.

Start II-75 Biff: I'll go in the morning. Put him - put him to bed
                    Includes:
                              Linda's quick change

Stop R-1 All in place for the Requiem

Cut to R-3 Happy: All right, boy.

                  Thru the end of the Requiem

TECHNICAL WEEK SCHEDULE

The following schedule, prepared for *Accomplice*, focuses on the tech week. It attempts to give the actors an idea of what section of the script will be teched (Act 1 or 2) and what level of technical readiness they should expect (full dress or props only). If a show is technically complex, it may not be possible to schedule accurately (*see* Thurs. April 5).

```
2/22/90                  ACCOMPLICE SCHEDULE


MON. MARCH 19-FRI. MARCH 30:  Load-in, Hang and Focus on a
                              basic 8:00-12:00, 1:00-5:00 day
                              schedule at theater

          Actors will continue to work 10:00 to 5:30 at
          890 Studios. Basic concept will be work and
          notes: AM; run-thru: PM. Understudies begin
          attending rehearsals March 26.

SATURDAY MARCH 31   (if possible technically)
    8:00- 6:00   Finish Focus, Dressing and Clean-up at Theater
   11:00         Actors: Notes and Run-Thru at 890
    3:00         Break Actors/Take Furniture, etc. to theater
    6:00         Break all crew, but house heads on at 7:00
    7:00         Cast on stage: Props and work light only;
                 adjust blocking, check sightlines, answer all
                 "Is this the way it's going to be?" questions.
   11:00         BREAK

SUNDAY APRIL 1   DAY OFF

MONDAY APRIL 2/ TUES. APRIL 3
    8:00-12:00   Crew time as needed
    1:00- 6:00   Technical rehearsal    (COSTUME PIECES AVAILABLE
    7:00-11:00   Technical rehearsal       as needed for Tech)

WEDNESDAY APRIL 4
    8:00-12:00   Crew time as needed
   12:30         Half-Hour for actors and dressers
    1:00         Crew call/ Full dress/Tech of Act One
    5:30         Actors Break
    6:00         Crew Break
    6:30         Half-Hour for actors and dressers
    7:00         Crew call/Full dress/Tech of Act Two
   11:00         Break
```

2/22/90   ACCOMPLICE SCHEDULE   p. 2

THURS. APRIL 5
    8:00-12:00   Crew time as needed
    1:00- 6:00   Notes, fixes and any remaining tech with actors
                  OR First full non-stop dress
    7:00   Half-Hour
    7:30   First or second full non-stop dress rehearsal
    11:00   Break

FRIDAY APRIL 6
    A.M.   Clean up and clear house/Any remaining crew work
    1:00   Actors called either for work and fixes or
                  full dress
    6:00   Break
    7:30   Half-Hour
    8:00   Preview #1

SATURDAY APRIL 7
    12:00   Actors called for notes
    1:30   Half-Hour
    2:00   Preview #2
    7:30   Half-Hour
    8:00   Preview #3

SUNDAY APRIL 8   DAY OFF

THE REMAINDER OF THE PREVIEW SCHEDULE ALLOWS FOR AFTERNOON
REHEARSAL FROM 1-6 ON ONE SHOW DAYS

PERFORMANCE SCHED. FOR PREVIEWS AND RUN:

MON.	TUES.	WED.	THURS.	FRI.	SAT.	SUN.
8:15	8:15	2:15	8:15	8:15	2:15	DAY OFF
		8:15			8:15	

OPENING NIGHT: THURS. APRIL 26 @ 6:45

ANY ADDITIONS, CORRECTIONS, OR CONFLICTS, PLEASE NOTIFY:
    THOMAS KELLY, PSM XXX-XXX-XXXX or XXX-XXX-XXXX

                         THANK YOU!

9. Cue Lights

It is amazing how a technically intricate production can be executed by a simple system consisting of a half-dozen light switches, some colored bulbs, and a set of carefully planned cue sheets. This appendix provides an example of how a cue-light (often written as "Q-light") panel, a set of cue sheets, and a script with all the cues carefully included can make a splashy industrial run smoothly. In this case, the industrial was a show in which Oldsmobile's new car models were introduced to dealers from across the country. It was performed at Radio City Music Hall in 1984 and featured the Rockettes. Fred Travalena and Terri Klaussner were the performers/ spokespersons.

CUE-LIGHT PANEL

The cue-light panel is placed on the stage manager's desk. It consists of a row of light switches, each with an indicator light underneath that becomes lit when the switch is flipped on. Every switch should be clearly marked. The cue-light panel for the Oldsmobile industrial was configured and labeled as in Figure A-1.

FLY	#1 TRAV	#2 TRAV	TT (Turntable)	COND.	SL	WORK LITE	WORK LITE
⊡ ●	⊡ ●	⊡ ●	⊡ ●	⊡ ●	⊡ ●	⊡ ●	⊡ ●

FIGURE A-1 *Cue-Light Panel*

This particular set includes a "FLY" cue light. The switch will turn on a light(s) on the fly rail from where the flymen will fly scenery in or out. On complicated shows, there may be several fly cues in close succession, necessitating simultaneous warnings and cues. In that case, the stage manager will have various colored lights on the rail and label his or her panel accordingly RED FLY," "BLUE FLY," and so on). When these lights are turned on, the crew is warned, and when turned off, they execute the cue (bringing in or taking out a drop or curtain). In the stage manager's cueing script, he or she will write exactly what is done with the cue light.

In other words, a warning for a fly cue in the book would read, "FLY ON," meaning turn on the fly-cue light, and underneath that might be the number of the cue and what move is being warned. For example, the written warning for a cue to bring in the set piece for a scene that takes place in the county jail might look something like this in a stage manager's script: FLY ON (Q3/Jail Drop In).

When the point arrives in the script or song for the jail to drop in, the cueing script should read "FLY OFF." This indicates that the stage manager should turn off the cue light, signaling the flyman to execute the move. This basic means of backstage communication can allow huge sequences of events to happen without the stage manager having to give any spoken cues, freeing him or her to continue verbally calling the lighting cues.

The rest of the panel indicates similar cueing switches: for two travelers (#1 TRAV, #2 TRAV), a turntable (TT), the conductor (COND), and stage left (SL). The conductor's cue light allows the stage manager to begin a show on the same beat or count as the music. The stage left cue light, in this case, was used to signal the opposite side of the stage. Often this is referred to as the OP (opposite portal) cue light or position.

The preceding sample cue-light panel also has two switches devoted to work lights. This configuration allows the stage manager easy access to the lights that are used to illuminate fast changes that occur as soon as a curtain, drop, or traveler is in. However, never place work-light switches in the middle of a cue-light panel. It makes it too easy to cause accidental flashes of light onstage during a performance. Always keep them to one end, and if they are not needed during the running of the show, tape them in the off position.

FLYMAN'S CUE SHEETS

Notice that the flyman has three different drops—a movie screen, a scrim, and a show drop.

OLDSMOBILE—1984		1
FLY Q's	**MOVE**	**NOTES**
PRESET	RADIAL ↓ LO SHOW DROP ↓ LO SCREEN ↓ ½ WAY SCRIM ↑ HI	
DURING 1ST Q TAPE 1 (LITE) (8 MINS)	SCREEN ↓ LO	EASY
END SANCHEZ Q 2 (LITE) (4 MINS)	SCREEN ↑ HI	EASY
AFTER 1ST CAR Q 3 (LITE) (IMMED.)	SCREEN ↓ LO	MEDIUM
Q 4 (LITE) (IMMED.)	SCREEN ↑ HI	FAST
Q 5 LITE	SCREEN ↓ LO	MEDIUM

FLYMAN'S CUE SHEETS (CONT.)

OLDSMOBILE—1984		2
FLY Q's	MOVE	NOTES
END FILM Q 6 (LITE) FAST	SCREEN ↑ HI	FAST
↓ Q 7 (LITE) 10 SECS	SCRIM ↓ LO	FAST
END FILM Q 8 (LITE) – LONG TIME –	SCRIM ↑ HI	FAST
AFTER 88 REVEAL Q 9 (LITE) – IMMED –	SCREEN ↓ LO	MEDIUM
AFTER FILM Q 10 (LITE)	SCREEN ↑ HI	FAST
DURING FRED – PRESET W/ WORK LITES ON	SHOW DROP ↑ HI SCREEN ↓ LO	WAIT FOR CAR MOVES Q FROM TOM OR LEE

TURNTABLE OPERATOR'S CUE SHEETS

OLDSMOBILE—1984		1
TT Q's	**MOVE**	**NOTES**
PRESET	WAGON w/ COVER	US FULL RAMPS IN
FIRST SONG FLASHDANCE 20 MIN IN SHOW	1) WAGON EXIT 2) TERRI EXIT 3) WAGON RESET	ADJUST FOR CAR IF NEEDED
END ROCKS I LOVE N.Y. Q1 LITE	3/4 DS + REV SR	DS LIMIT # 1
DURING REVOLVE Q2 LITE FLASH WILL STAY ON: WARN US + REV.	STOP AT :	
30 SECS. Q3 LITE	US + REV.	
TRAV. CLOSE WORKS (1 MIN)	REV TO: WAGON OFF SL SUPREME ON FROM SR ROCKETTES ON TT	1 MIN. FOR THIS

TURNTABLE OPERATOR'S SHEETS (CONT.)

OLDSMOBILE—1984		2
TT Q's	MOVE	NOTES
END FILM ROCKETTES EXIT Q4 LITE	DS (SUPREME →)	LIMIT 1
END FILM Q5 LITE IMMED.	REV. SL 360°	
END JOHN Q6 LITE (8 MINS)	US	TRAY CLOSE W/ CLEAR
DURING PIANOES	1) SUPREME OFF SL 2) WAGON OVER + OFF SR to SL 2) 88 ON SR (88 ←) + REV. TO ↩	
END PIANOES Q7 LITE	DS/REV. 180 SR to (88 →)	
"FLASH" LEAVE ON WARN REV. 180 (IMMED)	STOP AT 88 →	

SAMPLE OF FIRST TRAVELER OPERATOR'S CUE SHEETS

The light for traveler #1 was also used to cue the prop and carpentry departments at several points in the presentation.

OLDSMOBILE—1984		1
#1 TRAV (DS) Q's	MOVE	NOTES
PRESET	CLOSE	DURING ½ HR WAIT FOR Q WHEN PRESET READY
END 1st SPEECH Q1 LITE (8 MINS)	OPEN	FAST (NOT IN VIEW OF AUD.)
1) SONG 2) ROCKETTES 3) CAR Q2 LITE (1 MIN)	CLOSE	FAST
END FILM Q3 LITE — 3 MINS —	OPEN	MED. FAST
FOR PROPS Q4 LITE —6 MINS—	SET PIANOS	
END PIANO # FOR PROPS Q5 LITE (5 MINS)	STRIKE PIANOS	

SAMPLE OF SECOND TRAVELER OPERATOR'S CUE SHEETS

OLDSMOBILE—1984		1
#2 TRAV (US) Q's	MOVE	NOTES
PRESET -12 MINS -	OPEN	ON STAGE MARK (EDGE OF TT)
DURING FIRST SONG— "FLASHDANCE" Q1 LITE (30 SECS)	CLOSE	FAST WAGON OFF
Q2 LITE (10 SECS)	OPEN	FAST TO ON STG MARK
Q3 LITE (2 MINS)	CLOSE	FAST GIRL ON TT
END ROCKETTES Q4 LITE (2 MINS)	OPEN	RESET WAGON FAST REVEAL WAGON
END CAR + Q5 LITE (1 MIN)	CLOSE	MEDIUM WAIT FOR CAR US + WORKLIGHT

SAMPLE PAGES—OLDSMOBILE CUEING SCRIPT

The following are sample pages taken from the stage manager's actual cueing script for the Oldsmobile industrial. The sections filled with numbers represent the bars in the musical dance segments.

TERRI

"WHAT A FEELING"

FIRST, WHEN THERE'S NOTHING BUT A SLOW   SPOT TO PARTY
GLOWING DREAM
THAT YOUR FEAR SEEMS TO HIDE DEEP INSIDE   WARN   SPOT TERRI
YOUR MIND   LQ 105.5
ALL ALONE I HAVE CRIED SILENT TEARS FULL OF   106
PRIDE
IN A WORLD MADE OF STEEL-MADE OF STONE
TEMPO CHANGE
       1 2 3 4 5 6 7 8

       1 2 3 4 5 6 ↑7 8   ⌐LQ 105.5
                 TERRI POINTS   ⌊SPOT TO TERRI
WHILE I HEAR THE MUSIC CALL ME
FULL OF RHYTHM
WRAP AROUND   #2 TRAV. ON
TAKE A HOLD OF MY HEART   5 6 7 8   (Q1 / CLOSE)

WHAT A FEELING
BEIN'S BELIEVIN'
I CAN HAVE IT ALL
NOW I'M DANCING FOR MY LIFE
TAKE YOUR PASSION
AND MAKE IT HAPPEN
PICTURES COME TO LIFE
NOW YOU DANCE RIGHT THROUGH YOUR LIFE

BAR_____   **1**   2   3   4   5   6   7   8 ⌐LQ 106
              2   ②   3   4   5   6   7   8
                         CAR #5 (ON #2 SL) BACKS IN #4 SL
              3   ②   3   4   5   6   7   8
                         CAR #2 (ON #2 SR) BACKS IN #4 SR
              4   2   3   4   5   ⑥   7   8
                                                  ⌐#2 TRAV OFF
I HEAR THE MUSIC CALL ME   CARS CLEAR   (Q1/CLOSE)
I AM RHYTHM
IN A FLASH
IT TAKES HOLD OF MY HEART

WHAT A FEELING
BEIN'S BELIEVIN'
I CAN HAVE IT ALL
NOW I'M DANCING FOR MY LIFE

WARN: LQ 108 109   2

BAR _____ <u>1</u>   2   3   4   5   6   7   / 8

<u>2</u>   2   3   4   5   6   7 ↓ 8

<u>3</u>   2   3   4   5   6   7   8   #2 TRAV ON (Q2/OPEN)

<u>4</u>   2   3   4   5   6   7   8

WHAT A FEELING
(I AM MUSIC NOW)
BEIN'S BELIEVIN'
(I AM RHYTHM)

PICTURES COME ALIVE
YOU CAN DANCE RIGHT THROUGH YOUR LIFE
WHAT A FEELING
I CAN REALLY HAVE IT ALL
WHAT A FEELING

BAR _____ <u>1</u>   2   3   4   5   6   7   8

<u>2</u>   2   3   4   5   6   7   [8]   #2 TRAV ON

<u>3</u>   2   3   4   5   6   7   8   (Q3/CLOSE)

<u>4</u>   2   3   4   5   6   7   8

BAR _____ <u>5</u>   2   3   [4]   5   6   7   8   LQ 108 #2 TRAV OFF (Q3/CLOSE)

<u>6</u>   2   3   4   5   6   7   [8]   LQ 109

<u>7</u>   ROCKETTES ENTER (WITH ROX ANNOUNCER)
2   3   4   5   6   7   8   'LADIES +

<u>8</u>   I LOVE N.Y.
2   3   4   5   6   7   8   GENTLEMEN, THE RADIO CITY MUSIC HALL ROCKETTES

ROCKETTE'S I LOVE NEW YORK

BAR _____ <u>1</u>   2   3   4   5   6   7   8

<u>2</u>   2   3   4   5   6   7   8   RESET WAGON ON TT

<u>3</u>   2   3   4   5   6   7   8   WARN LQ 110

<u>4</u>   2   3   4   5   6   7   8   #2 TRAV ON (Q4/OPEN)

BAR _____ <u>5</u>   2   3   4   5   6   7   8   TT ON (Q1/DS, ¾ SR)

<u>6</u>   2   3   4   5   6   7   8

<u>7</u>   2   3   4   5   6   7   8

10. Actors' Equity Association Work Rules

AEA, the actors' union, puts out pamphlets detailing the "agreement and rules governing employment" for every type of union contract under which their members work. Included here is a sampling of some of the work rules concerning Rehearsals and Safe and Sanitary Places of Employment in effect at the time of publication of this book. Any stage manager wishing to work professionally would do well to read through all the rules contained in the various AEA pamphlets.

58. REHEARSALS.

(A) Beginning of. Rehearsals begin with the date when the Actor is first called. If the Producer chooses to start with a reading to or by the Company or a part thereof, said reading is a part of and shall begin the rehearsal period. If the Producer wishes to employ an Actor for such a reading and the Actor's contracted rehearsal period has not yet commenced, the Producer may offer the Actor the opportunity to participate in the reading provided the Actor is paid not less than two-sixths of minimum rehearsal salary and the Actor's participation is strictly voluntary. It is expressly understood that the Actor's participation in the reading may not be a condition of employment. (For requirement of Stage Managers at rehearsals see Rule 68, STAGE MANAGERS.)

(B) Rehearsals Continuous. It is agreed that rehearsals shall be continuous from the date of the first rehearsal to the date of the first public performance of the play as stated on the face of the Contract of Employment.

(C) Rehearsal Salary, Payment of.

(1) Beginning with the first day of rehearsal the Producer agrees to pay the Actor rehearsal salary as set forth in Rule 63, for a period of up to eight weeks for Principal Actors and Chorus in dramatic productions; up to nine weeks for Principal Actors in musical productions and revues; and up to 10 weeks for Chorus in musical productions and revues. For partial weeks, one-sixth of weekly rehearsal salary shall be paid for each day of rehearsal or part thereof except that the last seven days of any rehearsal period (see Rule 61(B)(1)(a)) shall be at the rate of one-seventh for each day or part thereof.

(2) Rehearsal salaries are to be paid before noon on the day before the last banking day of the week, but no later than Thursday.

(3) During any week in which there are rehearsals and performances and in which performance salary is paid pro-rata, the Actor shall be paid no less than one week's minimum salary.

(4) Compensation subsequent to permitted rehearsal periods shall be at not less than full contractual salary.

(D) <u>Rehearsal Hours, Breaks and Overtime</u>. (See also Rule 61, REST PERIODS AND DAYS OFF.)

(1) <u>Rehearsal Hours</u>.

(a) <u>Prior to First Paid Public Performance</u>. Except for the final seven days of rehearsal prior to the first paid public performance, rehearsal hours shall not exceed seven out of eight and one-half consecutive hours per day (including breaks required by Rule 58 (D)(2)(a) below). However, Producer may elect, at Producer's sole option, to rehearse eight out of nine and one-half consecutive hours per day in lieu of the seven out of eight and one-half hour schedule provided the Actors receive two days off in each week. These days off need not be consecutive. If the Producer elects a five-day schedule, pro-rated calculations shall be made in fifths for partial weeks. The Producer will be entitled to switch schedules only twice during the permitted rehearsal period. The Actors must receive at least one week's notice for any such change in schedule.

(b) <u>Final seven days of rehearsal prior to First Paid Public Performance</u>. During the final seven days of rehearsal prior to the day of the first paid public performance, rehearsals shall not exceed 10 out of 12 consecutive hours per day (including breaks required by Rule 58 (D)(2)(a) below). On the day of the first paid public performance, rehearsals and performance may exceed 10 hours and may encompass more than 12 consecutive hours so long as applicable rest period and breaks requirements are met. If a pre-Point of Organization tryout does not use all seven days of the "ten out of twelve" hour rehearsal days provided for in this paragraph, it may, when it returns to the Point of Organization, use the remainder of those seven days prior to the first paid public performance at Point of Organization. On a day of travel, rehearsal and travel time combined shall not exceed 10 hours excluding rest periods.

(c) <u>Rehearsal and Performance Hours During Tryout Away from Point of Organization and Previews at Point of Organization</u>. For any 10 out of the first 12 weeks after the First Paid Public Performance during tryout away from Point of Organization and/or Previews at Point of Organization but before the Official Opening at the Point of Organization, rehearsal, travel, and performance shall not exceed 10 out of 12 consecutive hours in any one day, except as follows:

(i) Once per week during any five of the 10 "10 out of 12 hour" weeks, each Actor may be called for 10 out of 13 consecutive hours. This may not be done on a two-performance day.

(ii) If the Actor is called as provided in (i) above, there shall be a rest period of not less than 11 hours between the end of the Actor's employment on the preceding day and the Actor's call on the "10 out of 13 hour" day.

(iii) It is understood that the "10 out of 13 hour" day, if used, need not be on the same day for all Actors, but that each Actor may be called for no more than five such days.

During the remaining two weeks of such 12 week period, rehearsal, travel and performance may not exceed seven hours out of eight and one-half consecutive hours in any one day (including breaks required by Rule 58 (D)(2)(a) below).

(d) Following the first 12 weeks after the First Paid Public Performance, rehearsal hours shall be governed by Rule 58 (D) (1)(e) below, with the following exception: If Producer uses "10 out of 12 hour" days (as described in (c) above) during no more than nine out of the first 12 weeks after the First Paid Public Performance, up to a maximum of six such days may be used within any single week before the Official Opening at Point of Organization, provided that in special circumstances the Producer may use them within a two week period with the consent of Equity, which consent will not be unreasonably withheld.

(e) <u>After Official Opening at Point of Organization or First Paid Public Performance on Tour</u>. Rehearsals after Official Opening at Point of Organization or First Paid Public Performance on Tour shall be limited to eight hours weekly, except that Actors signed to understudy may be called to rehearse their own understudy assignments for an additional four hours per week. Rehearsals shall be limited to two hours on two-performance days; however, absent special circumstances, there shall be no rehearsal between the matinee and evening performances except for understudy rehearsal and/or emergency cast replacements.

(f) Overtime shall be paid for all rehearsal hours in excess of those permitted herein.

(g) <u>Rehearsals after Performance</u>. Rehearsals shall not be scheduled after an evening performance. However, notes may be given for a period not to exceed one hour after curtain, such time to be chargeable as rehearsal hours.

(h) Rehearsal hours for each Actor shall be computed from the time of rehearsal call for that Actor.

(i) Absent special circumstances, rehearsals may be called only upon 24 hours' written notice.

(2) <u>Breaks</u>

(a) There shall be a recess of one and one-half hours after a period of not more than five consecutive hours of rehearsal and/or performance combined. In addition, there shall be a break of five minutes after each 55 minutes of rehearsal or 10 minutes after each 80 minutes of rehearsal for each Equity member. These break requirements are also applicable during technical rehearsals except for the last three days prior to the first preview. However, during that period, Producer shall use best efforts to comply with these requirements. (See also Rule 61, REST PERIODS.)

(b) Where rehearsal is consecutive with the half-hour call, the time from the call for rehearsal and the end of the performance shall not exceed five consecutive hours.

62. SAFE AND SANITARY PLACES OF EMPLOYMENT.

(A) The Producer agrees to provide the Actor with safe and sanitary places of employment.

(1) All stages shall be clean and properly heated. The Producer shall use best efforts to provide air-conditioning when necessary to insure comfortable healthful temperatures at all times. In New York, Chicago and Los Angeles, the Producer shall provide air-conditioning and heat in all dressing room areas when necessary to insure a reasonably comfortable and healthful temperature by the time of the Actor's call.

(2) Treads on backstage stairways shall be maintained in a safe condition. Stairways shall be provided with adequate lighting and adequate hand-rail supports.

(3) The Producer shall exercise best efforts to keep alleyways leading to stage doors of theaters accessible, properly lighted, free of debris and protected from trash or litter from overhead.

(4) At Point of Organization, Producer shall engage the services of a professional exterminator who shall treat the theater on at least a monthly schedule. Whenever feasible, such treatments shall be made on the company day off.

(5) Producer shall post such notices as are required by the regulations of the Occupational Safety and Health Administration.

(B) <u>Dressing Rooms</u>.

(1) Assigned dressing rooms shall be maintained for the exclusive use of the Actors. In Point of Organization cities, the Producer shall use best efforts to ensure that any rooms originally intended to be dressing rooms shall be assigned to the Equity Company, with special consideration for proximity to the stage. Curtained partitions shall not be deemed adequate separation to provide exclusive use of the space with respect to other backstage activities. Adequate table space for each Actor shall be allocated to all members of the Company, including Understudies and Swings, for makeup and dressing purposes.

(2) All dressing rooms shall be properly heated and shall have adequate lights, mirrors, shelves and wardrobe hooks for Actor's makeup and dressing equipment.

(a) Use of fluorescent lighting for makeup purposes is prohibited unless the fluorescent lighting is specifically warranted by the manufacturer to be for makeup purposes.

(b) All dressing rooms shall be maintained in a clean and sanitary condition and painted and maintained as necessary. Peeling paint and loose plaster shall be repaired. Floors shall be washed or vacuumed at least once each week and dressing rooms cleaned at least once each working day.

(c) Ventilation of dressing rooms and of all change rooms provided in basement areas, shall meet the standards set by municipal health codes.

(d) If an Actor with a physical disability is employed, reasonable accommodations, as defined by the ADA, shall be provided.

(3) Where more than three costume changes are required during a performance, a change room shall be maintained within two flights of the stage if space is available. Where adequate or proper space is alleged to be unavailable, such fact must be reported to the Producer and Equity by the Stage Manager and verified by a Deputy.

(4) Separate dressing rooms for male and female Actors will be provided.

(5) In New York City theaters in which performances are given during the summer, all dressing rooms and change rooms provided in basement areas will be air-conditioned. In all other theaters the Producer shall use best efforts to provide air-conditioning when necessary to insure comfortable healthful temperatures at all times.

(6) In theaters where smoking is permitted by law, assignment of dressing room space to Principals shall be made, in part, on the basis of each Actor's smoking habits. Where possible and where space limitations permit, a non-smoking Principal Actor will not be assigned a dressing room in which smoking is permitted. Where possible, Chorus dressing room assignments will be made on the same basis.

(C) Lavatory and Toilet Facilities.

(1) Each dressing room shall contain at least one washstand which shall provide hot and cold running water for each six Actors assigned therein, within the reasonable requirements of dressing room assignments. Sink stoppers and paper towels must be provided.

(2) Toilet facilities, sinks and showers shall be thoroughly cleaned at least once each day and shall be kept clean, sanitary and maintained in good working order at all times. Toilet paper must be provided. In New York City theaters, these facilities shall be on each dressing room floor except that where existing facilities are currently provided on alternate floors, additional facilities will be installed when reasonably feasible. In all other theaters they shall be on each dressing room floor where reasonably feasible.

(3) All theaters that house musical productions shall provide separate showers for men and women within a reasonable distance from or within the dressing rooms.

(D) <u>Cots</u>. The Producer shall provide at least two cots for every 10 cast members at the theater and at all places of rehearsal.

(E) <u>Rehearsal and Performance Surfaces</u>.

(1) Actors shall not be permitted to rehearse dances or to perform on concrete or marble floors or on wood or any other substance which does not provide adequate resilience.

(2) Where a portable stage is used, platforms must be securely fastened and the stage completely covered by a single deck of such material as wood or Masonite. The edges of all decks must be clearly visible or, if not, guard rails fastened in order to preclude the possibility of injury. Pits not in use shall be completely covered by a non-flexible material.

(F) <u>First-Aid Kit</u>. First-aid kits stocked with adequate supplies shall be available and easily accessible at all times whenever the Actor is required to rehearse, dress, or perform.

(G) <u>Drinking Water</u>. Ample, pure, cool drinking water shall be provided wherever the Actor is required to rehearse or perform.

(H) <u>Inherently Dangerous Conditions Prohibited</u>.

(1) No Actor shall be required to perform any feat or act which places Actor in imminent danger or is inherently dangerous, nor shall any Actor be required to perform in a costume or upon a set which is inherently dangerous. It is not the intent of Equity to interfere with proper artistic judgments of the Producer but only to protect the Actor from injury which may jeopardize or terminate a professional career. The Producer shall advise Equity as soon as possible when,

in Producer's judgment, there is a potentially dangerous situation. If Equity deems the situation to be one which should be prohibited by this section and the Producer does not agree, the matter shall be submitted for prompt consideration by an industry committee composed of the Executive Director of the League of American Theatres and Producers, or his designee, representing the League and the Executive Director of Equity, or his designee, representing Equity. If the two cannot agree, the matter shall promptly be submitted directly to arbitration.

(2) <u>Smoke and Fog</u>. Producer may not use any stage smoke or fog not already approved by Equity and the League. Adequate ventilation and exhaust equipment must be operating and in working order when smoke or fog is used. In addition, the Producer agrees to the following terms and conditions:

(a) Smoke machines shall be located so as to minimize Actors' exposure to the concentrated aerosol as it first exits the machine.

(b) The quantity and frequency of use of the various Equity/League approved fogs during a performance should be minimized in consultation with Equity, the Producer and the artistic personnel.

(c) An Equity/League fog committee shall review the use of all stage fogs whenever necessary.

(d) Right-to-know seminars shall be conducted each year for those shows utilizing fog and smoke. Said seminars shall be considered a required rehearsal call but its duration, not to exceed one hour, shall not be counted toward the maximum permitted rehearsal hours for that day or week. A production's first right-to-know seminar shall take place within two months of the first public performance. Material Safety Data Sheets shall be made available for each approved fog. Actors shall not be required to attend more than one right-to-know seminar per production provided there has been no change in the use of onstage fogs or other chemicals. The individual engaged to conduct the seminars shall be determined by the mutual agreement of Equity and the League.

(e) Juvenile Actors' exposure to stage fog shall be minimized in accordance with Paragraph (b) above.

(f) Only small amounts of refined, white and additive-free mineral oils may be used.

(g) Actor shall be advised by contract rider if fog or smoke will be utilized in the production.

(h) The foregoing provisions shall not apply to any form of carbon dioxide (e.g., dry ice) or liquid nitrogen. Fogs composed entirely of either substance shall be deemed pre-approved.

Any disagreement under paragraph (2), Smoke and Fog, shall be resolved by expedited arbitration pursuant to Rule 4(C).

(3) Firearms. Whenever firearms are used in a production, there shall be a safety demonstration for the entire company, prior to the first paid public performance, or use of firearms onstage, whichever occurs first. Thereafter, safety demonstrations and/or instructions will be required for all affected replacement Actors as well as Swings and Understudies, before their first paid public performance. Brush-up safety demonstrations and/or instructions shall be required at least once each year.

(4) Flash Photography. Flash photography during a performance is prohibited. The producer shall post the international symbol prohibiting photography prominently in the lobby. In addition, a printed announcement prohibiting flash photography shall be included on either the cast or synopsis page of the playbill or program. If a chronic pattern of flash photography develops, an announcement identifying its prohibition shall be made prior to each performance until the problem is corrected.

(I) Raked Stage. Prior to the construction of any raked stage where the incline will be greater than three quarters of one inch per foot, the Producer shall promptly notify Equity in writing of such plans and provide such information as Equity may reasonably request. It is understood that when a Producer is utilizing a set from a prior production, said notice may not be possible and the Producer agrees to notify Equity as soon as a determination is made that such set will be utilized. When a raked stage is used, a qualified instructor will give instructions to the cast, prior to opening, as to how to perform on the rake in order to avoid the risk of injury. Thereafter, brush-up instructions will be provided at least once each year. Instructions will also be provided for all replacement actors, as well as Swings and Understudies, before their first paid public performance.

(J) The safe and sanitary provisions set forth above are intended to bind only the Producer and Theatre Owners who are members of the League. With respect to other theater owners, however, the League and Equity agree that all booking contracts shall contain a mandatory clause stipulating that the theater must comply with the standards set forth above.

(K) Actor's Responsibility. It is the Actor's obligation to respect the physical property of the theater. It is agreed that the Actor shall be responsible for any damage to the theater willfully caused by Actor if the Producer is held responsible to the owner of the theater for such damage.

(L) Inspection and Compliance. Equity shall have the right at reasonable times to inspect all theaters at which Equity members are employed to determine whether the theaters are complying with this rule. If alleged violations are found, Equity shall notify the theater owner and the League immediately and a representative appointed by the League shall have an opportunity to inspect the theater.

(1) If Equity and the League agree that a violation exists, they shall notify the theater owner that unless the violation is corrected or that satisfactory assurances are given that it will be corrected promptly, the theater shall be certified as unauthorized for rehearsal and/or performance. If the League fails to avail itself of its right of inspection within 48 hours of receipt of notification, then Equity alone may so inform the theater owner.

(2) If Equity and the League do not agree, then the matter shall be submitted to arbitration in accordance with Rule 4 and the arbitrator may, in his discretion, suspend performances until the theater complies with this rule.

(M) Equity and the League agree it is their mutual intent that the theater be a working environment free of hazardous and toxic materials. To this end the parties commit to meet jointly with such experts as are necessary to identify materials and procedures which may be found in the theatrical environment which are hazardous, toxic, or otherwise unsafe and to seek means by which to eliminate them from the Professional Theatre.

11. Performance Report and Schedule

Here are two examples of New York City Opera paperwork. First is a weekly schedule with running times. It is vital that the PSM keeps this up-to-date, as so many people rely on it: ushers, parking garages, all crew and staff. It also forewarns staff and crew of when a show is close to or planned to go into overtime, so everyone steps up their attention and doesn't waste a minute. This schedule also gives you a look at a repertory schedule; remember that between each of these performances, the crew must change the set, refocus lights, reset props and costumes, etc. Sometimes this is compounded by the rehearsal of the next opera during the day.

The second form is a standard opera performance report, this one for *Carmen*. Note that injuries are fully detailed, as this serves as proof for any later Worker's Compensation claims that the accident did happen onstage. Also notice the detail with which the times are recorded; both artistically and due to union overtime rules, the timings are of utmost concern and must be recorded accurately.

NEW YORK STATE THEATER - NEW YORK CITY OPERA

APPROXIMATE RUNNING TIMES - APRIL 1 - APRIL 6, 2008

Tuesday Evening, April 1   NO PERFORMANCE

Wednesday Evening, April 2

FALSTAFF	ACT I	(34)	7:36 - 8:10 PM
(2 Hours, 42 Minutes)	Intermission	(20)	8:10 - 8:30
	ACT II	(43)	8:30 - 9:13
	Intermission	(20)	9:13 - 9:33
	ACT III	(45)	9:33 - 10:18

Thursday Evening, April 3

TOSCA	ACT I	(45)	8:06 - 8:51 PM
(2 Hours, 40 Minutes)	Intermission	(25)	8:51 - 9:16
	ACT II	(39)	9:16 - 9:55
	Intermission	(25)	9:55 - 10:20
	ACT III	(26)	10:20 - 10:46

Friday Evening, April 4

MADAMA BUTTERFLY	ACT I	(50)	8:06 - 8:56 PM
(2 Hours, 51 Minutes)	Intermission	(19)	8:56 - 9:15
	ACT II	(50)	9:15 - 10:05
	Intermission	(19)	10:05 - 10:24
	ACT III	(33)	10:24 - 10:57

Saturday Matinee, April 5

TOSCA	ACT I	(45)	1:36 - 2:21 PM
(2 Hours, 40 Minutes)	Intermission	(25)	2:21 - 2:46
	ACT II	(39)	2:46 - 3:25
	Intermission	(25)	3:25 - 3:50
	ACT III	(26)	3:50 - 4:16

Saturday Evening, April 5

FALSTAFF	ACT I	(34)	8:06 - 8:40 PM
(2 Hours, 42 Minutes)	Intermission	(20)	8:40 - 9:00
	ACT II	(43)	9:00 - 9:43
	Intermission	(20)	9:43 - 10:03
	ACT III	(45)	10:03 - 10:48

Sunday Matinee, April 6

MADAMA BUTTERFLY	ACT I	(50)	1:36 - 2:26 PM
(2 Hours, 51 Minutes)	Intermission	(19)	2:26 - 2:45
	ACT II	(50)	2:45 - 3:35
	Intermission	(19)	3:35 - 3:54
	ACT III	(33)	3:54 - 4:27

NYCO STAGE MANAGER PERFORMANCE REPORT

DATE: 07/04/06

PRODUCTION: **CARMEN**

PUBLISHED START TIME: 8:00

CONDUCTOR: Pelto

STAGE MANAGEMENT:
Calling: Kelly

Other: Duvall

Stage Right: Lazar
Stage Left: Wheeler
Guns: Haines

ASSISTANT DIRECTOR(S) ON DUTY: Moffit
REHEARSAL ASSISTANT ON DUTY:
PERFORMANCE DUTY STAFF: Lippiello

| | Published Start Time | 8:00 | | |
	Previous Performance	START	FINISH	ELAPSED
Act I		7:36	8:19	0:43
Intermission:		8:19	8:38	0:19
Act II		8:38	9:18	0:40
Intermission:		9:18	9:38	0:20
Acts III & IV		9:38	10:29	0:51
Total		xxxxxxxxxx	xxxxxxxxxx	2:53
Conductor Bow Complete		xxxxxxxxxx	10:30	2:54
Bows Complete		xxxxxxxxxx	10:32	2:56
Performance Total		xxxxxxxxxx	xxxxxxxxxx	**2:56**
Total From Published Start		xxxxxxxxxx	xxxxxxxxxx	2:32

HELD START OF SHOW FOR:

OPENED HOUSE AT: 7:06. Front scroller lights missing, had to be replugged.

ANNOUNCEMENTS: Normal Cell Phone Announcement.

PERFORMANCE AND / OR OVERTIME NOTES:
Good performance
Deb Williams inadvertently kicked by unknown other chorus or super during Manuelaita fight in ACT I. Ice applied, and she went to hospital for X-rays.

REPAIRS:
Screws out of one column in ACT... repaired.

Strange light up at top of ACT III on the curtain, killed soon after discovery.

(Over)

rev 3/30/99

NYCO STAGE MANAGER PERFORMANCE REPORT (CONT.)

> **THIS PORTION COMPLETED BY PERFORMANCE DUTY STAFF**

CONDUCTOR and/or ASSISTANT CONDUCTOR COMMENTS:

DIRECTOR and/or ASSISTANT DIRECTOR COMMENTS:
Deb Williams injured during fight sequence resulting in her early departure. Aimee Thompson covered her business in ACT III. Adrian Gans had some issues with his cape in ACT II (it became knotted and he had to step out of it as if it were a dress); he had some concerns/issues which I will discuss with Cindy Edwards and get back to him about prior to our next performance on 10/18. B. MOFFIT

CHORUS MASTER and/or ASSISTANT CHORUS MASTER COMMENTS:
Deb Williams injured in ACT I fight and went to hospital after ACT II. Good show from chorus, lots of energy.

PERFORMANCE DUTY COMMENTS:
Wonderful performance

FRONT OF HOUSE PROBLEMS:
none

SIGN-IN OF ARTISTS:
All signed in

COVERS AVAILABILITY:
All accounted for

Stage Manager TAK_____   Assistant Director: __B.M._____

CC: PKellogg, JGullong, RThompson, GManahan, SWoelzl, CGiles, TKelly, JHarris, JBeeson, DTitcomb, DDavis,
      GWedow, CKubala, TPiccolo, SAlvarez, MLonergan, MHollingshead, JD'Asaro, KWhite, TYoung, AJacob, KGarver,
      CEllison, CKeenen, CHough, CLippiello, IDerrer, House Management, SHOW A.D., CALLING S.M.

rev 3/30/99

12. Production Schedules for Touring/Closing a Show

The following production schedules are more detailed than the one in Appendix 2. The first is for the national tour of *A Day in Hollywood/A Night in the Ukraine*. The schedule covers the load-out from the New York scenic shops; the load-in to the theater in Wilmington, Delaware; and the subsequent move to Toronto. It serves to illustrate the complexities of

TOURING PRODUCTION SCHEDULE

```
                                                    11/12/81

              A DAY IN HOLLYWOOD/A NIGHT IN THE UKRAINE
                         National Company
                      PRODUCTION SCHEDULE

THURS NOV 12    8:00 am    TRUCK LOADS OUT NEW SET, UNIT DECK,
                           CRATES, ETC. FROM METRO SCENIC AND
                           NOLAN'S.

                9:30 am    ERIE TRUCK BRINGS ROAD BOXES TO
                           ROYALE FOR REPAIR WORK

                10:00 am   COMPANY REHEARSAL/ROYALE THEATRE

                1:00 pm    BREAK

                2:00 pm    RUN-THRU/ROYALE THEATRE

FRI NOV 13      8:00 am    LOAD OUT ROYALE-PIANO CRATES
                  to       DELIVERED BY PROPIANO-TRUCK #1-UNIT,
                5:00 pm    DECK, DOORS & CRATES TO WILMINGTON
                           TRUCK #2-HANGING GOODS & PROPS,
                           WARDROBE, PORTALS TO WILMINGTON
                           TRUCK #3-ROYALE UNIT, DECK &
                           PORTALS TO METROTRUCK #4- PICK UP
                           4-STAR FOR WILMINGTON-PICK UP
                           MASQUE FOR WILMINGTON

                10:00 am   COMPANY REHEARSAL AT 890 STUDIOS
                  to
                6:00 pm

SAT NOV 14      10:00 am   COMPANY REHEARSAL AT 890 STUDIOS
                  to
                10:00 pm   MID-DAY PRODUCTION CREW TRAVELS TO
                           WILMINGTON

SUN NOV 15      NOON       SPOT CREW/WILMINGTON

                3:00 pm    ELECTRIC CREW-UNLOAD TRUCK #4 AND
                  to       HANG OVERHEAD ELECTRICS AND START
                MIDNIGHT   SOUND
                           PERFORMING COMPANY/DAY OFF

MON NOV 16      10:00 am   COMPANY REHEARSAL AT 890 STUDIOS-
                  to       JOE CRANZANO TO MEET WITH COMPANY
                10:00 pm   AT 10:00 am RE: MAKE-UP

                8:00 am    LOAD-IN FULL CREW/WILMINGTON TRUCK
                  to       #2 UNLOAD FIRST TRUCK #1 SECOND
                MIDNIGHT   UNLOAD BY MIDNIGHT SHOW HUNG, DECK
                           DOWN/ASSEMBLING UNIT
```

HOLLYWOOD/UKRAINE (National Company) - PRODUCTION SCHEDULE

TUES NOV 17	10:00 am to 6:00 pm	COMPANY REHEARSAL AT 890 STUDIOS T. TUNE AT REHEARSALS/T. KELLY & L. BALL IN WILMINGTON
	6:00 pm	JIM DAWSON STRIKE ANKLE STAGE AT 890 STUDIOS
	8:00 am	CONTINUE SET-UP AND ASSEMBLING UNIT, ETC. PM-START FOCUS AS EARLY AS POSSIBLE ON ACT I SET BY MIDNIGHT-FINISH ACT I FOCUS
WED NOV 18	8:30 am	CAMPUS COACH BUS LOADED AT 890 STUDIOS
	10:30 am	KING DISPLAYS DELIVER CUT-OUTS, ETC. TO SHUBERT ALLEY
	NOON	COMPANY TRAVELS TO WILMINGTON- ASSEMBLES 45TH STREET SIDE OF SHUBERT ALLEY
	8:00 am	FINISH ANY ACT I FOCUS-ASSEMBLE ACT II UNITS-SHIFT TO ACT II AND FOCUS ACT II
	10:00 am	LEONARD HARTZELL-PIANO TUNER IN TO WORK ON PIANOS
	4:00 pm	FINISH FOCUS ACT II-SHIFT TO ACT I, DRY TECH TRAVELLERS, SET FOCUS AND ACT I LITE Q's.
	6:00 pm	LATEST BREAK LOAD-IN CREW
	7:00 pm to 11:00 pm	COMPANY CALLED-ACT II SET ON STAGE RUNNING CREW-TECH AND RUN ACT II WITH COMPANY
	11:00 pm to MIDNIGHT	COMPANY NOTES/SHIFT TO ACT I BREAK
	MIDNIGHT	FLAMEPROOFING BEGUN BY CHARLES BRANCH-4 to 5 HOURS TO COMPLETE, HOWEVER, STILL TO BE DETERMINED IF IT WILL ALL BE DONE ONE NIGHT OR CONTINUED THURSDAY NIGHT.
THURS NOV 19	8:00 am to NOON	FINISH & CLEAN-UP ON ACT I SET

stage managing a production on the road. The second schedule, starting on page 268, is for the closing and subsequent move of *I'm Not Rappaport*. Although the play closed only to move from an Off-Broadway theater to a Broadway theater, several blocks away in New York, it also demonstrates the careful planning necessary for such a seemingly simple move.

TOURING PRODUCTION SCHEDULE (CONT.)

```
                                                        Page 3
HOLLYWOOD/UKRAINE (National Company) - PRODUCTION SCHEDULE
```

	NOON	COMPANY CALLED/INTO COSTUME & MAKE-UP
	1:00 pm to 5:00 pm	TECH/DRESS ACT I
	5:00 pm	ACTORS BREAK, CREW NOTES, TOUCH UP, ETC.
	7:30 pm	RESUME TECH ACT I
	10:00 pm to MIDNIGHT	FINISH ACT I TECH & RUN ACT I AND CHANGE SET TO ACT II
FRI NOV 20	8:00 am	CREW NOTES & CLEAN UP AS NEEDED ON ACT II SET
	1:00 pm	WORK AS NEEDED IN ACT II SET WITH COMPANY
	2:00 pm	SET-UP ACT I
	2:30 pm	DRESS REHEARSAL ACT I
	3:30 pm	CHANGE TO ACT II
	4:00 pm	DRESS REHEARSAL ACT II
	6:00 pm	BREAK (CHANGE TO ACT I END OF REHEARSAL, IF POSSIBLE)
	8:00 pm	FIRST PREVIEW
SAT NOV 21	2:00 pm	SECOND PREVIEW
	8:00 pm	THIRD PREVIEW
SUN NOV 22		COMPANY DAY OFF
MON NOV 23		TRUCK #3 LOADS OUT METRO & 4 STAR AND HEADS TO TORONTO WITH MANIFEST TO BE IN TORONTO READY TO UNLOAD SUNDAY, NOVEMBER 29 AT NOON
	8:00 pm	OPENING NITE PERFORMANCE/WILMINGTON
TUES NOV 24	8:00 am to NOON	WORK CALL—ALL DEPARTMENTS—DO FOCUS CHARTS
	1:00 pm to 5:00 pm	PICTURE CALL—ON STAGE—MARTHA SWOPE

HOLLYWOOD/UKRAINE (National Company) - PRODUCTION SCHEDULE

OUTLINE FOR TORONTO MOVE

SAT NOV 28	11:00 pm	LOAD OUT WILMINGTON (APPROXIMATELY 6 to 8 HOURS)
SUN NOV 29	5:00 am**	SPOT LINES
	1:00 pm* to MIDNIGHT	TORONTO—UNLOAD JUMP TRUCK, HANG OVERHEAD ELECTRIC & START DECK *(OR 9 HOURS FROM CONCLUSION OF "CHILDREN")
	2:00 pm	COMPANY DEPART WILMINGTON EN ROUTE TO TORONTO
MON NOV 30	8:00 am to MIDNIGHT	LOAD-IN CONTINUES
		COMPANY DAY OFF
TUES DEC 1	9:00 am	FINISH ACT I SET UP—SWITCH TO ACT II BEFORE LUNCH SET & FOCUS ACT II
	10:00 am	FINISH SET—BEGIN FOCUS ACT I
	1:00 pm	BREAK
	2:00 pm	SET ACT II
	3:00 pm	FOCUS ACT II
	4:00 pm	ACTORS ON ACT II SET
	5:00 pm	ACTORS ON ACT I SET
	7:00 pm	BREAK
	8:00 pm	HALF HOUR

** CREW TO DEPART ON A 9:40 AM FLIGHT OUT OF PHILADELPHIA

CLOSING AND MOVE PRODUCTION SCHEDULE

I'M NOT RAPPAPORT - SCHEDULE

MOVE AMERICAN PLACE TO BOOTH

Week Ending October 20th

1. Scenery shops begin
2. Electric shop bids finalized

Week Ending October 27th

1. Sound order complete and to shops for bids
2. Production Meetings with American Place regarding load-out and Electrics at Booth regarding load-in

Week Ending November 3rd

1. Electric shop begin work Monday, October 28th
2. Finalize all trucking
3. Finalize all Booth Theatre dressing room assignments and necessities (telephones, power, ice boxes, painting, furnishing and fixing)
4. Finalize load-out and load-in crews
5. Possible flame proofing at American Place

Week Ending November 10th

1. Sound shop pull equipment and dupe show tape
2. All boxes, crates, etc. for move delivered to American Place - Fri. by T. Kelly in van - Wardrobe boxes, Stage Manager desk, etc. Also deliver all tools and materials as discussed with T. Walsh and B. Scales to Booth for load-in and/or American Place for load-out
3. Friday, November 8th - Spotting call at Booth Theatre
   Joe McCarthy to set call and coordinate with Don Beck, etc.
4. Sunday, November 10th -
   3:00 FINAL AMERICAN PLACE PERFORMANCE
   6:00 - 12:00   Begin load-out American Place - Set & Electrics
       a. Re-wire lampposts
       b. Additional sound proofing underneath platform & steps
       c. Salvage deck carpet for bridge covering at Booth
       d. Wardrobe sent to cleaners for clean and store until delivery to Booth on Monday, Nov. 18th and/or packed in Wardrobe boxes in Wardrobe room. Shoes and supplies packed in Wardrobe room.
       e. All make-up, hair and personal dressing room supplies (refrigerators, phones, etc.) packed and stored in Wardrobe room

I'M NOT RAPPAPORT - SCHEDULE

MOVE AMERICAN PLACE TO BOOTH   2

    f. Portals #2 & 3 FIRST UPSTAIRS ready for
        shop pick-up MON. NOV. 11TH

    g. All props packed and stored in Wardrobe
        room. SAVE THE FLAMEPROOFED TRASH FROM
        TRASH CAN!

    h. Trees stored in safe place with
        extensions unbolted; to be walked over
        Tues. Nov. 12th

Monday November 11th

1. 9:00 - 1:00   Finish Load-Out American Place
   2:00 - 6:00   "   "   "   " - Later if
necessary

2. 9:00 - Shop pick up portals

3. 45-ft. truck arrive 10:00 A.M.
      LOAD - 1. All bridge & stone work BLANKETED
              2. Benches & lampposts & sewer pipes
              3. Portal #1, pipes and plexi-facing
              4. Deck & escape stair SL & backstage stairs
     STORE - 1. Steel Framework
     LOSE - Cyc, scrim, SR stairs & SL platforms

4. 12:00 Production Arts Truck start electrics pick-up

BY 6:00 - (Later if necessary)
       1. 45-ft. truck loaded and parked, either on 46th Street or
         in lot next to theatre
       2. Electrics returned
       3. Steel framework, props, wardrobe, personal make-up &
         dressing room boxes, Stage Manager's desk, etc. in
         loading dock ready for 9:00 A.M. TUESDAY Walton truck #2

Tuesday, November 12th

8:00 Walton truck #1 at Electric Shop, pick up electrics
9:00 - 12:00 - Load-In begin at Booth Theatre
    1. Electric truck (Walton #1)
    2. Shop truck #1 with Portal #2 (new) and all additional set
       pieces and new pipes
    3. Shop truck # 2 with cyc and scrim
    4. 45 ft. truck from 46th St. - at Booth by 9:30
    5. Walton #2 at American Place - 9:00 - Load steel, props,
       wardrobe, etc. - deliver to Booth, then pick up sound &
       deliver to Booth
    6. Begin Electrics, cyc, scrim & portals hung on stage
    7. During morning - trees walked to Booth

12:00 - 1:00 - BREAK AT BOOTH
            Completely out of American Place

13. The Who/What/Where: *Il Matrimonio Segreto*

Similar to a production analysis, it gives everyone involved in an opera a guide or map to exactly who will be doing what in what clothes and with what props on what scenery at what time in the act.

BAM May '08 Director: Jonathan Miller Score: Ricordi	Il Matrimonio Segreto Who/What/Where					ASM: Francesca DeRenzi SM: Tom Kelly June 4, 2008 Page 1 of 3 Final Version

Placement	Time	NT/xt	Who	Props	Wardrobe	Notes
Overture & Act I (75:00)						
14/2/3	5:15	1st NT SL Door	PAOLINO C. Johnson CAROLINA H. Stober	Letter	Costume #1 Costume #1	Pao closes door behind them
34/2/1 after "presenter"	11:35	Offstage Noise SR	GERONIMO C. Coad			Grumbling & stomping
43/3/5	14:40	xt Caro Door	CAROLINA H. Stober			Caro closes door
46/1/2	14:45	1st NT SR Doors	GERONIMO C. Coad MALE SERVANT T. Cowdery		Costume #1 Costume #1	M Serv auto XTs, closing doors
46/2/1	14:50	xt SL Door	GERONIMO C. Coad			Ger leaves door open
46/3/2	14:55	Offstage singing SL	GERONIMO C. Coad			
46/4/1	15:00	NT SL Door	GERONIMO C. Coad			Ger leaves door open
50/4/2	16:10	xt SR Doors	PAOLINO C. Johnson			Pao leaves doors open
51/3/2	16:20	NT Caro Door 1st NT Elis Door	CAROLINA H. Stober ELISETTA G. Jarman		Costume #1	Caro & Elis close doors
51/3/2 end	16:22	NT SR Doors	MALE SERVANT T. Cowdery			M Serv leaves doors open
51/3/1	16:25	1st NT UL Doors	FEMALE SERVANT M. Peinado		Costume #1	F Serv closes doors
51/4/2	16:28	Offstage singing SL	FIDALMA F. Brillembourg			
51/3/4	16:30	1st NT SL Door	FIDALMA F. Brillembourg	Small Book, Glasses	Costume #1	Fid leaves door open
64/4/2	21:30	xt SL Door	GERONIMO C. Coad	Letter		Ger closes door behind him
		xt SR Doors	MALE SERVANT T. Cowdery			M Serv closes doors behind him
		xt UL Doors	FEMALE SERVANT M. Peinado			F Serv closes doors behind her
85/3/1	27:00	xt SL Door	CAROLINA H. Stober			Caro closes door behind her, xt to 5 min. QC on SL

103/4/2	32:30	xt SL Door	FIDALMA F. Brillembourg ELISETTA G. Jarman			Close door behind them, both xt to 1:45 QC on SL
104/1/1	32:45	NT UL Doors	FEMALE SERVANT M. Peinado CAROLINA H. Stober		Costume #2	F Servant opens & closes doors

EXITS are indicated in ITALICS

May '08
Director: Jonathan Miller
Score: Ricordi

Il Matrimonio Segreto
Who/What/Where

ASM: Francesca DeRenzi
SM: Tom Kelly
June 4, 2008
Page 2 of 3
Final Version

Placement	Time	NT / xt	Who	Props	Wardrobe	Notes
			GERONIMO 　　　　C. Coad		Costume #1a	
107/1/1	33:40	NT SR Doors	PAOLINO 　　　　C. Johnson MALE SERVANT 　　　　T. Cowdery			Pao leaves doors open
107/1/2	33:45	*xt SR Doors*	*PAOLINO* 　　　　*C. Johnson*			*Pao leaves doors open*
107/3/1	34:00	NT SR Doors	PAOLINO 　　　　C. Johnson			Pao leaves doors open
108/1/4	34:10	NT UL Doors	FIDALMA 　　　　F. Brillembourg ELISETTA 　　　　G. Jarman		Costume #2 Costume #2	F servant opens and closes doors for Fid & Elis
108/1/5	34:12	Offstage Singing SR	CONTE 　　　　J. Best			
108/2/4	34:15	1ˢᵗ NT SR Doors	CONTE 　　　　J. Best	Tiny Book	Costume #1	Con leaves doors open
110/1/1	35:00	*xt UL Doors*	*FEMALE SERVANT* 　　　　*M. Peinado*			*F Serv closes doors behind her*
		xt SR Doors	*MALE SERVANT* 　　　　*T. Cowdery*			*M Serv closes doors behind him*
123/5/3	38:30	*xt UL Doors*	*GERONIMO* 　　　　*C. Coad* *PAOLINO* 　　　　*C. Johnson*			*Close doors behind them*
154/3/1	47:10	*xt SR Doors*	*CONTE* 　　　　*J. Best*	*Tiny Book*		*Con leaves doors open*
		xt Elis Door	*FIDALMA* 　　　　*F. Brillembourg* *ELISETTA* 　　　　*G. Jarman*			*close doors behind them, both xt to 13:00 change on SL*
154/3/4 end	47:15	NT SL Door	PAOLINO 　　　　C. Johnson			Pao closes door behind him
158/4/3	48:10	*xt Caro Door*	*CAROLINA* 　　　　*H. Stober*			*Caro closes door behind her, xt to 4:45 QC on SR*
158/4/3 end	48:12	NT SR Doors	CONTE 　　　　J. Best			Con leaves doors open
180/4/5	53:25	*xt SR Doors*	*PAOLINO* 　　　　*C. Johnson*			*Pao leaves doors open*
182/1/1	53:30	NT Caro Door	CAROLINA 　　　　H. Stober		Costume #3	Caro closes door behind her
199/4/2	59:20	*xt Caro Door*	*CAROLINA* 　　　　*H. Stober*			*Caro closes door behind her*

EXITS are indicated in ITALICS

14. Site Survey for an Event at Yankee Stadium

This simple site survey for an event to be held at Yankee Stadium points out some of the variables that must be addressed when planning an event for a space never used before for a "show." It is doubly interesting historically because of the fact that the survey took place on a day when everyone in the building was frantically trying to get the stadium reopened after a beam had fallen in left field!

SITE SURVEY

EVENT: SANITATION DEPT. AT YANKEE STADIUM
DATE OF SURVEY: APRIL 22, 1998
TYPE OF EVENT: Breakfast with speakers, Video presentation, speakers
　　　　　　　　Event will be videotaped, entertainment by 4 person
　　　　　　　　comedy troupe, Chicago City Limits

DATE OF EVENT: June 16 + 17　　　　TIME: 9AM-12 Noon
LOAD IN AND SET UP: DATE: June 15　TIME: TBD
REHEARSALS: TBD

EVENT REQUIREMENTS:
　　1: SOUND
　　　　　4 wireless mics for Chicago City Limits performers
　　　　　　　Can they be run thru room system? Rented?
　　　　　Podium with mics/ Supplied by Yankee Stadium?
　　　　　Small electronic keyboard amplified and mixed?
　　　　　Playback for video
　　　　　Speaker and Video Monitor position indicated on badly
　　　　　drawn floor plan, left and right of stage area
　　　　　There is a small amplifier and cassette tape player in the
　　　　　　　room with overhead speakers built into ceiling.
　　　　　There is a mic jack built into the wall behind the stage
　　　　　area, presumably for the Podium mic

　　2: LIGHTS
　　　　　Room is lit with overhead small spots built into ceiling
　　　　　Control is non-dim and switched off in sections
　　　　　Will need small light package with booms and 9 foot
　　　　　pipes in center section for speakers and show
　　　　　Lights could also possibly be hung from pipe behind stage
　　　　　　　area with drape and sign

　　3: PROJECTION
　　　　　No Projection
　　　　　2 Video playback monitors, Left and Right of Stage Area
　　　　　　　Desired equipment: 45" flat Phillipps monitors, or does
　　　　　　　　　Yankee Stadium have a system for the room?
　　　　　Video Camera and taping equipment for Event taping

4: STAGING
No Staging risers
Stage area to be defined by 12' x 12' Carpet, possibly
Astroturf in keeping with Stadium.
Tables (25) to be set out from stage in "chevron" style

5: PIPE AND DRAPE
12' W x 9'6" H Drape against wall behind speaker/
stage area. Color and material TBD.
WE CAN DO IT sign to be hung on Drape

SPACE/ ROOM: The room is long and narrow, approx. 125' x 19'.
It has a slightly curving wall that follows the contour of
the stadium. It is carpeted in the dining/ stage area and tiled in the
entrance bar area.
There is a dropped ceiling with acoustical tile throughout.
6' from the wall, on one side, the ceiling is 7"6". The remainer of
the ceiling (13') is at 9'6" cut every 12' by a 1' wide beam at 8' high.
There are no hanging points.

FLOOR PLAN: None was available; I have made a
VERY rough sketch

DIMENSIONS: 9'6", 8', 7'6" H X 19' W X 125' L

HANGING   DROPPED CEILING? yes
BEAMS ABOVE? no
ANY PERMANENT HANGING POSITIONS? no
LOADING DOORS
DIMENSIONS: 5' W X 7'6" H
DOCK HEIGHT: Street
SCHEDULE/ ELEVATORS/ FORK LIFTS AVAILABLE? ETC.
Elevator from ground level/ Doors 5' W X 7'H
POWER
PANEL AND SERVICE/ Could not find/ Not available today

PROVIDE BREAK OUTS? They will

HOUSE ELECS? Yes, there is a Union Room electrician

SEPARATE SOUND, LITE AND PROJ. FEEDS? No

FLOOR is CARPET

NOTES:
Due to current situation at Stadium, no one available today with full
knowledge and technical details on room.
It is a full union venue, but Sean, our guide, did not know which
unions.

15. Basic Guide to a Site Survey for an Outdoor Event

This basic guide to a site survey for an outdoor event covers the basic questions that must be answered before a production manager can get on with his or her work planning for the event.

OUTDOOR EVENT
Basic Guide to Site Survey
Questions

1. UNIONS
   Who is involved?
   Jurisdictions?
   a. Staging
   b. Electrics (Stage and Power seperate? Television Remotes?)
   c. Rigging/ High Steel
   d. Loaders/ Teamsters?
   e. Sound (Show PA, Communications, Telephones/ Page?)
   f. Audio Visual (Jumbo Trons, Television Monitors/ Plats)
   g. Wardrobe
   h. Crane Operators (Heavy lifting and television/ sound booms)
   i. Forklift Ops (Equipment also)
   j. Spot Lite Ops
   k. Board Operators/ Vari Lite, etc.
   Full details on work rules, meals, benefits, safe and sanitary, etc. for any unions
   Names and contacts for all labor contractors

2. SCOPE OF JOB
   What is size of event/ Production, estimated crowd, lenght of time to set up and strike, cooperation of city, parks, conservancy, etc.

3. SECURITY
   Before during and after event
   Include first aid personnel, any Secret Service or special police squads involved

4. Who is in charge of total event?

5. Rain and weather contingencies for load in and performance

6. Permits and Workers Compensation
   All city, park, sidewalk, truck, noise permits discussed and assigned
   If large structure/ Building Permits and Architects Public Assembly permits
   Generator power permits and limits, etc.

7. Vendors/ Who is providing all equipment and how is it getting to the site
   Dates/ Trucking limitations of weight or height or time of delivery?

8. Personnel Needs/
   Food/catering w/ tents, Toilets, Lockers for tools, etc/ Trailers/ Power/ Phones

16. Scheduling and Running Events in Hotel Situations

"Pamway Dinner at Waldorf Astoria" shows the basic ideas behind scheduling and running one-night events in hotel situations. Note the compressed schedule, which includes working all night at the hotel. This often happens because hotel ballrooms or dining halls are rented out on such a regular basis that one show/event will be going out as the next is coming in. It is always important to check out the hotel's scheduling in that regard. You should also make sure the hotel has loading elevators and engineers available to help you.

PAMWAY DINNER AT WALDORF ASTORIA
Nov. 23-25, 1996
Production Schedule and Crew Calls A/O Nov. 16
Please call **Tom Kelly, Production Manager** with any questions,
additions, corrections or schedule conflicts @ 914-XXX-XXXX

THUR. 11/21	8am HEAD + 1 ELEC	Bash Lighting/ Prep
FRI. 11/22	8am HEAD + 1 ELEC	Prep Lights
SAT. 11/23	6pm 4 LOADERS	Waldorf Loading Dock
	6pm 1 ELEVATOR OP.*	Load in elec. equipment
Waldorf Dock is on 50th St. between		Trav. tracks, Drapes to
Park and Lexington (closer to Lex.)		Grand Ballroom
Grand Ballroom is on third floor		
	6pm HEAD + 5 ELECS	Hang Lights
	6pm HEAD + 2 CARPS	Hang Travellers/ Drapes
	6pm Waldorf CARP/ ELEC*	*Tie in power/ Run pipes
		*Provide Waldorf Lift
	10pm DINNER BREAK/ LOADERS END OF DAY	
	2am FULL CREW BREAK FOR DAY	
SUN. 11/24	10AM-1PM/ AVAILABLE FOR EMERGENCY ONLY	
	2pm HEAD + 2 ELECS	1 Board Op/ 2 Spot Ops
	HEAD + 1 CARP	Trav. and Fly Cues
	2pm Waldorf Carp/ Elec Crew Call/ As needed*	
	2-6pm Touch up focus/ Run all cues/ Preview Videos	
	Sound check	
	6pm CREW DINNER/ GUEST RECEPTION IN LOBBY	
	7pm FULL CREW/ BALLROOM OPEN	
	DINNER	
	8:30pm PROGRAM BEGINS	
	11PM-3AM LOAD OUT/ **Add** 3 ELECS/ 1 CARP/ 4 LOADERS	
	WALDORF CARP/ ELEC/ FREIGHT ELEVATOR OP*	

CC:	Jules Fisher/ Barbara Handman	Producers
	Gail Mehado	Asst. to Producers
	Jack Jacobs	Lighting
	Josh Weitzman	Electrician
	*Gary Merjian * (all Waldorf crew and equip.)	Waldorf Manager
	Bestek Co.	Staging
	Stage Right Co.	Crewing
	Jane McGivena	Production Coordinator

17. Discussion Agenda for Planning and Producing a Performance in a Nonperformance Space, Along with Load-In and Trucking Schedule

These lists provide a detailed overview of a production in its planning stages, along with the final schedule for load-in and trucking. The production is *Madison Scare Garden*, a "spooktacular" event held at Madison Square Garden in New York every fall for several years now. Both the discussion agenda and the load-in/trucking schedule show the inherent problems encountered in producing a performance event in a nonperformance space.

MADISON SCARE GARDEN /DISCUSSION AGENDA/ WEEK OF 7/29-8/2
9/20/98   4:41 PM   1

These are topics in each category that need discussion, resolution and/or a plan for work to continue.
SCENERY
        Description and verbal outline of 10 scares per house and 3 scares
          for Labyrinth to finalize design and propping
        Discuss and get final word on neccessary building materials or
          flameproofing requirements for ROTUNDA/MSG from Nat
          Silberman that differ from ESH's standard building/ fireproofing
        Discuss all "Outside of Rotunda" scenic treatments
             i.e. Merchandising, Ticket windows, displays,etc.
        Finalize designs and materials for all facades
        Final paint elevations and drawings, sketches discussed and assigned
        Finalize entrance position and treatment
        Discuss CIRCUS position or shape to increase backstage area
        New schedule for completion and reviews in Dallas due to late start
        Discuss sound speaker placement in rooms
        Discuss emergency exits
        Finalize interior of theater:
          Dropping seats? or other effects that require resetting/ crew, etc.
          Stage show and operator/ performer requirements
          Seating/standing
          General decor and direction
        Finalize Pumpkin Patch and Performing Stage look and concept
        What is wall texture and load limit on hanging in Labyrinth?
LIGHTING/ EFFECTS
        All grid, ceiling and lighting possibilities discussed for code
        considerations
        Feasibility and fire code stipulations for raising the false ceiling
          for lighting positions, effect on sprinkler systems,
          emergency lighting, etc

MADISON SCARE GARDEN   LOAD IN AND TRUCKING SCHED/a/o 10/5

10/5/96   1.

MON. 10/7   9AM   Event Staff signing in Green Room

WED. 10/9   8AM   LOAD IN COMMENCES/Carps, Elecs, Riggers, Forks
                     1. CENTERLINE/   1   48" Trailer with Scenery
                     2. PRODUCTION ARTS/   2 24" with lighting equip
                     3. ELM ST./   3   48" Trailers, 1 53' with scenery
                     Start Elecs hang, Rigging, Scenery install
                     12 Noon   LUNCH
                     Continue Elecs, Rigging and Scenery
                     Hang Skylight, Truss and Sign
                     Lay out all attractions with plywood base and carpets
                     Begin assemble attractions
                     Begin assemble Pumpkin Patch, Windows, Theater
              5 Rolls Vinyl Blackout Material from Proflex due at loading dock
                     5PM   BREAK (6 PM if needed)

THU. 10/10   8AM   Continue Hang Elec/ Power
                     Continue Ceiling hanging treatment/ Rigging
                     Set Install
                     5PM   Break (6 PM if needed)
                     On Retail Lobby/ Install Window Black out treatment behind BATIQUE
                                          if delivered Wed.

FRI. 10/11   8AM   Continue set and Lights
                     Hang Tower entrance scenery and Black window treatments
                     1PM   Begin Lighting of completed units
                     5PM   Break for Day/   Facade, 2 Attractions Built/ Lighting Started
                             (6 PM if needed)
                On Retail Lobby/ Deliver and Hang BAT/ Time TBD
                     1 24' Truck/ CENTERLINE
                     Pipe and Drape delivered and set by NY Decorating
                     Complete all install of BATIQUE/ Bat, Window, Pipe and Drape/
                             OPEN BATIQUE

SAT. 10/12   8AM   Set Installation Continues
                     SOUND delivers/ MASQUE SOUND/ 1 or 2 24" Truck
                     Lighting Continues on Finished Sets/ Rooms
                     Sound and Communications Begin set up
                     5PM   Break (6 PM if needed)

SUN. 10/13   Contingency Work Day, if Neccessary Only/ Possibly Sound only?

18. Costume Breakdown

This form serves many purposes at once. It gives the stage manager a basic concept of who is in what scene to keep the director abreast of his or her needs for rehearsal. It gives the wardrobe personnel an immediate outline of their needs for quick changes and preparation. If you want my humble opinion, this particular breakdown shows a ridiculous number of costume changes, many unnecessary and difficult for the singer to have to worry about. It seems there was a budget surplus on the first production of the opera, so they spent it on the wardrobe!

BAM May 2008 Director: Jonathan Miller	Il Matrimonio Segreto Costume Breakdown	ASM: Francesca DeRenzi SM: Tom Kelly June 4, 2008 Page 1 of 2 Final Version

ACT I

Principals	Act I, Scene 1	Act I, Scene 2	Act I, Scene 3	Act I, Scene 4	Act I, Scene 5	Act I, Scene 6	Act I, Scene 7	Act I, Scene 8
Carolina Heidi Stober	Cost #1		Cost #1	Cost #1 (exit to 5 min change)		Cost #2	Cost #2	Cost #2
Elisetta Georgia Jarman			Cost #1	Cost #1	Cost #1 (exit to remove apron, ADD hat)		Cost #2 (w/Hat)	Cost #2 (exit to change)
Fidalma Fredrika Brillembourg			Cost# 1	Cost #1	Cost #1 (exit to ADD jacket/hat)		Cost #2 (New jacket)	Cost #2 (exit to change)
Conte Robinson Jonathan Best							Cost #1	Cost #1
Geronimo Conal Coad		Cost #1	Cost #1 (exit to waistcoat change)			Cost #1a	Cost #1a	
Paolino Chad A. Johnson	Cost #1	Cost #1					Cost #1	
Male Servant Todd Cowdery			Cost #1				Cost #1	
Female Servant Melinda Peinado			Cost #1			Cost #1	Cost #1 (exit to apron change)	

BAM May 2008 Director: Jonathan Miller	Il Matrimonio Segreto Costume Breakdown	ASM: Francesca DeRenzi SM: Tom Kelly June 4, 2008 Page 2 of 2 Final Version

Principals	Act I, Scene 9	Act I, Scene 10	Act I, Scene 11	Act I, Scene 12	Act I, Scene 13	Act I, Scene 14	Act I, Scene 15	Total/Act
Carolina Heidi Stober	Cost #2 (exit to 5 min. change)		Cost #3		Cost #3	Cost #3	Cost #3	3
Elisetta Georgia Jarman				Cost #3		Cost #3	Cost #3	3
Fidalma Fredrika Brillembourg				Cost #3		Cost #3	Cost #3	3
Conte Robinson Jonathan Best		Cost #1	Cost #1		Cost #1	Cost #1	Cost #1	1
Geronimo Conal Coad				Cost #2 (New waistcoat)		Cost #2	Cost #2	3
Paolino Chad A. Johnson	Cost #1	Cost #1		Cost #1		Cost #1	Cost #1	1
Male Servant Todd Cowdery				Cost #1			Cost #1	1
Female Servant Melinda Peinado							Cost #1a (New apron)	1

19. Costume Run Sheet: *Il Matrimonio Segreto*

The important considerations here are time, where the entrances and exits happen, and where a costume and hair change or fix-up can happen. This then guides the deck SM's as to where to keep room and privacy for quick changes backstage and also supplies an accurate time to warn or call the dressers or have prop men set up the change booths.

BAM May 2008 Director: Jonathan Miller	Il Matrimonio Segreto Costume Run Sheet	ASM: Francesca DeRenzi SM: Tom Kelly June 4, 2008 Page 1 of 4 Final Version

FIRST ENTRANCE TIMINGS

05:00	Heidi Stober (*Carolina*)
05:00	Chad Johnson (*Paolino*)
14:30	Conal Coad (*Geronimo*)
16:15	Georgia Jarman (*Elisetta*)
16:15	Fredrika Brillembourg (*Fidalma*)
18:30	Melinda Peinado (*Female Servant*)
18:30	Todd Cowdery (*Male Servant*)
34:15	Jonathan Best (*Conte Robinson*)

Bold & *Italics* indicate Quick Change   *Italics indicate an Exit into Costume Change*

ACT I (75:00)

Exit Time	Exit Locale	Who	Change Location	From/To	Enter Time	En / Re-En Locale	Total Time
		Carolina (H. Stober)		1st Entrance Costume #1	05:00	SL	
		Paolino (C. Johnson)		1st Entrance Costume #1	05:00	SL	
		Geronimo (C. Coad)		1st Entrance Costume #1	14:55	SR	
		Elisetta (G. Jarman)		1st Entrance Costume #1	16:15	SR	
		Fidalma (F. Brillembourg)		1st Entrance Costume #1	16:20	SL	
		Male Servant (T. Cowdery)		1st Entrance Costume #1	18:30	SR	
		Female Servant (M. Peinado)		1st Entrance Costume #1	18:30	SL	
20:30	SL	*Geronimo* (C. Coad)	SL	*FROM Cost #1 to Cost #1a* *(New Waistcoat)*	32:30	SL	12:00
27:00	SL	**Carolina** **(H. Stober)**	SL	**FROM Cost #1 TO Cost #2** **(w/ Hat)**	32:30	SL	5:30
32:30	SL	**Fidalma** **(F. Brillembourg)**	SL	**FROM COST #1 TO Cost #2** **(New Jacket, ADD Hat)**	34:15	SL	1:45
32:30	SL	**Elisetta** **(G. Jarman)**	SL	**FROM Cost #1 to Cost #2** **(Remove Apron, ADD Hat)**	34:15	SL	1:45
		Conte Robinson (J. Best)		1st Entrance Costume #1	34:20	SR	

<table>
<tr><td colspan="3" rowspan="2">
May 2008
Director: Jonathan Miller</td><td colspan="3" rowspan="2">Il Matrimonio Segreto
Costume Run Sheet</td><td colspan="2">ASM: Francesca DeRenzi
SM: Tom Kelly
June 4, 2008
Page 2 of 4
Final Version</td></tr>
</table>

35:00	SL	Female Servant (M. Peinado)	SL	From Cost #1 to Cost #1a (New Apron)	61:30	SL	26:30
38:30	SL	Geronimo (C. Coad)	SL	FROM Cost #1a TO Cost #2 (New Waistcoat)	59:30	SL	21:00
47:00	SR	Elisetta (G. Jarman)	SL	FROM Cost #2 TO Cost #3 (w/ Hat)	60:00	SR	13:00
47:00	SR	Fidalma (F. Brillembourg)	SL	FROM Cost #2 TO Cost #3	60:30	SR	13:30
48:15	SR	Carolina (H. Stober)	SR	FROM Cost #2 TO Cost #3	53:30	SR	4:45
63:00	SL	Fidalma (F. Brillembourg)	SL	ADD Rust-Colored Jacket	65:00	SL	2:00

INTERMISSION (20:00)

Who	Change Location	From/To	Enter Time	En/Re-En Locale	Total Time
Geronimo (C. Coad)	Dressing Room	FROM Cost #2 TO Cost #3	Preset	On Stage	20:00
Conte Robinson (J. Best)	Dressing Room	FROM Cost #1 TO Cost #2	Preset	SR	20:00
Paolino (C. Johnson)	Dressing Room	FROM Cost #1 TO Cost #2 (No coat)	9:30	SR	29:30
Fidalma (F. Brillembourg)	Dressing Room	FROM Cost #3 TO Cost #4	10:00	SL	30:00
Carolina (H. Stober)	Dressing Room	FROM Cost #3 TO Cost #4	14:15	SL	34:15
Elisetta (G. Jarman)	Dressing Room	FROM Cost #3 TO Cost #4 (w/ Hat)	24:00	SR	44:00

GLOSSARY

act curtain The front curtain in a proscenium theater, usually raised when the show begins and brought in for the end of each act; also referred to as the "grand drape."

arena stage Any stage setup or configuration that places the audience on all four sides of the stage action.

banda The banda is a small contingent of the orchestra set offstage to perform either effects or accompaniment, like the brass at the bullfight in *Carmen* or the strings playing offstage love songs in Mozart. There are also sometimes onstage bandas where the musicians appear in or accompany a scene onstage, requiring costume, etc. Offstage, the banda always need stands, chairs, and lights, and it is often a stage manager's challenge to figure out where, when, and how these set ups can be made and struck with the amount of traffic and changes going on.

bits The term used to describe small pieces of stage action that often do little to advance the plot or play but may enhance character or relationships. They might include little foibles that a character develops due to being short-sighted, hard of hearing, or clumsy. Quite often bits are added by the actors during the course of a run to keep their creative juices flowing at best and to get a cheap laugh at worst. There are also "bit parts," which refer to characters—a messenger or delivery boy, for example—that only have one or two lines.

blackout The moment at which the entire playing area goes dark, usually in a sudden fashion, often to mark the end of a scene or musical number.

blocking The term given to the staging of the actual movement of each cast member actor; it is the stage manager's responsibility to carefully record the blocking and see that it is strictly followed during performances.

bow warning lights A valuable tool for curtain calls. Simply place two red cue lights on the orchestra pit rail where the cast can easily see them. When turned on, they are warned not to come downstage again for a bow; the curtain is coming in, or the lights are going to black out, etc.

boxes The seats on the sides of a theater that may hang over the edges of the seats in the orchestra; they have separate entrances and usually seat six to eight people. They often have poor sightlines and offer a limited view of the stage.

breakaway Costumes that are designed to do just what the word describes, allowing a fight scene to include a shirt or a jacket or dress to be ripped and then repaired easily because the tear is already built into the garment by the use of either Velcro or loose stitching. Breakaway clothes are also designed and used for quick changes so costumes can be switched in an instant.

bridge A term left over from the days of theater/ship vocabulary, it usually refers to a level backstage that is maybe ten feet off the deck (stage level) and often holds dimmer or sound racks.

brush-up rehearsals Rehearsals often used to take out the actors' "bits"; on a long-running show these rehearsals seek to return the play or musical to its original form or intent, sometimes involving the whole cast, sometimes just one or two actors or scenes.

cables There are all kinds of cables backstage: electric cables powering lights and dimmers, sound cables connecting microphones and communication systems, and steel cables that support huge pieces of scenery.

call The time at which performers or crew members must arrive for a rehearsal or performance.

callboard The place in the theater where the sign-in sheet, all schedules, and any other vital information for cast and crew are posted.

chorus master The "musical director" of the chorus, responsible for their rehearsal preparation vocally, working to ensure with director and stage management that they are grouped onstage and offstage for maximum vocal effect and that correct voices are placed next to each other. There are also assistants who sometimes conduct chorus singing in the wings or from the wings when the singers cannot see the conductor or monitors from the stage. Children's choruses will have their own chorus masters.

clip lights These are used to provide illumination necessary to run a performance backstage. Usually rigged with low-wattage blue bulbs, they are aimed down at the floor and away from the stage, helping to light the backstage passages for actors and crew. The "clip" is a strong clamp that allows these lights to be placed anywhere—on scenery, the edges of curtains, stair railings, etc.

contact sheets The address book of a production, comprising sheets that contain the phone numbers and addresses of everyone working on a show.

costume plot A list and description (breakdown) of every costume piece worn by every actor and character in a play.

covers Actors or singer-dancers who "cover" certain scenes, songs, or small parts for absent performers. Covering is simpler than understudying; a cover may already be in the scene or number and, when covering, perform additional lines or movements for the absent performer.

crossover A passageway behind the set used by actors to cross the stage unseen by the audience. On Broadway sets, often there isn't one, and crossovers must be made through the theater's basement.

cue Technically, a cue is the execution of a move or effect in lighting and sound. For the actors, a cue is the line that immediately precedes a line of their dialogue. As a verb, the word may be used by the stage manager, who cues all technical personnel either verbally or on a light and cues actors by giving them their lines when they have forgotten them.

cue light A light that when turned on functions as a warning to a crew member to perform a cue or to an actor to make an entrance and when turned off signals them to go.

cue sheet The written record of every technical cue in each department; it should include the cue number or letter of each cue, how the cue will be called (either verbally or on a cue light), and what will happen in the cue (either scenery move or light or sound effect).

cue-to-cue A technical rehearsal that focuses on getting the physical production caught up with the acting by skipping over scenes or dialogue that have no technical cues in them to run the next cue.

cyc Short for "cyclorama," it refers to a large drop or curtain that usually hangs at the back of a set and is often used by the lighting and set designers to represent the sky.

dance numbers On a wide white tape downstage in rehearsal room, mark the center line and every two feet out from center to right and left. This gives an easily found spacing mark for the singers, chorus, dancers, etc. to find when they are staged. The downstage of your playing deck should also have these numbers so that the spacing worked out in the room can be quickly repeated and then adjusted as needed. Be sure the numbers remain visible after the floor and footlights are completely installed. It is very valuable to have a large set of the numbers made on cards that can be put across the front of the stage facing the director and choreographer for technical and staging rehearsals, then they can move individuals or groups to numbers easily from the house.

deck The stage level, derived from ship terminology.

deck cues The cues that happen on the stage level—i.e., the moving of scenic elements, platforms, etc. onto and off the stage.

dressers The wardrobe crew members who actually help actors in and out of their costumes and supervise the cleaning and distribution of the costumes on a regular basis. They also organize and assist all quick changes that happen backstage when there is no time for returning to dressing rooms.

drops Pieces of scenery that are hung over the stage and often "fly" in and out; often painted but can also be full wall units with doors, windows, etc.

dry tech Basically a "cue-to-cue" carried out without actors.

escape stairs The steps, unseen by the audience, that an actor uses to "escape" after an upper-level exit; also used to get in place for an entrance from upper platforms or doors.

fight director The person who stages, with an eye for safety and the actors' ability to repeat the actions, any fight scenes, duels, etc. in a play or musical.

first-call sheet A cast list with the first time every actor is called for rehearsal or performance.

flash-pot A small box that will cause a noisy explosion of smoke; it is set by crossing two wires with opposite polarity that then short out when cued, igniting a gunpowder-type substance with the spark.

floor plan The accurate, detailed diagram of the way the set lays out on the stage, with all walls, platforms, stairs, furniture, and moving pieces indicated; also called the "ground plan."

fly floor The level from which the "flies" or flown scenery and drops are run.

focus The period of time during which the lighting designer instructs the electric crew where to aim and shutter (focus) each lighting instrument. Lighting instruments can be focused to illuminate a small or large area of the stage. For an actor or director, "focus" refers to where the audience's attention should be during a scene, often called the "point of focus." In large scenes it is important to watch that crowd-scene actors don't "pull focus" with some "bits" they may have devised.

gels In the old days the color filters for stage lights were made of a gelatin substance, and hence the term "gels" for these filters used to create dramatic lighting effects.

greenroom This is a room or area in the theater in which the actors may relax and gather before and during a rehearsal or performance; the term harkens back to the Greeks, who would go off to a leafy bower or grove to relax when offstage.

grid A matrix of iron or heavy wooden beams at the top of every theater building from which the hanging pipes for lights and scenery are suspended.

ground plan See **floor plan**.

hanging plot This refers to one of two plots. There is the lighting designer's hanging plot that shows where every lighting instrument is to be hung, either backstage or in the house; and there is the master hanging plot that assigns pipes and hanging positions to every lighting, sound, and scenic element in the show.

hospitality The basic care and comfort offered by the stage manager to the cast and crew on as high a level as can be squeezed from the budget. If you don't know how to offer this, don't be a stage manager.

house The term used to describe the area of a theater where the audience customarily sits.

house lights The lights used to illuminate the audience areas, they are dimmed out as the show begins and the stage lights take over, drawing focus to the stage.

light board The control board run by the electrician that cues the lights; most are computerized these days and involve nothing more complex than pushing a button . . . until something goes wrong.

load-in/load-out The time a show goes into or out of a theater; also called "take-in/take-out." Large crews are usually assembled just for this period.

maestro This is the term used for the conductor. It also distinguishes his equipment and needs such as a maestro stool, being the stools set backstage for assistant conductors to stand up on to conduct offstage chorus or banda.

maestro pit door There is usually a door that swings open into the house built into the orchestra pit railing. This is how the maestro can easily get in and out during rehearsals. It must be checked before performance that it is bolted shut so that in leaning back on it during the performance, the maestro does not end up in the audiences' lap.

monitors There are sound and visual monitors, both stationary and moveable, so that singers and chorus can follow the conductor at all times.

It is the development of this technology that allowed operas to break away from the old forms of staging where everyone singing had to be facing exactly downstage to see the conductor. Now in a standard opera house you will see conductor monitors permanently affixed to the balcony, maybe to the closest boxes to the stage, on the proscenium, and in every wing. Sound monitors are vital for singers getting pitch; in opera these have only the orchestra, no vocal, and certain instruments may be amplified higher than others. *Rovers* are monitors on rolling stands that can be moved into different positions depending on the scenery or staging of singers and chorus.

notes The endless process of recording comments on performance quality, technical conditions, etc.; making sure they are communicated clearly is the stage manager's continuing job from beginning to end of a show. *Notes* is also the term given to the period of time when the director gathers the cast together to discuss a performance or rehearsal. It is vital that the stage manager be at every note session to record the notes to avoid any confusion later.

off-book The term used to describe when the actors put down the script in the tenuous but brave belief that they now know their lines well enough to perform their parts without benefit of reading dialogue.

pace The speed at which a play is performed. The pace can be speeded up or slowed down by actors speaking the lines faster or slower or by their cutting down the time between lines (also called "picking up the cues") or increasing it.

palette A thin piece of plywood or Masonite (upon which often rests a section of a room covered by a rug with furniture on it) that can be used to quickly change sets without having to handle each piece of furniture separately.

perishables Props that must be replaced constantly—food, broken bottles or glasses, ripped-up documents, or anything else that "perishes" on a nightly or weekly basis.

pipes Long pieces of iron, usually three-quarters of an inch or one inch in diameter, that hang above the stage from the grid and from which are hung lights and scenery.

places The term used backstage to announce to the company that an act or scene is beginning. It literally means, "Kindly come to your places for the commencement of the act or scene about to be run or performed." In England the term *beginners* is used.

practical props/appliances Any object actually used by an actor on the set—a lamp, a stove, a cigarette lighter, etc.

preproduction The planning period that takes place before rehearsals begin.

preset The preshow setting of all physical elements of the production before the action begins. There is usually a lighting preset that warms the curtain or, in situations with no curtain, highlights the set slightly. Onstage, the preset is the positioning of all scenery and props for the opening of an act.

preview A performance before the official opening; often these are rehearsals with an audience and a time when new material is tested and tried out.

prompt What you hope actors are; also the act of giving a line to an actor when he or she goes "up" or forgets a line, which is also referred to as "drying."

props The elements on a stage that are not scenery or furniture, including everything that is handled and used by the actors, as well as all set "dressing" and ornaments.

prop tables Tables in the wings on which the actors' props can be preset for use during the performance and to which the actors should return the props when finished with them; the tables should be carefully marked and labeled so each prop has its proper place.

proscenium Latin for "in front of the scenery," the word refers to the arch or frame that actually goes around the stage.

quick-change booth A temporary backstage dressing room used for quick changes of costumes, wigs, etc.; it may be used by many different actors at different times during the course of a show.

raked stage The practice of setting the stage floor on a "rake" or incline, so that the downstage edge is considerably lower than the upstage edge; this aids with sightlines and also gives the set designer the opportunity to use the floor as a scenic element.

replacement Any performer who replaces another.

running crew The actual crew that is required for the operation of each performance.

running order The order in which a show's scenes and songs are performed.

run-throughs The first attempts at performing a show all the way through without stopping; after opening, they are used for brush-up or replacement rehearsals.

scene breakdowns Careful annotations of each scene in a play, with all necessary actors listed and some indication of the action and setting.

scrim A gauze-like curtain that, when lit from the front, is opaque (cannot be seen through) and when lit from behind becomes translucent and seems to disappear.

shops The various workplaces where the physical production is assembled or built; there are scenery, light, costume, sound, and prop shops.

Sitzprobe German term meaning a sit-down reading of the score with the singers. The maestro runs this completely and addresses both the orchestral balance and modulations for the vocalists and gives the vocalists a chance to hear the orchestration over which they will be singing.

special effects Any effect out of the ordinary—storms, fire, explosions, blood, etc.

stage combat Any stage fighting, from a slap to a battle.

Stagione Italian term used in opera for a "stand alone" production or series of productions that run one at a time, as opposed to "repertory," which indicates a company or schedule that will play several operas at the same time.

stand-by A performer who is an understudy but who does not report to the theater unless called to perform; he or she may perform one or two shows on a regular basis.

strike What the producers hope the unions never do; also, the term for the removal of any item of the physical production either temporarily between scenes or permanently (the load-out).

supers The short term for *supernumeraries,* sometimes also referred to as character mimes. These are performers who appear onstage in non-singing roles; these may be soldiers, footmen, waiters, crowd members, etc. who fill the stage picture and perform many small pieces of business that move the plot along.

tableaux A grouping of performers to make a pretty stage picture, often used for curtain calls.

tech rehearsal The rehearsal or rehearsals where the physical elements of a production are integrated with the performed elements.

theater-in-the-round Like arena stages, the audience sits on four sides of the stage, but the stage is round.

thrust stage Any configuration of the playing area in which the stage projects into the seating area.

title screen In most opera houses in America there are title screens that hang in front of the stage and give English translations of the vocal score being sung onstage. Stage managers usually have little to do with this other than warning the operator before starting and keeping a channel open to them for problems or when they need to hear a cue for a blackout. In a repertory house or when one opera may be rehearsing in the day while another plays at night, it is important to check that the screen is at the proper trim, or height, for the performance you are about to call.

trap doors Sections of the stage floor that open, allowing actors to enter or exit.

travelers Curtains that open as opposed to "flying" in and out.

truss An additional or extra system of pipes from which light and sound equipment can be hung.

tune light In calling an opera, the stage manager's final sequence for the start of the show starts with the orchestra tune. It is vital that the orchestra knows exactly when to do so, and a cue light is usually installed at eye level of the first violinist who leads the tuning of the orchestra. House is usually called to half of the available lighting power, and all announcements made before the tune. Then the maestro is sent into the pit, bows, and the opera starts. The tune light can often double as a conductor Q-light when needed to inform them to start in order to coordinate with cueing and technical effects.

turntable A section of the deck or stage that can turn, moving scenery and actors into or out of the audience's view.

understudy An actor who is prepared to go on for another actor in case of emergency.

wagon A rolling or tracked platform that goes on- and offstage with actors and/or scenery on it.

Wandelprobe German term for what we also call a stage orchestra rehearsal. In these rehearsals, the maestro is still in charge, but it will include staging and technical cues as well. However, the musical elements will come first, and the maestro will control the scheduling of the time, and any repeated parts of the opera will be at his request. It is specifically NOT a technical rehearsal.

wardrobe department The crew members who deal with costumes.

warning The stage manager "warns" all cues either verbally or by turning on a cue light.

winch The device by which wagons are moved onto and off the stage; basically, a large drum around which steel cables are wound or unwound by means of a crank.

wings The area directly offstage.

work call The time period during which the crew is called to work on any technical element of a production and that does not involve actors or rehearsal.

SUGGESTED READING

Stage managers should read anything about the theater, whether technical textbooks, design handbooks, guides to acting and directing techniques, or theater diaries and novels. You can go to Amazon Books and search under Theater, Broadway, Stage Management, Acting, etc. and find many more books than I can think of. Another valuable resource for learning about stage equipment, terms, etc. is to write away for catalogs from places like Productions Resource Group (PRG), I Weiss, Rosebrand, Mutual Hardware, and Sound Associates. Here are some basic reading suggestions:

DESIGN/TECHNICAL

The Backstage Handbook, Paul Carter. New York: Broadway Press, 1988. A basic guide to theatrical terms and backstage services.

The Dramatic Imagination, Robert Edmond Jones. New York: Theater Arts Books, 1969. My favorite theater "bible," this essay collection is filled with the author's vision of an ideal theater. Jones, one of the great twentieth-century theater artists (he designed many of O'Neill's plays and the set for John Barrymore's 1922 production of *Hamlet*), believed the art form should encourage the audience's imagination, not bombard it with excess.

A Method of Lighting the Stage, Stanley R. McCandless. New York: Theater Arts Books, 1978. The long-standing text that still offers the best basic information on how to design and execute theatrical stage lighting.

From Option to Opening: A Guide to Producing Plays Off-Broadway, Donald Farber. New York: Limelight Editions, 1988. An excellent text on the complexities of theater from the management perspective.

Scenery for the Theatre, 2nd, rev. ed., Harold Burris-Meyer and Edward C. Cole. Boston: Little, Brown and Co., 1971. The text that explains the fundamentals: stage terminology, basic building and rigging techniques, scenery construction and painting, and lighting rudiments. If you read only one technical book, make it this one.

Stage Lighting, Richard Pilbrow. New York: Applause Theatre Books, 1990. A good text with excellent insights into the use of lighting and its creation.

Stage Manager's Forms and Formats, Barbara Dilker. New York: Drama Book Publications, 1982. Many valuable forms and ideas for organization.

Stage Manager's Handbook, Bert Gruver and Frank Hamilton. New York: Drama Book Publications, 1972. Contains helpful hints on setting up and organizing a show. Mainly geared toward the commercial New York theater and touring.

A Stage Manager's Manual, Edward C. Cole. New Haven: Yale University Department of Drama, 1937. Old-fashioned and out of print, but pure gold and worth a trip to the library. The advice remains sound and the methods haven't changed that much, and because as the technical complexity of theater has grown, so has the need for clear, human leadership and organization.

Stage Manager: The Professional Experience, Larry Fazio. Oxford, UK: Focal Press, 2000. Excellent combination of teaching and sometimes hysterical, sometimes touching experience; a good read.

Stage Specs: A Guide to Legit Theaters. Available from League of American Theaters and Producers, 226 W. 47 St., New York, NY 10036. E-mail: webmaster@ilovenytheater.com. A thorough reference to theaters across the county, detailing dimensions, seating capacities, load-in and load-out procedures, union requirements, and more. A must for anyone considering touring a show.

ACTING AND DIRECTING

Actors on Acting, rev. ed., Toby Cole and Helen K. Chinoy, eds. New York: Crown Publishers, 1980. Interviews with many accomplished actors who discuss their approaches to the creation of a character.

Building a Character and *My Life in Art*, Constantin Stanislavsky. New York: Routledge, Chapman, and Hall, 1989. The architect of a new approach to theater at the turn of the century, Stanislavsky's thought became the foundation for Lee Strasberg's Method, as well as other acting techniques.

The Director's Voice, Arthur Bartow. New York: Theatre Communications Group, 1988. Interviews with many of the leading directors in the theater today.

A Dream of Passion: The Development of the Method, Lee Strasberg; Evangeline Morphos, ed. New York: New American Library, 1988. The authoritative text on the Method acting technique, developed by the author at the Actors' Studio.

Great Directors at Work: Stanislavsky, Brecht, Kazan, Brook, David Richard Jones. Berkeley: University of California Press, 1986. An examination of the director's art as practiced by four of the most accomplished directors of the twentieth century.

On Directing, Harold Clurman. New York: MacMillan, 1974. A detailed and illuminating discussion of the director's craft by one of the Group Theatre's founders.

Respect for Acting, Uta Hagen, with Haskel Frankel. New York: MacMillan, 1973. Excellent descriptions of sense memory work and exercises used by many actors.

Sanford Meisner on Acting, Sanford Meisner and Dennis Longwell. New York: Random House, 1987. Written by an original member of the Group Theatre and the founder of the Neighborhood Playhouse, this book details Meisner's influential actor training process.

Stage Directions, John Gielgud. New York: Theatre Arts Books, 1979. A great lesson in acting style and approach from a master.

The Technique of Acting, Stella Adler. New York: Bantam Books, 1988. One of the best acting texts, this is an in-depth study of behavioral acting.

BACKSTAGE ACCOUNTS AND FICTION

Act One: An Autobiography, Moss Hart. New York: Random House, 1976.

Diary of a Mad Playwright, James Kirkwood. New York: Dutton, 1985. Difficult stars, a play that isn't working, and the rigors of a national pre-Broadway tour. You can learn a lot here.

Peter Hall's Diaries, Peter Hall; John Goodwin, ed. New York: Limelight Editions, 1985. Incisive insights into the process of putting on plays, running a theater, and trying to maintain a life while existing on the creative edge.

Understudy, Elia Kazan. New York: Scarborough House, 1975. This novel uses the theater and its workings as the setting for its story. It offers a stage manager interesting insights into some of the emotional and philosophical motivations of theater people.

INDEX

C

ABOUT THE AUTHOR

Thomas A. Kelly has been a professional stage manager of opera, Broadway, Off-Broadway, and regional theater for over forty years. His Broadway career includes *Hair*, *The Wiz*, *Sugar Babies*, *The Merchant of Venice*; *Death of a Salesman* (with Dustin Hoffman), *Othello* and *Cyrano* (with Christopher Plummer), Tommy Tune's productions of *The Club* and *A Day in Hollywood/A Night in the Ukraine*, David Mamet's *Speed-the-Plow*, Herb Gardner's Tony Award-winning *I'm Not Rappaport*, and the John Guare/Peter Hall production of *Four Baboons Adoring the Sun* for Lincoln Center.

As a production manager and staging supervisor, Mr. Kelly worked on a diverse set of events and shows, from the Rock and Roll Hall of Fame to the Papal Mass in Central Park and from MTV's *Unplugged* and VMA shows to an outdoor production of *Peter and the Wolf*, with the Brooklyn Philharmonic, narrated by Dustin Hoffman and Ossie Davis. He has managed installations of everything from the scenarios and lighting for the Salem Witch Museum and *Madison Scare Garden* to Nickelodeon's Extreme Baseball at Shea Stadium, as well as King World Studios' *Rolanda Watts*, *Inside Edition*, and *American Journal* studio setups.

Mr. Kelly was the general/production manager for Center Line Studios, where he supervised the production and installation of scenery and technical support for shows on Broadway, Lincoln Center, Manhattan Theater Club, and the Public Theater in New York; the New York City and Chicago Lyric Opera Companies; the New York City and Milwaukee Ballet companies, and the Merce Cunningham Dance company; Fox Television and Madison Square Garden; and outdoor installations at the Wollman Rink Summer Night's Dance and Battery Park Summer Concerts in New York. From 2001 to 2008, Mr. Kelly was the production stage manager for New York City Opera at Lincoln Center's State Theatre, helping to mount over sixty operas—new, old, traditional, and modern.

A graduate of Trinity College in Hartford, Connecticut, Mr. Kelly is married to composer/musical director Memrie Kelly and has three children. He has been on the adjunct faculty of Rutgers, Columbia, and SUNY Purchase. In 2002, Mr. Kelly was awarded the Lifetime Achievement Award from USITT, and his work on *Between the Lions* for PBS earned him a Daytime Emmy Award.